Dimensions of Dignity at Work

Dimensions of Dignity at Work

Sharon C. Bolton

Routledge
Taylor & Francis Group

LONDON AND NEW YORK

First published 2007 by Butterworth-Heinemann
Published 2015 by Routledge

2 Park Square, Milton Park, Abingdon, Oxon, OX14 4RN
711 Third Avenue, New York, NY 10017

Routledge is an imprint of the Taylor & Francis Group, an informa business

Notice
No responsibility is assumed by the publisher for any injury and/or damage to persons
or property as a matter of products liability, negligence or otherwise, or from any use or
operation of any methods, products, instructions or ideas contained in the material
herein. Because of rapid advances in the medical sciences, in particular, independent
verification of diagnoses and drug dosages should be made.

British Library Cataloguing in Publication Data
A catalogue record for this book is available from the British Library

Library of Congress Cataloging-in-Publication Data
A catalog record for this book is available from the Library of Congress

ISBN: 978-0-7506-8333-3 (pbk)

Contents

Foreword

Sharon Bolton began this book with an investigation into why dignity at work matters, and her questions, *why dignity? why now?,* are tremendously fruitful. An important message to emerge from this book is that dignity and its absence are characteristics of humans working together; neither is inevitable, and our choices can make one more likely than the other.

A central trade union principle is that employment rights are human rights, and dignity at work is a foundational value for our movement. This follows on from an understanding of what the good life means for both individuals and societies. Dignity is inherent in the values that have inspired our civilisation. Aristotle argued that the highest good is the happiness people achieve when they realise their capacities for reason and virtue. Kant said that humans have an inherent worth and should never be treated just as a means, but also as ends in themselves.

There is no boundary fence round the world of work, with a notice that these values no longer apply. That is why the International Labour Organisation, in its 1944 Philadelphia Declaration, said that 'labour is not a commodity. . . all human beings, irrespective of race, creed or sex, have the right to pursue both their material well-being and their spiritual development in conditions of freedom and dignity, of economic security and equal opportunity'.[1]

Nearly all work depends on co-operation and co-ordination, and the ways in which this is organised – such as contracts, hierarchies or mutual aid – can all operate to promote or deny dignity. But not equally and not in the same ways. Unions have always denied the justice of contracts between unequal parties, and our daily practice is to challenge the inequality inherent in hierarchies. Voluntary work, mutual aid and co-operation have sometimes been promoted as answers to these problems, but can also fall foul of the human tendency to empathise most readily with those who are most similar to us.

Unions work to reduce and then eliminate characteristics that can make jobs themselves undignified: all unions aim to rid the workplace of overwork, dangerous work and dirty work – issues that form an integral part of contributions to this edited collection. And we help workers resist those managers and organisations that would deny their dignity as individuals through bullying, harassment and discrimination.

The larger task, however, is to generalise from these specific tasks. Relationships of power have an inherent tendency to deny autonomy to the majority in an organisation, and to do this regardless of whether the source of power lies in an employment contract, workplace status or force of personality. The soul of indignity is lost autonomy of the right to develop one's capacities or to make choices. And, as social scientists have pointed out for over a century, the resulting sense of being forced into immoral work encourages the notion that society's proclaimed values are a fraud.

Turning this analysis into a programme for action is notoriously difficult. Checks and balances, reducing the power imbalance in the workplace must be part of this work. Legislated rights – especially employment rights and anti-discrimination legislation – can play a double role; first, they can bring the state into the workplace as a countervailing power and second, the very existence of rights undermines claims that indignity is the natural state of affairs.

The strength of unity is, of course, one way in which unions help to restore the power balance, but trade unions are also a pro-dignity institution by virtue of the very way they operate. The experience of self-organisation and of resistance is a source of dignity in itself, even in defeat, and the experience of solidarity can convince sceptics that it is possible to adhere to values that are not hypocritical.

For unions, dignity at work is a right, and it is the centrepiece of what we are about. It is the product of our work and the way we work, and the goal for workplace reform. The new debate on dignity at work is well-begun with the questions raised by Sharon and fellow contributors to this book.

Brendan Barber,
TUC General Secretary

Preface

Exploring dimensions of dignity

Many people have talked about dignity at work, though there are very few contemporary studies that directly address the issue. The topic tends to be disguised under headings such as citizenship, satisfaction, mutuality, pride in work, responsible autonomy and a secure sense of self, and the term tends to be related to a focus on mismanagement, over-long hours or a poor working environment. At the present time, there are also some high-profile campaigns, notably in the UK and USA, which concentrate on workplace bullying and harassment as the central facilitator of indignity at work. However, though the topic of dignity at work is linked to many important work and employment issues, it has received little attention as a distinct topic meaning that it now has an almost taken-for-granted quality. Apart from isolated texts (see Hodson, 2001), there is nothing that is available or readily accessible that a diverse audience may access and engage with. As a result, there are no available insights into what dignity might mean to managers and workers in their day-to-day working lives, how this impacts upon their experiences of work, how it might impact upon the consumers of their goods and services and how it might enable (or prevent) an organisation from carrying itself with dignity in the local community and the global marketplace. This book aims to address the current gap.

To form a basis of understanding dignity in the contemporary workplace requires that the voices of various stakeholders who are interested and implicated in the issues involved in creating and maintaining dignity at work are heard. An Economic and Social Research Council (ESRC)-funded one-day workshop (June, 2005) was a first step in this process.[2] Leading academics, trade unionists, charity groups and practicing managers presented their views and empirical research on dignity. An equally diverse audience participated in the further development of ideas presented. This edited collection of papers draws on some of the discussion of that day and further contributions since in order to investigate the concept of dignity at work. The book aims to stimulate an exploration of the concept of dignity and what it means to people in their working lives. Its central purpose is to open the doors to a broad understanding and bring some clarity to the notion of dignity *in* and *at* work. That is, dignity *in* the nature of the work we do, linked with the notion of 'good work', and dignity *at* work linked with our workplace experiences: how we are perceived and valued as a person in the workplace.

The range of contributions to this collection suggests that dignity at work is a far more complex phenomenon than current studies tend to represent. For instance, the notion of dignified work is about much more than escaping mundane or 'dirty' work and attaining a state of 'self-actualisation'. For how is it that a work situation may be deemed undignified but people are able to carry themselves with dignity nonetheless? Clearly, it is not enough to rely on the image of the autonomous craft-worker as the last bastion of dignity at work or to suggest that dignity at work is an unachievable aim due to the competitive pressures of a global economy. There can be little doubt that the economic, political and social frameworks that may enable the achievement of dignity are being re-drawn; nevertheless, the papers featured in this collection suggest the consequence may be not that dignity is necessarily destroyed but rather, that it becomes re-ordered and experienced in different ways.

This is a timely contribution as there is growing interest in the concept of dignity and respect at work which is closely associated with high-profile management issues such as work–life balance, diversity, empowerment, employee involvement and bullying and harassment. The book's originality rests with the broad spectrum of contributors who offer views and empirical work on dignity from a wide range of perspectives and backgrounds. As a whole, the chapters address important core issues involved in understanding dignity at work:

- What is dignity *in* and *at* work?
- How is it experienced differently by different groups of working people?
- Do patterns emerge from empirical studies to suggest enduring *divisions of dignity*, that is, unequal access to what is accepted to be a fundamental human right?
- To what extent has dignity come under pressure and what are the consequences of a breakdown in dignity at work – for individuals, the workplace and society?
- How can we ensure that opportunities are available for the creation, maintenance and/or restoration of dignity at work?
- What role does management practice play in the creation and maintenance of dignified workplaces?

This edited collection will offer a comprehensive review of prevailing views on the topic of dimensions of dignity at work, exploring how dignity may be defined, what is the relationship between dignity and the economy, and dignity in workplace practice.

Sharon C. Bolton

Contributors

Stephen Ackroyd is Professor of Organisational Analysis at Lancaster University Management School. He is perhaps best known for his work in organisational behaviour, and especially, organisational mis-behaviour which was completed whilst a consultant to several large engineering firms. After spending much time subsequently researching public sector organisation and the professions, his current research is concerned with the activities and strategies of the largest British companies still involved in manufacturing. When time allows, he enjoys working with hand tools (especially the mattock and the pick) described in the current chapter. His recent books include: '*Realist Perspectives on Management and Organisation*' (2000) (written and edited with S. Fleetwood); *The Organisation of Business* (2002). 'The New Managerialism and the Public Service Professions, (2004 with Ian Kirkpatrick). Recently, he has co-edited and co-authored with R. Batt and others '*The Oxford Handbook of Work and Organisations*'.

Sharon C. Bolton is Professor of Organisational Analysis in the Department of Management at Strathclyde University Business School. Sharon moved to Strathclyde University in March 2007. Prior to this, she spent six years in the Department of Organisation, Work and Technology at Lancaster University Management School, and her first academic position was as Simon Marks Research Fellow in the Department of Sociology, University of Manchester. She completed her PhD in May 1999 in the Department of Behaviour in Organisations, University of Lancaster. In her previous life, Sharon worked as a Senior Administrator in the public and private sectors. Her research interests include the emotional labour process, public-sector management, the nursing and teaching labour process, gender and the professions, the human in human resource management and dignity in and at work in a moral economy. Sharon's work is published widely in leading academic and practitioner journals along with a sole authored book *Emotion Management in the Workplace* (Palgrave, 2005), and she has recently co-edited *Searching for the Human in Human Resource Management* with Maeve Houlihan (Palgrave, 2007).

David Coats has been Associate Director of Policy at The Work Foundation since February 2004. He is responsible for The Work Foundation's engagement with the public policy world, seeking to influence the national conversation about the world of work. Recent publications include *Who's Afraid of Labour Market Flexibility* (2006) and *Raising Lazarus: The Future of Organised Labour* (Fabian Society, 2005). From 1999 to 2004, he was Head of the TUC's Economic and Social Affairs Department. He served on the Low Pay Commission from 2000 to 2004 and is currently a member of the Central Arbitration Committee.

Niall Cooper has been National Coordinator of Church Action on Poverty since 1997 and has been responsible for piloting a number of new approaches to anti-poverty work in the UK, drawing on international development experience, as well as running high-profile campaigns on poverty, debt and asylum-related issues. Prior to joining Church Action on Poverty, he worked as a community worker in Hulme, Manchester, for five years and set up and ran a national churches campaign coalition focused on housing and homelessness issues. In 1999, he co-founded the Debt on our Doorstep network for fair finance. In 2000, he chaired the UK Coalition Against Poverty's Commission on Poverty Participation and Power and, in January 2004, joined the Government Advisory Group on Over-indebtedness. In 2004/2005, he was jointly responsible with Catherine May for a research project exploring dimensions of the informal economy in the UK.

Corry de Jongh is Dutch, working and living in Ireland for 30 years. She has worked for 15 years as an Employee Assistant programme (EAP) consultant. As part of the Clanwiliam Institute, Corry will develop and reorganise the Corporate Department in the near future. She has a first degree in clinical psychology and has recently graduated with a first in a management consultancy masters from UCD. Corry intends to broaden her focus of interest into organisational relationships and dynamics.

Bill Doolin is Professor of Technology and Organisation at Auckland University of Technology, New Zealand. His research focuses on the processes that shape the adoption and use of information technologies in organisations. This has involved work on information systems in the public health sector and electronic commerce applications and strategies. His work has been published in journals such as *Information Systems Journal*, the *Journal of Information Technology*, *Accounting, Management and Information Technologies*, *Public Management Review*, *Organization and Organization Studies*.

Adele Geoghegan has lectured at European Business School (EBS) Dublin since September 2005. She holds a first-class honours Bachelor of Business degree in Management from ITT Dublin (2005) and is currently completing a Masters Degree at the UCD Michael Smurfit Graduate School of Business. Prior to joining EBS, Adele spent four years as Telesales Manager at GE Money Ireland, a General Electric business. Before that she spent three years at Lufthansa's Dublin call centre as Customer Service Manager, leading the business' European Frequent Flyer reservations division. She has also worked in Recruitment, sourcing senior call centre professionals for contact centres and shared services centres.

Randy Hodson is Professor of Sociology at Ohio State University, USA. His research interests include worker citizenship and resistance, management behaviour and co-worker relations. He has recent articles appearing in *American Journal of Sociology*, *American Sociological Review*, *Organization Science*, and *Journal of Contemporary Ethnography*. His recent books include *Dignity at Work* (2001, Cambridge University Press) and *Worlds of Work: Building an International Sociology of Work* (co-authored with Daniel B. Cornfield, 2002, Kluwer/Plenum). He is co-author with Teresa A. Sullivan of *The Social Organisation of Work*, 4th edition (2007, Wadsworth). His most recent book is *Social Theory at Work* (co-edited with Mareck Korczynski and P.K. Edwards, 2006, Oxford University Press). He is currently the editor of the *American Sociological Review*.

Frank Hogan is People and Organisation Development Adviser at the Royal Mail, Manchester. He has held a range of operational, personnel management and industrial relations roles with Royal Mail. Frank has also acted as principal consultant to Moscow International Post Office and in other international projects. He has an MBA with distinction from Lancaster University Management School. He is a director and trustee of Skylight Circus Arts, a charity, and sits on the Executive Board of the Chartered Institute of Personnel and Development.

Maeve Houlihan lectures in Organisational Behaviour and Work at UCD Business Schools, University College Dublin, Ireland. Her

research focuses on contemporary working lives, management practices and their links with society. Maeve completed her doctoral studies
at Lancaster University where her PhD involved a participant ethnographic study of the experience of working and managing in call
centres. Maeve's research is published in leading journals such as
*Human Resource Management Journal and Work, Employment and
Society* and she recently co-edited *Searching for the Human in Human
Resource Management* with Sharon Bolton (Palgrave Macmillan,
2007). Current projects include the Ireland Study for the Global Call
Centre Project, the UCD Egalitarian World Initiative and searching for
dignity in a busy academic life.

Amanda Jones has been Head of Diversity for the Co-operative Group
since June 2004. The Co-operative Group is the UK's leader in top-up
shopping, the UK's largest funeral director, the UK's fourth largest
pharmacy and manages a significant number of other retail businesses.
Since joining, Amanda has developed a Diversity Strategy for the
Group that reflects the commitment to engaging the talent in our diverse
employee base, responding to the diversity of our customers and recognising Diversity within the communities we serve. This strategy has
been supported by the implementation of a number of programmes
such as *Respect Works* which is designed to build the right kind of culture and strongly reflects the ethical principles of the Group. Amanda
was previously Head of Diversity for the Royal Bank of Scotland
Group and, prior to that, a senior IT manager within the Financial Services sector managing both UK and global infrastructure operations.
Amanda is also a winner of two *Opportunity Now* awards (1995 and
1998) and a *Wainwright Trust* winner for personal commitment to
equal opportunities.

Catherine May has worked on issues relating to livelihoods, gender
and participation issues in England since joining Oxfam's UK Poverty
Programme in 2001. Projects have included working with partner
organisations campaigning for the rights of home workers to receive
equal employment status and for fairer access to affordable credit.
Current projects also includes the delivery of a programme of work
to support migrant workers in England, the development of a holistic
sustainable livelihoods analysis in a town in the North East and support to organisations working on rural poverty issues. Catherine has
a background in anti-poverty work in England and Northern Ireland
and has a Masters in Social Policy and Social Development from the
Institute of Development, Policy and Management at the University of

Manchester. Catherine is currently working as the Programme Coordinator for the UK Poverty Programme and has written her contribution to this chapter in a personal capacity.

Laurie McLeod is currently a PhD candidate at Auckland University of Technology, New Zealand. After working for a number of years as a research scientist, she is now undertaking interpretive research into the detailed processes of interaction that occur in and around information systems development. Recently, she has worked as a usability engineer at the University of Waikato, New Zealand. Her usability work has been presented at international computer science conferences.

Marina Meehan is currently employed as the Learning and Development manager for PayPal, based in their European Headquarters, Dublin. In her spare time, she studies for a second masters in Law with Leicester University, which she hopes to complete in the next 12 months. Marina has enjoyed a career in Human Resource Management (HR) that spans 25 years, with a demonstrable track record of success working in the global arena in the private and public sectors, at a senior and middle manager level, as a direct contributor or as an independent consultant.

John Philpott has been Chief Economist at the Chartered Institute of Personnel and Development (CIPD) since November 2000. He holds a first-class honours degree in Economics from the University of Sussex (1980), a Doctorate from the University of Oxford (1985) and is Visiting Professor in Economics at the University of Hertfordshire, a Fellow of the RSA and a member of the Society of Business Economists. Prior to joining the CIPD, John was, for thirteen years, Director of the Employment Policy Institute (EPI), an independent policy think-tank. Before that, he spent four years as a post-doctoral researcher and lecturer in labour economics.

Charlotte Rayner is Professor of Human Resource Management at Portsmouth Business School. She has been in academic research since the mid-1990s when she completed the first major UK survey on workplace bullying for the BBC. Clients include The Work Foundation, NHS Trusts, UNISON, AMICUS and smaller unions, as well as local councils and the private sector. Research topics have included stress, bullying and harassment, communication strategy appraisal, local residents' opinion surveys and service performance measurement as judged by customers. Much of her work has been confidential. Charlotte is currently managing the research component of the £1.8m

DTI/AMICUS-funded project Working Together to Tackle Bullying and Harassment at Work. She has a PhD from Manchester, an MBA from Cass Business School, a first degree in Psychology from Newcastle. She writes on the topic of bullying at work and negative behaviour for professional and academic publications. She is particularly interested in prevention strategies and lectures internationally.

Andrew Sayer is Professor of Social Theory and Political Economy in the Department of Sociology, Lancaster University, UK. His books include *Microcircuits of Capital* (with K.J. Morgan, Polity, 1988), *Method in Social Science* (Routledge, 1992), *The New Social Economy* (with R.A. Walker, Blackwell, 1992), *Radical Political Economy: A Critique* (Blackwell, 1995), *Realism and Social Science* (Sage, 2000) and *The Moral Significance of Class* (Cambridge UP, 2005). He is currently working on 'moral economy' and a critique of social science's treatment of values in everyday life and in its own research. Other interests: making music, cycling, walking and having a life.

Anastasia von Mende is a PhD student in business management at University College Dublin, Ireland. She holds a bachelor's degree in business administration from Simon Fraser University in Burnaby, Canada. For her doctoral thesis, she is studying foreign workers in Ireland and exploring their role in the creation of multicultural organisations.

Terry Wallace is Reader in Organisational Analysis at Edge Hill University College. He worked as a truck driver until he was 34. After completing his PhD he worked at the Universities of Manchester, Central Lancashire, Leeds Metropolitan and Cardiff. His research interests include: industrial relations, organisation theory, industrial heritage and history.

Gemma Wibberley has worked in several research roles, collecting and analysing various forms of data, contributing towards agency and university projects. Her most recent role was as research assistant for the ESRC-funded project 'Dignity *in* and *at* Work', working with the principal investigator, Professor Sharon Bolton, based in the department of Organisation, Work and Technology, Lancaster University Management School. Gemma is now working towards her PhD examining the growing demand for domestic service workers, what she describes as the 'servant class', and their role and status in the new economy.

Acknowledgement

It is something of an irony that academics are quite so vocal on the topic of dignity at work, as though somehow we occupy the intellectual high ground and are immune from colleagues' bad behaviour and institutional failings. This is far from reality as increasingly harsh performance measures combined with longstanding macho cultures create competitive, rather than collective, communities that stifle creativity and deny difference. However, academic work holds many possibilities for the achievement of dignity, opportunities to pursue projects such as this book for instance and for special friendships and working partnerships to flourish – my pal Maeve Houlihan springs to mind. There are also some wonderful colleagues who offer support, lively discussion, shared laughter and human connection that cushion us from the harsher elements of academic life. For this, I thank Stephen Ackroyd, Jean Yates, Daniel Muzio and Steve Fleetwood; my friends and former colleagues in the department of organisation, work and technology at Lancaster University. I look forward to more of the same with my new colleagues at Strathclyde University.

This book represents collective enthusiasm for a very basic idea – the achievement of dignity at work. Together, the range of contributions to the book forms a powerful voice that will serve to significantly advance the debate on human dignity and work. A heartfelt thanks go to all the book's contributors for sharing their thoughts, ideas and ongoing research and responding so well to my, not so subtle or gentle, editorial prompts. Brendan Barber's foreword sets the tone for the book beautifully; the TUC's enthusiastic endorsement of the notion of *dimensions of dignity* is very much appreciated. I would also like to thank Stephanie Sparrow for introducing me to Butterworth and the editorial team for their endless patience and support. When speaking of enthusiasm and commitment to the topic of dignity at work, I would like to express gratitude for the huge contribution Gemma Wibberley made to the research project overall.[3]

And, finally, this book is dedicated to Steve, Jack and Geordie, who help keep life in perspective.

Sharon C. Bolton, 2007

Part One: Defining Dignity

1

Dignity *in* and *at* work: why it matters

Sharon C. Bolton

Why dignity? Why now?

Throughout the history of social science, dignity is a word that is continually used to express concern about various aspects of work. Within these concerns, we see a set of implicit understandings of what dignity is, and what it does, and profoundly, dignity as an essential need of the human spirit. Beginning with some of the earliest insights that inform contemporary analyses of work, we can see that, in different ways and relating their concerns to different eras, the founding fathers of the sociology of work each conceptualise increasing industrialisation as entailing a possible denial of dignity: Marx' focus on alienation and capitalism as a threat to our 'species being', Durkheim's concern that the relentless drive towards economic efficiency leads to a state of *anomie* (normlessness) and Weber's pathos for the individual trapped in excessive bureaucratic rationality. Similarly, early writings on the human aspects of management briefly refer to the possibilities of dignity at work via a recognition of the need for self-esteem in work (Maslow, 1965) and, later, impassioned pleas for the 'humanization of work' are early precursors to new softer management practices leading to job enlargement, teamwork, industrial democracy and responsible autonomy (Freidman, 1977; Gemmill, 1977; Khan, 1981; Rosow, 1979; Ryan, 1977; Schumacer, 1979). Very recent prescriptions from high-profile management gurus mirror early human relations writings and call for management practice to create the conditions for dignity at work (Peters, 1995; Reeves, 2001), which reflect more critical accounts that focus on requirements for more interesting and meaningful work as a route to dignity at work (Agassi, 1986; Fox, 1994; Hodson,

1996, 2001; Hodson and Roscigno, 2004). As Matthew Fox eloquently states:

> 'Our jobs are too small . . . Our work is not revelatory. For too many of us, work contains no mystery, no deep passion, no real truth. It is drudgery without meaning, sweat without purpose, duty without play, toil without learning. Worst of all, our work lacks dignity and hope for the future. And when our work lacks dignity and hope so do we' (Fox, 1994, p. 122).

The focus of many of these studies has been almost entirely on the subjective elements of dignity at work, that is self-esteem, autonomy and meaningful work. This aspect of the dignity at work debate has most recently been colonised by the focus on bullying and harassment. The high-profile campaign for 'dignity at work' (cf. AMICUS and Andrea Adams Trust) draws attention to the everyday bullying behaviours that occur in the workplace serving to intimidate and oppress employees, coming both from the workplace hierarchy, and, whether through cultural consensus or individual mal-intent, from peers. This reflects a feeling that some fundamental rights are coming under pressure. The proposed UK 'Dignity at Work Act' advises that 'every employee shall have the right to dignity at work'. However, in this framing, dignity at work is defined in very specific terms:

> 'an employer commits a breach of the right to dignity at work of an employee if that employee suffers during his employment with the organisation harassment or bullying or any act or omission or conduct which causes him to be alarmed or distressed' (Dignity at Work Act, 2001).

Linked to the focus on bullying, there have been varied calls for building cultures of respect (Ishmael, 1999; Rennie Peyton, 2003; Tehrani, 2004; Wright and Smye, 1997), where some of the core concerns of this campaign are clearly related to substantive structural matters not dissimilar to earlier concerns relating to autonomy and worth. Nevertheless, the campaign for 'dignity at work' focuses very much on indignities caused by intimidation from over-zealous managers or competitive colleagues and tends to miss that dignity at work is related to a wide range of issues not always linked to bullying.

At a broader level, there are valuable critiques of contemporary work that highlight the inequalities in access to well-paid work and safe and secure working conditions, specific tangibles of the achievement of dignity at work. Polly Toynbee's popular study of the working poor spans 30 years (1975, 2003) and highlights how structural inequalities have changed little over that period, with people working for barely, if not less than, the minimum wage whilst carrying out work that should be socially valued but is not and attracts poor material rewards. Similarly Abrams' (2002) account of living 'below the breadline' points out that often it is only the non-material rewards – for example, the social connections and moments of humour and humanity – that make work bearable.[1] These accounts reflect growing concerns about the general availability of 'good work' (Coats, 2005b; Moynagh and Worsley, 2005; Powell and Snellman, 2004; Thompson, 2005). And yet despite reported disquiet about widening divisions in the labour market, policy makers continue to propose a narrow vision of equality of opportunity in a high-skill, high-reward economy (Department of Trade and Industry, 2004) – the widely invoked vision of a brave new world of 'better' work:

> 'few people now toil under arduous or hazardous conditions. Most people work in safe, clean environments. Modern workplaces are a long way from the dark satanic mills of industrializing Britain. Increasingly, work environments look, feel, sound and even smell great. . . Toynbee and others are fighting the industrial battles of the past, when poorly paid workers were forced to work long hours in terrible conditions at jobs they hated. Work is not like that anymore' (Reeves, 2001, pp. 70 and 140).

This upbeat theme is represented by the focus on the 'high road' of management, which promises a 'softer' style of management and includes the development and utilisation of new skills. Such a focus relies on an increasing availability of 'good' work created in a service producing economy which in turn relies on the utilisation of soft, tacit knowledge and promises a long overdue recognition of 'people skills' as a quantifiable expertise (Bolton, 2005; Coats, 2005a; Department of Trade and Industry, 2004; Westwood, 2002). Unfortunately, what many of these accounts appear to miss is that the new forms of work, which represent the largest growth in employment in the Knowledge Economy, may be cleaner and physically safer but have gruelling and monotonous aspects in the same way as the 'dirty' jobs they have replaced (Bolton and Houlihan, 2005; Boyd, 2002; Bunting, 2004; Callaghan and Thompson, 2001; Houlihan, 2002; Taylor et al., 2002; Thompson, 2005). That is not to say, however, that 'dirty work' has disappeared. On the contrary, the growth in 'personal services'[2] partially represents a new 'upstairs and downstairs' where the 'cash rich but time poor' contract out domestic work – cleaning, gardening and child care – and a twenty-first century servant class emerges who regularly earn less than the minimum wage and have no employment rights or protection (Gregg and Wadsworth, 1996; Philpott, 2000; The Work Foundation, 2005).

Contemporary critical accounts of work offer a balance to the hyperbole of the knowledge economy rhetoric and question what the realities of work are for the majority of people. Whilst recognising that 'bad' work is unlikely to disappear (Coats, 2005a; Philpott, 2000; Taylor, 2002), there is a call to ensure that policy makers and companies recognise what the ingredients of good work might be – a recipe that clearly reflects the International Labour Organisation's (ILO) definition of 'decent work' in its emphasis on equality of access, employee voice and just reward (Coats, 2005b; Moynagh and Worsley, 2005; Taylor, 2002; Westwood, 2002). Given the focus on 'good work', and the growing concerns regarding its lack, an examination of work in the knowledge economy through the holistic lens of dignity at work seems timely.

Defining dignity and work

Human dignity is a concept that has been of central importance to western thinking and civilisation for centuries. For many, dignity is a matter of status and honour, free will and autonomy – indeed contemporary dictionary entries still fall back on the notion of dignity as 'dignified status' (Ackrill, 1981; Hampton, 1986). The concept of 'dignity' is what makes us human and separates us from animal life; it is something that we possess by virtue of our shared humanity (Pico della Mirandola, 1965; Sacks, 2002; Soyinka, 2004). Kant (1964) picks up on this latter theme in his secular account of people as 'ends in themselves' rather than a means to an end; he sees this as a principle of humanity that should be protected. Though often dismissed as a 'soft-headed attitude' that naively attempts to replace 'political with ethical ideas' (Weber, 1947), Kantian thinking is built into moral and political philosophy and enshrined in international constitutions as a necessary commitment to the equal worth and dignity of all of humanity:

> 'According to the morality of human rights, because every human being has inherent dignity, no one should deny that any human being has, or treat any human being as if she lacks, inherent dignity' (Perry, 2005, p. 101).

A principal feature of this commitment is the central role work plays in human dignity as in 'dignity in labour', the right to decent work and the contribution that the possibilities for dignity contribute to a 'moral economy' and an equal and stable society (Durkheim, 1971; Lutz, 1995; Sayer, 2000; Smith, 1976; Veblen, 1994; Weber, 1947). And this remains the case in contemporary accounts of work and society, as dignity is closely associated with issues of respect, worth, esteem, equality, autonomy and freedom (Bourdieu, 1999; Charlesworth, 2000; Hodson, 2001; Personnel Today, 2005; Rayman, 2001; Sayer, 2005; Sennett, 2003). As such, the one word 'dignity' encompasses issues that have exercised scholars of work for decades and offers a holistic lens through which workplace issues might be examined. As Lutz eloquently states when speaking of human dignity and economics:

> 'we now have a human standard that is strongly critical of any socioeconomic thought embodied in theory or institutions that either denies human equality, autonomy and responsibility, or otherwise encourages the disrespect or degradation of the humanity in others by manipulating or exploiting them' (Lutz, 1995, p. 179).

This 'human standard' is now widely recognised, and the relationship between dignity and work and its realisation as a collective achievement rather than an individual attribute is enshrined in international constitutions (United Nations, 1948). Campaigning organisations such as the ILO's (2005) call for an international standard for 'decent work', clearly linking the concept with the achievement of human dignity. Nevertheless, despite a common association, there is little doubt that dignity at work remains an elusive subject. There is general consensus, though originating from many different perspectives, that dignity is an essential core human characteristic. It is overwhelmingly presented as meaning people are worth something as human beings, that it is something that should be respected and not taken advantage of and that the maintenance of human dignity is a core contributor to a stable 'moral order'. However, when entering the realms of work and the complexities of exchanging labour for a wage, the definitions become much less clear. In selling one's labour does one also relinquish autonomy, freedom, equality and, often, well-being – the very ingredients of life that have been most commonly associated with human dignity? Or, is it the case that paid work can provide the means for all of these core elements of a quality life to be realised? For Marx, the selling of one's labour leads to alienation and loss of dignity and yet he, and many others, suggests there is a fundamental dignity in labour.

Hodson's insightful analysis of classic workplace ethnographies attempts to deal with these complexities within a framework of the 'four faces of dignity'. He suggests there are four principal challenges to the achievement of human dignity in the workplace: 'mismanagement and abuse, overwork, limits on autonomy and contradictions of employee involvement' (Hodson, 2001, p. 5). Turning to the essences of it, Rayman (2001, p. 4) proposes that there are 'three pillars of dignity at work – livelihood, self-respect, and social responsibility'.

From this, it becomes apparent that dignity at work is a multifaceted phenomenon. Hodson, as many others, talks of meaningful work as a major source of dignity at work. However, he also adds economic and political dimensions to the topic when he talks of democracy, justice and equality. Likewise, Rayman (2001) speaks of a 'dignity spectrum' where people are placed depending on their ability to survive in conditions of global capitalism, underscoring the reality of the relative but deeply systemic and socially impacting dynamics of dignity. It is therefore important to see that it is not a mere case of dignity existing as a core human characteristic that is realised through fulfilling labour, but that various organisational structures and practices will impact on how dignity is realised and that the overarching structural relations of a capitalist economy in which organisations must operate and survive will, in turn, impact on how these organisational practices are shaped and implemented. We cannot therefore view dignity as an individual and situational thing, but must see its global relationships and consequences.

Building on this foundation, it might be suggested that dignity can be more clearly explored if its multidimensional character is highlighted. Despite the difficulties of arriving at a clear definition of dignity at work, there appears to be defining features that are widely recognised as necessary contributors. There are the objective factors of security, just reward, equality, voice and well-being, but there are also the subjective factors inherent in an understanding of human dignity, as presented in moral and political philosophy, of autonomy, meaning and respect. These objective and subjective factors might be usefully thought about as *dimensions of dignity*. Dignity in labour via interesting and meaningful work with a degree of responsible autonomy and recognised social esteem and respect may be understood as *dignity in work;* structures and practices that offer equality of opportunity, collective and individual voice, safe and healthy working conditions, secure terms of employment and just rewards would lead to workers attaining *dignity at work*. Thinking in terms of dimensions allows for a detailed analysis of dignity at work that covers many important issues in the world of work and how experiences may differ. For example, many people enjoy *dignity in work* as they have some autonomy and/ or meaning in the type of work they do but not *dignity at work* in the sense they do not enjoy good terms and conditions of employment, or respectful social relations. Yet others may carry out mundane and monotonous work but benefit from *dignity at work* in that they gain from a physically healthy working environment and secure terms and conditions. Combined, dimensions of dignity represent a useful opportunity for a holistic analysis of work in its blend of the inherent dignity of the human person with the political economy and conditions that may deny this basic human right.

Dimensions, divisions, denials and development of dignity

A focus on dignity at work is hardly a new way of looking at work – the concept of dignity lies at the heart of the study of work and has informed endless studies of humanity and work. But what is different about this edited collection is the way it reflects the different dimensions of dignity, how divisions and denials can occur and also how there are many developments in the workplace that attempt to create and support dignity in and at work. The book is presented in three parts: *Defining Dignity*; *Dignity, Work and the Political Economy* and *Dignity in Workplace Practice*.

Part One, *Defining Dignity*, includes this chapter and two other contributions – reflective pieces offered by Andrew Sayer and Stephen Ackroyd. Andrew Sayer considers how respect and recognition contribute significantly to the achievement of human dignity. He feels that dignity at work is about respecting people *as people* and not merely as a means to an end, though he questions how this may be put into practice due to the instrumental nature of organisational life. However, at the heart of Andrew's analysis is his emphasis on the importance of human relationships that acknowledge the contribution people make, that engage in the minor courtesies of social exchange, that offer people autonomy and do not treat people as mere objects or instrument – in other words, relationships that recognise humanity and the importance of respect, esteem and dignity. An element of Andrew's scrutiny of what creates and maintains dignity centres on the status that is attached to work; this is also a theme that is at the heart of Stephen Ackroyd's chapter. He focuses on the relationship between dirt, work and dignity and ponders how it is that some occupations may be potentially deemed undignified due to their involvement with certain pollutants and yet are not; somehow dignified work is achieved and the status of the worker maintained despite unsavoury and socially taboo aspects of the work itself. Stephen considers three different work groups – labourers, miners and abattoir workers – as a means of understanding the connection between dirt and society and what this means for dignified work.

Chapters focusing on *Dignity, Work and the Political Economy* make up the second part of the book. In Chapter 4, David Coats asks 'just how good are British workplaces?' David uses the concept of respect at work to persuasively argue that the employment relationship today remains characterised by imbalances of power despite any claims to the contrary based on the changing nature of work and employment and enlightened people management practice. In the same vein as Andrew Sayer, David contends that work is an activity that should engage all that it is to be human and the employment relationship cannot be viewed as a mere economic transaction if Human Resource Management claims of happier workers and increased productivity are to be realised. He goes on to set out a realistic agenda for positive change based on the importance of the availability of 'good work' that is recognised and endorsed by government regulation. In the following chapter, John Philpott takes a different stance and reasons that the economic case and the social justice case for humanistic approaches to people management can be successfully combined into a form of 'shared interest capitalism', with the result that productive work can also be good work. However, whilst John sets out a positive case for how this can be achieved he recognises the difficulties involved when cost-based business models are still widespread in the UK and the take-up of high-performance people management practices is low. Nevertheless, he advocates a gradualist approach to policy and business engagement rather than what he describes as 'quick fix' solutions that he argues can alienate those who need to be fully involved and also create social and economic costs as well as benefits. Chapter 6 moves from an analysis of possibilities for good and dignified work in the formal economy to an exploration of work in the informal economy. Niall Cooper and Catherine May address a relatively unexplored area and present a compelling examination of the diverse nature of the informal economy and the difficulties involved in capturing people's experiences of work in this area. Despite these difficulties, Niall and Catherine offer valuable insights into what they call the 'Cinderella subject' of the labour market – 'a badly dressed, poor relation' – and call for more research and effective policy intervention that will help to transform exclusionary mechanisms into ones of inclusion.

The third section of the book offers a range of perspectives centred on *Dignity in Workplace Practice*. Randy Hodson's insightful analysis of managerial behaviours that might support working with dignity is the first contribution in this section. Randy presents a sophisticated methodology which uses a combination of survey and ethnographic methods. He 'measures' dignity across three facets: the opportunity to engage in organisational citizenship and the absence of excessive vertical and horizontal conflict. He concludes that management competence is far more important than many practitioners and organisational analysts currently recognise and argues that it needs to be more widely acknowledged just how much of an impact competent and respectful managerial behaviours have on widespread organisational well-being and the support of dignity at work. Chapter 8 also focuses on management practice as a mechanism for creating and supporting dignity at work. In their review of best practice people management (BPPM) and its utilisation in the top 10 companies proclaimed as 'best' in the *Sunday Times Top 100 Companies to Work For* list, Sharon Bolton and Gemma Wibberley offer a holistic analysis of the relationship between BPPM and dignity at work. They find that in assessing 'best' companies, an emphasis is placed on the softer aspects of management and intrinsic reward for employees, to such an extent that it is difficult to find companies that offer 'bundles' of best practice management. Sharon and Gemma conclude that lack of age and gender diversity and poor material reward is a feature of some companies proclaimed to be the best. However, despite this, there is evidence of companies investing in innovative people management practices and attempting to provide some elements of dignity at work via involvement and empowerment mechanisms. Information technology is the focus of Chapter 9. Bill Doolin and Laurie McLeod argue that technology permeates society and the organisation and process of work and, therefore, it is vital to address its implications for dignity at work. Bill and Laurie suggest that information technology is not neutral, but is imbued with social processes, norms and, ultimately, power that deeply affect people in organisations. They draw on the dimensions of dignity framework introduced earlier in this chapter to talk about the relationships between information technology and *dignity in work* as associated with autonomy and participation and *dignity at work* as related to electronic surveillance. Drawing on empirical examples, Bill and Laurie conclude that information technology can be enabling and empowering but only under conditions of shared trust where people are involved in decision making regarding its introduction and implementation and that technology is not seen as a replacement for human contribution but as a support mechanism. As a result, they suggest the need for reflection on the political nature of technology and its consequences for dignity in and at work.

The high-profile issue of bullying and harassment at work and its role in the denial of dignity is discussed by Charlotte Rayner in Chapter 10. Drawing on qualitative data collected from practitioners who had positive contributions to make regarding interventions, Charlotte highlights the difficulties in defining what behaviours constitute bullying at work and the complexities involved in dealing with the breakdown of relationships in the workplace. She goes on to discuss the challenges facing organisations in implementing effective policies that are able to cover a varied experience such as dignity at work but concludes that however difficult organisations must face up to the challenge, otherwise the line between interpersonal and institutional bullying becomes blurred by *organisational (in)action*. Chapter 11 once again addresses the notion of 'good work', but this time with a more focused analysis of workplace practice where Terry Wallace traces the development of work organisation in the Volvo Truck Corporation over a 35-year period from the 1970s. Terry, somewhat contentiously, argues that work has not experienced a fundamental shift away from the standardised and, some would describe, alienating production techniques associated with Fordism, despite many claims to the contrary. This is not to say, however, that there are not examples of 'good work strategies' to be found. Volvo is one such example. Nevertheless, Terry draws on data drawn from a longitudinal study of Volvo's Truck plant in Sweden to contend that such strategies are dependent on specific socio and economic conditions, meaning that the impetus to provide 'good work' is swamped by the competitive pressures of global capitalism. Diversity is the focus of Chapter 12 where Maeve Houlihan and Anastasia von Mende review the diversity debate and its relationship to dignity at work. Maeve and Nassia draw on empirical material to discuss the currently high profile, and relatively unexplored topic in the people management field, of migrant labour and they ask how diversity initiatives may be more clearly linked with a notion of dignity. Their argument concerning the mismatch between the rhetoric and reality of diversity policies is persuasively supported with compelling accounts from migrant workers which continually highlight the dignity and fragility of difference. Overall, the chapter offers an alternative to sanitised perspectives on what diversity management does and needs to do in order to support dignity at work.

The final chapter in the book is rather an unusual but very important contribution in that it comprises a selection of *short stories from industry*. This chapter supports the overall philosophy of the book in that it represents many different voices; a range of people involved in creating, maintaining and experiencing dignity at work. The *short story* chapter comprises of six individual reflective pieces that consider dignity and its role in corporate life. Four of the pieces are written from the perspective of people working in senior roles in various organisations who attempt to address issues involved in dignity in their own workplace, with the ultimate aim of creating 'cultures of respect'. Each contribution employs an informal and engaging style, presenting thoughts and feelings concerning not only the aims and objectives of various policies and practices but also the philosophy behind them and a consideration of their successes and failures and the difficulties involved in effective implementation. Amanda Jones talks about the Cooperative group's culture of respect policy, from the planning to the implementation stage; Adele Geoghegan persuasively argues that, based on her own management experiences, monetary reward is neglected as a core contributor to dignity at work; Corry de Jongh draws on her experience as counsellor to tell us 'Sean's Story' which reveals the very human consequences of bullying and harassment at work; Frank Hogan introduces empirical data drawn from an employee survey in order to explain how Royal Mail specified priority areas and set about building an organisation culture where people are recognised first and foremost as people requiring respect and recognition; Marina Meehana poignantly reflects on the paradox of being given the task of disseminating dignity at work polices whilst personally experiencing denials of dignity. The final section of the *short stories* chapter is made up of a selection of 'voices'; people from all walks of life talking about their experiences and definitions of dignity at work.

In total, the contributions to the edited collection *dimensions of dignity at work* bring together a broad range of ideas, experiences and possible agendas provided by a wide range of contributors. Whilst drawing on a diverse range of authors examining a multitude of different issues, all the chapters have a remarkable consistency – all express concern for the human condition and the ambition that dignity in the workplace will become an achievable aim. While a focus on dignity at work may not be a new way of looking at work, its emphasis has become too silent, and its importance too often overlooked. However, this book offers a unique opportunity to engage with the contemporary workplace in terms of the questions of *respect*, *good work* and ultimately *dignity at work*. Contributions to the book help to establish dignity at work as an issue to be taken seriously by business and policy makers and in doing so acts as a powerful representative of those who are regularly denied dignity at work.

References

Abrams, F. (2002) *Below the Breadline: Living on the Minimum Wage*, London: Profile Books.

Ackrill, J. (1981) *Aristotle the Philosopher*, Oxford: Oxford University Press.

Agassi, J. B. (1986) 'Dignity in the Workplace. Can Work be Dealienated?' *Journal of Business Ethics*, **5**, 4, 271–285.

AMICUS. http://www.amicustheunion.org

Andrea Adams Trust. http://www.andreaadamstrust.org

Bolton, S. C. (2005) *Emotion Management in the Workplace*, London: Palgrave.

Bolton, S. C. and Houlihan, M. (2005) 'The (Mis)-Representation of Customer Service', *Work, Employment and Society,* **19**, 4, 685–703.

Bourdieu, P. (1999) *The Weight of the World*, Cambridge: Polity Press.

Boyd, C. (2002) 'Customer Violence and Employee Health and Safety', *Work, Employment and Society*, **16**, 1, 151–169.

Bunting, M. (2004) *Willing Slaves: How the Overwork Culture is Ruling Our Lives*, London: Harper Collins.

Callaghan, G. and Thompson, P. (2001) 'Edwards Revisited: Technical Control and Call Centres', *Economic and Industrial Democracy*, **22**, 1, 13–57.

Charlesworth, S. (2000) *A Phenomenology of Working Class Experience*, Cambridge: Cambridge University Press.

Coats, D. (2005a) *Ideopolis: Knowledge Cities Working Paper 1: What is the Knowledge Economy?* The Work Foundation. http://www.theworkfoundation.com/pdf/Working_paper.pdf

Coats, D. (2005b) *An Agenda for Work: The Work Foundation's Challenge to Policy Makers*. Provocation Series, The Work Foundation. 1, 2. http://www.theworkfoundation.com/pdf/Agenda_for_work.pdf

Department of Trade and Industry (2004) 'Achieving Best Practice in Your Business. High Performance Work Practices: Linking Strategy to Performance Outcomes'. http://www.dti.gov.uk URN 05/665.

Dignity at Work Act (2001) http://www.parliament.the-stationery-office.co.uk/pa/ld200102/ldbills/031/2002031.pdf

Durkheim, E. (1971) *The Elementary Forms of the Religious Life*, London: George Allen and Unwin.

Ehrenreich, B. (2001) *Nickel and Dimed: Undercover in Low-Wage USA*, London: Granta Books.

Fox, M. (1994) *The Reinvention of Work*, San Francisco: Harper.

Freidman, A. (1977) *Industry and Labour: Class Struggle at Work and Monopoly Capitalism*, London: Macmillan.

Gemmill, G. (1977) 'Postscript: Toward the Person-Centred Organization', in *A Matter of Dignity: Inquiries into the Humanization of Work* (Heisler, W. and Houck, J., eds), London: University of Notre Dame Press, pp. 197–205.

Gregg, P. and Wadsworth, J. (1996) 'The Polarisation of Work', *Employment Policy Institute Employment Audit*, November.

Hampton, J. (1986) *Hobbes and the Social Contract Tradition*, Cambridge: Cambridge University Press.

Hodson, R. (1996) 'Dignity in the Workplace under Participative Management: Alienation and Freedom Revisited', *American Sociological Review*, **61**, 5, 719.

Hodson, R. (2001) *Dignity at Work*, Cambridge: Cambridge University Press.

Hodson, R. and Roscigno, V. J. (2004) 'Organizational Success and Worker Dignity: Complementary or Contradictory?', *American Journal of Sociology*, **110**, 3, 672.

Houlihan, M. (2002) 'Tensions and Variations in Call Centre Management Strategies', *Human Resource Management Journal,* **12**, 4, 67–85.

International Labour Organisation (2005) *Decent Work: The Heart of Social Progress*. http://www.ilo.org/public/english/decent.htm

Ishmael, A. (1999) *Harassment, Bullying and Violence at Work*, London: The Industrial Society.

Kant, I. (1964 [1785]). *Groundwork of the Metaphysics of Morals*. Translated by H.J. Paton. London: Harper and Row.

Khan, R. (1981) *Work and Health*, New York: Wiley.

Lutz, M. A. (1995) 'Centering Social Economics on Human Dignity', *Review of Social Economy*, **LIII**, 2, 171–194.

Maslow, A. (1965) *Management*, Homewood, IL: Irwin-Dorsey Press.

Moynagh, M. and Worsley, R. (2005) *Working in the Twenty-First Century*, ESRC and the Tomorrow Project.

Personnel Today (2005) 'New Pope will Defend Labour Rights', 19 July 2005. http://www.personneltoday.com/Articles/2005/07/19/30844/New+Pope+will+defend+labour+rights.htm

Perry, M. (2005) 'The Morality of Human Rights: A Nonreligious Ground?', *Emory Law Journal*, **54**, 97–150.

Peters, T. (1995) *The Pursuit of Wow*, New York: Macmillan.

Philpott, J. (2000) 'Behind the Buzzword: the New Economy', *Economic Report*, **14**, 8, Employment Policy Institute.

Pico della Mirandola (1965) *On the Dignity of Man*, Indianapolis/ Cambridge: Hackett Publishing Company Inc.

Powell, W. and Snellman, K. (2004) 'The Knowledge Economy', *Annual Review of Sociology*, **30**, 199.

Rayman, P. (2001) *Beyond the Bottom Line*, New York: Palgrave.

Reeves, R. (2001) *Happy Mondays. Putting the Pleasure back into Work*, London: Pearson Education Limited.

Rennie Peyton, P. (2003) *Dignity at Work: Eliminate Bullying and Create a Positive Working Environment*, Brunner: Routledge.

Rosow, J. M. (1979) 'Human Dignity in the Public-Sector Workplace', *Vital Speeches of the Day*, **45**, 6, 66.

Ryan, J. (1977) 'Humanistic Work: Its Philosophical and Cultural Roots', in *A Matter of Dignity: Inquiries into the Humanization of Work* (Heisler, W. and Houck, J., eds), London: University of Notre Dame Press, pp. 11–22.

Sacks, J. (2002) *The Dignity of Difference*, London: Continuum Books.

Sayer, A. (2000) 'Moral Economy and Political Economy', *Studies in Political Economy*, Spring, 79–103.

Sayer, A. (2005) *The Moral Significance of Class*, Cambridge: Cambridge University Press.

Schumacer, E. F. (1979) *Good Work*, New York: Harpur Colophon Books.

Sennett, R. (2003) *Respect: The Formation of Character in a World of Inequalities*, London: Allen Lane.

Smith, A. (1976) *The Wealth of Nations*, Chicago: University of Chicago Press.

Soyinka, W. (2004) *The Quest for Dignity: Reith Lectures 2004*, Lecture 4. http://www.bbc.co.uk/radio4/reith2004/

Taylor, R. (2002) *Britain's World of Work – Myths and Realities'*, Economic and Social Research Council. http://www.esrctoday.co.uk

Taylor, P., Mulvey, G., Hyman, J. and Bain, P. (2002) 'Work Organization, Control and the Experience of Work in Call Centres', *Work, Employment and Society,* **16**, 1, 133–150.

Tehrani, N. (2004) *Bullying at Work: Beyond Policies to a Culture of Respect.* http://www.cipd.co.uk/NR/rdonlyres/D9105C52-7FED-42EA-A557-D1785DF6D34F/0/bullyatwork0405.pdf

Thompson, P. (2005) 'Skating on Thin Ice: The Knowledge Economy Myth', Glasgow: University of Strathclyde.

Toynbee, P. (1975, 2003) *Hard Work. Life in Low Pay Britain,* London: Bloomsbury.

The Work Foundation (2005) *Domestics: UK Domestic Workers and their Reluctant Employers.* http://www.theworkfoundation.com/pdf/Domestics.pdf

United Nations (1948) *Universal Declaration of Human Rights,* General Assembly of the United Nations.

Veblen, T. (1994) *The Theory of the Leisure Class,* New York: Dover Publications.

Weber, M. (1947) *The Theory of Social and Economic Action.* Translated by Henderson, A. M. and Talcott Parsons, Talcott Parsons (ed.) New York: The Free Press.

Westwood, A. (2002) 'Is New Work Good Work?' *The Work Foundation.* http://www.theworkfoundation.com/publications/

Wright, L. and Smye, M. (1997) *Corporate Abuse,* New York: Simon and Schuster.

2

What dignity at work means

Andrew Sayer

For those in high-status professions, dignity and dignified treatment
can usually be taken for granted, but it is often at risk for workers lower
down the occupational hierarchy. If we are denied respect by others
or, through no fault of our own, lack the things that are respected,
it is hard to maintain our self-respect. Encountering disrespect can
be harder to bear and more troubling for workers than low pay or
job insecurity. As the historian E.P. Thompson (1963) argued, many
political struggles, including the rise of the labour movement itself,
were about gaining recognition and respect as much as about gaining
more material wealth (see also Sennett and Cobb, 1973). Still today,
many struggles which are presented as purely about remuneration
and job security are actually motivated significantly by the pursuit of
dignity and respect – better pay being taken to signify recognition.
Dignity at work therefore matters to both employees and employers
and needs to be discussed.

The most serious kinds of denial of workers' dignity have been
highlighted recently by campaigns such as that of Britain's AMICUS
union and the Department of Trade and Industry for 'dignity at work'
in response to bullying and harassment. However, as I shall try to
show, dignified work requires much more than just the absence of such
treatment. It involves workers being respected as people and not being
treated merely as means to others' ends, being allowed autonomy and
not having others take advantage of their vulnerability, being trusted
to act responsibly, being taken seriously and listened to, and having
types of work which are not themselves demeaning. These, I argue, are
the key elements or preconditions of dignity at work. In any situation,
they are precarious, but they are especially so where there are durable

inequalities of power – whether they involve the stigmatisation of particular groups (sexism, racism, homophobia, etc.) or the internal inequalities of organisations – and where the instrumental goals of organisations are pursued at the expense of employees' well-being.

In considering what dignity involves, it is helpful to discuss it in relation to a number of other feelings and conditions, all of which have major implications for our well-being. Some of these, such as integrity, respect, pride, recognition, worth and standing or status, are positively related to dignity. Others, such as shame, stigma, humiliation, lack of recognition or being mistrusted or taken for granted, are negatively related to it. Moral concepts like these are fuzzy and shade into one another; we can understand dignity better in relation to these other concepts than in isolation. My own interpretation of dignity at work is based on a combination of empirical research and personal observation regarding inequality, and philosophical analyses of recognition and respect. I shall first set out the key elements and preconditions of dignity, noting how the instrumental character of economic organisations puts the dignity of workers at risk. I shall then discuss how durable inequalities tend to undermine the dignity of those in subordinate groups. These inequalities are argued to be of two kinds – 'identity-sensitive', such as those deriving from sexism, racism, homophobia and ableism – and identity-insensitive, such as those deriving from the nature of economic organisations in capitalist society. I shall then discuss the kinds of work which are seen as inherently undignified and propose a distinction between servile and service work, and conclude.

Key elements of dignity

To be dignified or have dignity is first to be in control of oneself, competently and appropriately exercising one's powers. Most obviously, then, dignity is about self-command and autonomy. As with so many other matters relating to moral sentiments, dignity is partly consciously, partly unconsciously signalled through the body – in our bearing, in how we hold ourselves. The closely associated sense of respect also implies autonomy, for to respect someone implies refraining from attempting to colonise or control their lives, and keeping a certain 'respectful' distance from them. From a normative point of view, it is important that what is respected in the other person includes not only what they have in common with us but what is different. For an employer to refuse to recognise the religion or culture of minority ethnic workers – for example, the need of Muslim workers to observe Ramadan – would be an affront to their dignity.[1] To have dignity and to have one's dignity recognised is to be treated as an end in oneself, at least in part, and not merely as a means to someone else's ends, or as substitutable for someone else. It is hard to respect someone who has no autonomy, no distinctiveness or individuality, no will of their own and who passively obeys the will of others. They lack dignity.

It will already be apparent that dignity is an elusive quality depending not only on how an individual behaves but on how others treat her. It can therefore be a fragile thing because we are deeply *social* beings – vulnerable and dependent on others – physically, psychologically and economically – throughout our lives. If others treat us in an undignified manner, for example, by refusing to acknowledge us as ends in ourselves and treating us wholly as means to their own ends, then we may find we have to struggle to maintain our dignity in the face of this treatment, for example, by limiting acknowledgement of those who disrespect us, by concealing our hurt or by signalling our *indignation,* whether silently or verbally. If, on the other hand, they invariably respect our autonomy, then dignity may become something we can take for granted and do not have to work at. In both cases, dignity depends on both the actor and her others.

Second, to lack dignity is also to be unable to exercise the kinds of powers we associate with being a capable adult, both basic ones – controlling our bodies – and 'higher' ones involving complex tasks, especially in social situations.[2] Individuals who lose these powers, perhaps through illness or old age, may find it hard to maintain their dignity. We may also regard some practices which we are called upon to do as 'beneath our dignity', because they do not allow us to exercise those powers, or else are associated with bodily and other functions which are viewed with disgust or disdain; at worst, they might reduce us to no more than our animal status.[3] Being 'above' such things is a source of dignity.

Third, maintaining our dignity depends not only on how we conduct ourselves and whether others accord us respect for this, but on whether we *have* things which others regard as essential or normal ['the social bases of self-respect', as Rawls called them (Rawls, 1971)]. This is why people who have little income often engage in quite expensive conspicuous consumption – to show that they are worthy of respect.

Fourth, dignity is also associated with seriousness and being taken seriously. Someone who is never serious lacks dignity; if they are serious but are never taken seriously by others, it is hard for them to maintain their dignity and self-respect.[4] This includes being able to speak out and be listened to and have their views taken seriously. It is important both for individuals' self-respect and welfare and for the success of organisations that disagreements and criticisms can be aired. An important aspect of dignity is being allowed to disagree (respectfully) with others without this undermining our position or inviting contempt from others. Allowing people to lose arguments or admit mistakes without loss of face or humiliation (i.e., allowing them to maintain their dignity) is important both for morale and for organisational learning.

Related to these characteristics of seriousness and autonomy, acting in a dignified way implies a measure of self-control and composure, including limiting displays of strong emotions, whether happy or sad or angry. Such behaviour is especially expected of professionals, as it helps clients to put their trust in them because they seem in command of themselves, or 'together', and hence more likely to be competent. Those kinds of work which involve a closer emotional engagement with others, such as counselling and nursing, involve a difficult balance between avoiding coldness and insensitivity on the one hand, and an unwanted or premature familiarity and emotionality which would indicate disrespect towards the client on the other. Again, respect implies a certain distance. What is now termed 'emotional work' includes consideration of individuals' dignity. The case of nursing is particularly striking because of the difficulty for nursing auxiliaries in maintaining their own dignity while carrying out tasks which would normally be regarded as undignified, such as wiping bottoms, and maintaining the dignity of patients whose autonomy and capacities are impaired. Sometimes, doing such undignified but necessary jobs may win them respect.[5]

Being treated not purely as a means to someone else's ends or as invisible, but as an end in oneself, a person in one's own right, is thus crucial. Yet of course in employment, the employee is not hired out of respect for them or charity but because of their usefulness to the employer. At the same time, earning an income is itself a source of dignity, in that it demonstrates autonomy and self-reliance, rather than dependence on others. The valuation of 'the dignity of work' and 'social usefulness' (Sennett and Cobb, 1973, p. 266) is a crucial motivation, one neglected by economists who imagine that it is in the self-interest of people to free-ride on others' efforts wherever possible.

In any relation of economic exchange, the purpose of interacting with others is in order to exchange money for goods or services. The instrumental nature of these relationships can threaten the dignity of the worker or seller unless respect for them as persons is signalled in some way. At the minimum, we may do this by simply saying 'hello'. Precisely because they signal respect, 'pleasantries' are not trivial and taking time out from the pursuit of the organisation's goals to acknowledge workers as persons with their own concerns can make an important difference to the experience of work. To treat others as merely an object or instrument, as in the case reported by Hodson of managers who would take products out of the hands of the workers working on them without saying anything to acknowledge them, is to undermine their dignity (Hodson, 2002). Of course such 'courtesies' can be given merely instrumentally in order to gain favours, but recognition is valued precisely where the other does not have a personal instrumental interest in giving it.

In all these aspects, we see the way in which dignity is established through a relation between the individual and others, and that while it depends to some extent on how the individual behaves, it can be confirmed or undermined by others. It exemplifies both our vulnerability and dependence on others on the one hand and our capacity for autonomy and self-direction on the other. Our self-respect is strongly dependent on whether others treat us with respect. It is both a highly personal matter and a matter of social standing. Dignified relations involve respect both for others' autonomy *and* their dependence on us, so that we do not take advantage of their vulnerability.

The relation between autonomy and vulnerability is evident in the way in which being trusted enhances our dignity: others allow us autonomy and discretion on the assumption that we will not betray their trust by taking advantage of the fact that they have made themselves vulnerable precisely by putting their trust in us. Trust signals recognition of our competence and probity. Refusal of trust, on the other hand, erodes dignity. In her report on undertaking low wage jobs in the USA, Barbara Ehrenreich notes the humiliating character of practices such as searching employees' purses (legal in workplaces in the USA) to make sure they have not stolen anything, and of requiring employees to take random drug tests. As she points out, many forms of surveillance of workers, or restrictions such as being banned from talking with other workers, are indignities (Ehrenreich, 2001, p. 211). They signal lack of trust in workers' competence and probity, and lack of respect for them as persons. To be told how to do things that one would in any case do perfectly well of one's own volition, and to be constantly under surveillance, may be humiliating. This is one reason why service workers may resent having to use scripted conversations in dealing with clients. The refusal of trust and discretion is itself an indignity.

Lack of trust may 'crowd out' trustworthy behaviour, reducing people's willingness to make an effort to work well. Further, to assume, as management often does, that people will only work well for rewards, rather than doing a good job for its own sake, is demeaning and fails to respect their dignity. It overestimates their dependence on others as a source of motivation and underestimates their capacity for acting responsibly. This is not to say that people will always be trustworthy, or that recognition and rewards are unimportant, but to treat an employee's actions as purely motivated by the expectation of reward is to reduce virtue and integrity to instrumental action for the purposes of exchange, and may have a demotivating effect (Brennan and Pettit, 2004; Frey, 1997; Le Grand, 2003). Doing some things for their own sake (e.g., working extra time to finish a job because it needs finishing) also seems more dignified and virtuous than doing them purely out of self-interest precisely because it implies treating those for whom the job is done as ends in themselves.[6] Of course, the point of employment for employees *is* to get an income, but it is not necessarily the only point. Their dignity also matters, and in being trusted to act well they are also being valued as persons, and not merely for carrying out some task properly. People need recognition too, but as responsible, capable people and not merely for specific actions that are useful to the organisation: if the recognition is given in a way which seems controlling by gearing it too closely to specific actions, as in rewarding a dog with a biscuit for obeying an order, it may seem demeaning rather than dignifying (Brennan and Pettit, 2004).

Although, from a normative point of view, respect for individuals' *rights* should be unconditional, respect for behaviour and character has to be conditional.[7] Making respect for others obligatory, no matter how they behave – the customer is always right, even when abusive – rather than conditional, devalues it completely and is hardly dignified or dignifying. To respect people's dignity is to treat them as responsible for their actions, and to respond positively or negatively towards them according to what we consider they deserve. It is not about engaging in compulsory niceness and refraining from judgement. 'A person who is punished for his [sic] misdeeds is held responsible for them in a concrete way' (Rachels, 1978, p. 159). Conversely, to treat them as not responsible for what they say and do is to undermine their dignity by refusing to acknowledge their ability to think and act for themselves, indeed it is insulting.

People may manage their emotional interactions with others, but this does not necessarily mean they are manipulative or taking advantage of them; indeed it may be intended respectfully, altruistically or 'philanthropically' (Bolton, 2005). But often, in work situations, workers are indeed expected to exercise their emotional labour in a more instrumental way for the good of the company ('pecuniary emotion management', to use Bolton's term) rather than the good of the customer or client. As Bolton suggests, because attending to people's needs and wants is a highly complex and subtle business, attempts to control and script this may be clumsy and ineffective. By contrast, it may be service workers' gift of philanthropic emotion management, drawing upon tacit social skills and emotional intelligence, which actually enables good service. Suppressing the worker's scope for discretion in such cases may be undignified for both worker and customer.

Dignity in and against inequality

The word 'dignitary' hails from an earlier age of aristocratic privilege and authorised inequality, but it reminds us that dignity was once seen as the preserve of the dominant. While that privilege no longer has authority, current forms of inequality, equally undeserved, have taken its place, such as those of class, gender and race, and obstruct the pursuit and maintenance of dignity.

There are two kinds of inequality that are relevant here. The first, 'identity-sensitive', exemplified by sexism, racism, homophobia and ableism, are forms of unwarranted unequal treatment which respond to certain constructions of people's identities (Sayer, 2005). A crucial element of all these ills is treatment of members of the relevant groups in ways which are undignified: typical forms are mistrust, underestimation of their ability and probity, refusal to take them seriously, and worst of all, taking advantage of their vulnerability, including the special vulnerability which derives precisely from their stigmatisation, as in sexual and racial harassment. In addition, these social groups are often denied normal access to the 'social bases of respect' – the resources and practices which are seen as valuable in the wider society.

The second kind of inequality is structural to modern economies in both the nature of the employment relation itself and the internal hierarchies or inequalities of economic organisations. Although these inequalities may correlate with, respond to and reinforce inequalities arising from identity-sensitive mechanisms of sexism and racism, they can exist even in the absence of the latter. They are products of 'identity-insensitive' economic mechanisms (Sayer, 2005). The employment relation is itself unequal in that the employee usually has fewer options than the employer, and the latter is dominant and indeed normally dominates. In turn, there are inequalities among employees in terms of pay, security and working conditions, and indeed in all the respects which we noted as important for dignity. There are further inequalities in relation to consumers and clients, often but not always in favour of the latter. The very existence of inequalities and relations of domination means that, objectively, individuals' autonomy and dependence are unequal, and although this does not rule out the possibility of dignified employment, it means that some will find it easier to maintain their dignity than others.

There is a world of difference between claiming or being accorded respect for one's conduct and claiming or being accorded it merely for one's social position, particularly where we do not deserve that position, or 'deserve' it as a result of having taken advantage of an inherited advantageous social position. (Inherited advantages are not a thing of the past: no-one deserves the class position that they are born into, yet it has a considerable effect on their life chances and the kind of people that they become.) Amongst equals, the granting or refusal of respect is responsive to how people actually behave. But where there is inequality, respect may be demanded by the dominant, and refused to the subordinate, irrespective of whether such expectations are merited in terms of behaviour. Inequalities of power distort and inhibit recognition, for as Hegel identified in his discussion of master–slave relations, the dominant can never get adequate recognition from subordinates, because the latter are not in a position to give their honest view without prejudice to their own security, and are also likely to lack the information and training to be able to give an informed opinion. Their expressed opinion therefore cannot be taken seriously. Recognition is most valuable when it comes from equals who are free to say what they really think, and/or from those who have the expertise to evaluate the behaviour in question. Deference to superiors that is expected and merely based on undeserved differences in standing is, at least to some degree, humiliating for the subordinate, though they may become thoroughly accustomed to it. If the service worker cannot treat the customer as an equal, which implies being able to sanction rude and unreasonable treatment, and has to accept uncritically whatever they say or do, then this may be seen as sacrificing their dignity. 'Where the customer is king, unequal exchanges are normal, and from the beginning customer and client assume different rights to feeling and display. The ledger is supposedly evened by a wage' (Hochschild, cited in Bolton, 2005, chapter 1). Conversely, where the employee is in a position of authority or expertise in relation to the user (as in the case of lecturer–student or doctor–patient relations), it may require some care to make sure the user is respected at the same time as he or she is evaluated or advised.

Further, where there are durable inequalities, double standards often appear, so that the same behaviour (e.g., absenteeism and theft of company property) is seen more critically in the subordinate than the dominant (Sayer, 2005). Often the double standards are gendered, so that what is seen as beneath the dignity of men (e.g., simpering compliance and making the tea) is expected of women. When we criticise someone for imagining that some task is 'beneath their dignity', while others do the same thing without complaint, it is because they assume that they are somehow more worthy than others, indeed 'above' them. In other words, we suspect them of arrogance, snobbery or sexism. Again, dignity can easily be confused with rank and dominance.

However, equality or inequality of respect and access to respect is not just a matter of expressions of attitudes and interpersonal relations. If employers make pronouncements about treating everyone with equal respect, but in their actions, and in the conditions which they provide for their employees, treat them unequally, then their words are likely to be seen as hollow, as being contradicted by their deeds. Expressions of equality of recognition which are not backed up by equality of treatment and distribution of resources, including job security and the provision of working conditions, are likely to appear hypocritical. Again, these are part of the social bases of self-respect. The micro-politics of distribution and recognition are thus intimately related (Honneth, 1995; Sayer, 2005).[8]

We might say that it ought to be possible for all to be treated with dignity *despite* inequalities, but the 'despite' is significant. And just because people at the bottom often do not complain does not mean that there's no problem; the effects may be embodied in the form of low self-esteem and low expectations. Alternatively, they may resist, as Hodson (2001) emphasises, and this may help them maintain their dignity, though it is important not to romanticise the picture by overlooking cases where resistance is absent. Even where dignity derives from sustained resistance to disrespect, it is clearly a compensatory assertion of dignity, in that it substitutes for the absence of respectful treatment. Without palpable recognition, reflected in circumstances and treatment as well as verbal expressions, maintaining one's dignity is merely a way of holding oneself in the face of indignities – a matter of fortitude and forbearance. This may itself elicit respect, but then that respect may also reduce feelings of guilt or shame on the part of those who benefit from such inequality (echoes of the noble savage sentiment).

Sometimes the resistance may be direct and explicit but often it takes the form of increased efforts to assert autonomy, self-control and respectability as in the moral self-discipline and valuation of hard work of the American working men studied by Lamont, though as in all pursuits of respectability, it can involve a kind of self-repression too – a theme often noted in literature on working-class life. Alternatively, resistance may take the form of pursuit of status in spheres the dominant cannot affect, such as efforts to dress up where the dominant dress down and to demonstrate pride, style and 'class' (Lamont,

2000; Skeggs, 1997). However, for those who adopt this strategy, it is often not only a matter of establishing worth relative to the dominant but about distinguishing themselves from those who are even more disadvantaged (showing they are 'above' them); snobbery, racism and other forms of undignified treatment are not limited to those at the top. In either case, those in subordinate positions may be in a Catch-22 situation, where maintaining their dignity allows the more fortunate to assume that there is nothing wrong with their situation, while failing to maintain their dignity invites contempt and casual assumptions that they deserve their fate.

If we take matters of dignity and respect seriously, then because of the way in which recognition of worth and distribution of wealth are so closely related, we have at some point to confront the problem of undeserved inequalities. Expressions of respect between dominant and subordinate which merely accommodate these inequalities are devalued and deferential for the former and condescending and consolatory for the latter (Sayer, 2005). Without tangible improvements in the distribution of the social bases of respect – which must mean both significant reductions in economic inequality and restraints on the tendency of instrumental behaviour in economic life to override respect for persons – demands for recognition of dignity risk inviting facile, token responses in the form of mere espousals of equality.

Dignified and undignified work

Particular kinds of work may be seen as dignified or undignified in themselves, or at least, in the latter case, as difficult to do in a dignified way. The distribution of dignified and undignified work varies strongly by class, gender and race and tends to be taken as confirming the status of those who do it. Again, just what is seen as dignified or undignified tends to be seen in terms of double standards based on class, gender and race; for example, serving others may be seen as undignified in men and as dignified in women.

Whether work seems dignified or undignified is also related to skill and the difference between service and servility. The dignity of skilled work derives from the respect and self-respect which is conditional on proficiency in carrying out demanding tasks that those who need them doing could not do themselves. Other things being equal, a skilled job brings more respect and is a stronger source of dignity than one which anyone can do. Imagine I were to hire a cleaner, despite being an able-bodied person capable of doing the same work myself. On the same day that the cleaner comes, I hire a plumber to deal with a burst pipe.

I may treat both civilly, with unconditional respect for them as persons, but the plumber finds it easier to maintain a sense of dignity because he or she[9] is doing something we both know I cannot do. Although the cleaner might find some respect in doing the job well, it is more difficult, because we both know that I could also do the job as well or nearly as well, and the only reason I am not doing it myself is that our incomes are sufficiently unequal for me to be able to afford to pay them to do it. Thus, low-skilled work that is done for others who could perfectly well do it themselves is not in general a source of dignity, beyond that which derives purely from having a source of income rather than being dependent on state benefits. The household cleaner's job signals *servility* – and is properly called servant labour – while the plumber is providing a specialist, skilled service (see Cox, 2005; Ehrenreich 2001; Ehrenreich and Hochschild, 2002; Tronto, 2002). However, serving others may be a source of dignity where it provides something for others that they could not easily provide for themselves and where it does not require compulsory deference.

There are also more problematic forms of indignity deriving from work involving dirt or practices which have some kind of taboo or stigma attached to them. With regard to the example of gynaecology nursing, Sharon Bolton comments:

> 'In its connection with 'dirty work', the work of the gynaecology nurse can be classified as 'physically, socially and morally tainted' . . . Physically tainted due to its association with the body, death and abnormality (in the form of aborted foetus); socially tainted through the regular contact with patients who are stigmatised for choosing to terminate a pregnancy, and morally tainted because what should remain private and invisible is made public and rendered visible' (Bolton, 2003, p. 8).

Those who have to do undignified work often try to distance themselves from the task and, as we have already noticed, engage in what might be termed 'compensatory respect work', making an effort to maintain their dignity and standing in the eyes of others. They may also use various coping mechanisms such as humour and other ways of 'letting off steam' when out of the gaze of supervisors and clients (Bolton, 2003).

The crucial issues here are: first, just what tasks should properly be regarded as undignified; second, if they are indeed properly regarded as undignified, whether they are avoidable (can they be eliminated or at least ameliorated); and third, if they are unavoidable, that they should not become the special preserve of a particular social group, thereby reinforcing their disadvantage with the stigma of dirty or servile work.

Conclusion

Maintenance of dignity is far from being a minor concern in daily life, and employment in particular, and for those for whom employment is an undignified experience this may trouble them more than other, more economic circumstances like low pay and lack of job security, although these too tend to be seen by others as indicators of lack of worth. Workers' dignity can be supported where they have autonomy and trust, are respected and not bullied, harassed or otherwise have their vulnerability taken advantage of and where they are taken seriously and listened to. The elimination of sexism, racism and equivalent forms of discrimination is important in this regard, but economic organisations are in any case unequal and structured by relations of domination and subordination which distribute the social bases of respect unequally. Further, such organisations are instrumental in character, not only inevitably treating their employees as means to their own ends but frequently, especially under pressure of competition, allowing this to result in lack of respect for their dignity. As I hope to have shown, both of these fundamental characteristics mean that for many employees, dignity at work is lacking or can only be maintained by strategies of resistance which by their very existence acknowledge the problem.

Finally, there is a more radical implication. As Samuel Scheffler has put it, 'equality is not, in the first instance, a distributive ideal [. . .] It is, instead, a moral ideal governing the relations in which people stand to one another' (Scheffler, 2003). Partial or wholesale refusal of dignity seriously contravenes this moral ideal, and within contemporary society this happens on a large scale. But if the whole structure of the formal economy is based on forms of organisation which reproduce inequalities in the relations in which people stand to one another, then that implies a complete solution must lie in the development of a different economic system, one founded on equality. That we do not have an available alternative that is clearly feasible and less bad than capitalism does not invalidate the critique which we have developed, and there is still room within a capitalist framework to make significant improvements in the enabling of dignity at work.

Acknowledgement

Thanks, with the usual disclaimers, to Sharon Bolton, Phil O'Hanlon and Steve Fleetwood for comments on earlier drafts and to Sharon for getting me interested in this topic in the first place.

References

Bolton, S. C. (2003) 'Women's Work, Dirty Work: The Gynaecology Nurse as "Other" ', *Gender, Work and Organisations*, **19**, 2, 5–23.

Bolton, S. C. (2005) *Emotion Management in the Workplace*, London: Palgrave.

Brennan, G. and Pettit, P. (2004) *The Economy of Esteem*, Oxford: Oxford University Press.

Cox, R. (2005) *The Servant Problem*, London: Tauris.

Ehrenreich, B. (2001) *Nickel and Dimed: On (Not) Getting by in America*, New York: Metropolitan Books.

Ehrenreich, B. and Hochschild, A. R. (eds) (2002) *Global Woman: Nannies, Maids and Sex Workers in the New Economy*, London: Granta.

Frey, B. (1997) *Not Just for the Money: an Economic Theory of Personal Motivation*, Cheltenham: Edward Elgar.

Gorz, A. (1983) *Critique of Economic Rationality*, London: Verso.

Hodson, R. (2001) *Dignity at Work*, Cambridge: Cambridge University Press.

Hodson, R. (2002) 'Demography or Respect?: Work Group Demography Versus Organizational Dynamics as Determinants of Meaning and Satisfaction at Work?' *British Journal of Sociology*, **53**, 2, 291–317.

Honneth, A. (1995) *The Struggle for Recognition: The Moral Grammar of Social Conflicts*, Cambridge: Polity.

Lamont, M. (2000) *The Dignity of Working Men*, Cambridge, MA: Harvard University Press.

Le Grand, J. (2003) *Motivation, Agency and Public Policy: Of Knights, Knaves, Pawns and Queens*, Oxford: Oxford University Press.

Rachels, J. (1978) 'What People Deserve', in *Justice and Economic Distribution* (Arthur, J. and Shaw, W. H., eds), Englewood Cliffs, NJ: Prentice-Hall, Inc., pp. 150–163.

Rawls, J. (1971) *A Theory of Justice*, Oxford: Oxford University Press.

Sayer, A. (2005) *The Moral Significance of Class*, Cambridge: Cambridge University Press.

Scheffler, S. (2003) 'What is Egalitarianism?' *Philosophy and Public Affairs*, **31**, 1, 5–39.

Sennett, R. and Cobb, J. (1973) *The Hidden Injuries of Class*, NY: Alfred A. Knopf.

Skeggs, B. (1997) *Formations of Class and Gender*, London: Sage.

Smith, A. (1984 [1759]) *The Theory of Moral Sentiments*, Indianapolis: Liberty Fund.

Taylor, C. (1994), 'The Politics of Recognition', in *Multi-Culturalism: Examining the Politics of Recognition* (Gutmann, A., ed.), Princetown, NJ: Princetown University Press.

Thompson, E. P. (1963) *The Making of the English Working Class*, Harmondsworth: Penguin.

Tronto, J. (2002) 'The "Nanny" Question in Feminism', *Hypatia*, **17**, 2, 34–51.

3

Dirt, work and dignity

Stephen Ackroyd

One broad category of things we devalue is dirt. If it gets on us, we may feel polluted or devalued too. This is unfortunate because work tends to be dirty: it creates (or otherwise involves handling) a great deal of extraneous or displaced matter.[1] Manual work involves moving material around, shaping and transforming things, creating useful products on the one hand and dirt, dust and detritus on the other. Hence, if dirt gives rise to indignity, much work is likely to be found undignified also. And this is the case despite claims that new forms of work are cleaner and unpolluted, rendering an analysis of dirt and work unmeaningful (Reeves, 2001). This chapter explores the conceptual connections between work, dirt and dignity by comparing and contrasting responses to three occupations that have typically produced a good deal of dirt. It is argued that, against expectation, exposure to dirt in daily work is not necessarily or intrinsically undignified. Considering the circumstances in which dirty work need not be undignified as well as the circumstances in which it becomes so is the rationale for this chapter.

Some different examples of manual work are considered by looking at what ethnographic and other sources have to say about them. The aim is to identify key similarities and differences in the ways these occupations have been organised, and in the ways in which the members of these occupations have responded to the experience of different kinds of work. First, the traditional occupation of agricultural labouring using hand tools is considered. This is a type of work that largely disappeared around the turn into the twentieth century in this country. From our contemporary conception of what was entailed in this job it was, fairly obviously, a dirty occupation. However, as we shall see, there are some aspects to this work that led to its being surprisingly free of any sense of pollution. Second, in contrast with agricultural labouring, the occupation of coal mining is analysed. To consider this, we shift our time location forward and focus on the period when coal was still largely hand got. In much of Britain, mining was not very mechanised well into the twentieth century; but, mechanised or not, it was spectacularly dirty. In contrast to manual work on the land, both the miners themselves and the general public clearly did regard the dirt that accompanied mining work as polluting. Third, in contrast to both labouring and mining, the responses of abattoir workers will be considered. Here again we shift our time frame forwards to look at an example of slaughterhouse work at the end of the twentieth century. This work, though also mostly manual as labouring and coal mining were, was and is regarded by many as grossly polluting. As a result, the abattoir worker sometimes goes to extraordinary lengths to avoid the effects of the dirt he handles.

These three occupations have been chosen for comparison for a number of reasons: First, despite their distinctiveness, they all involve the use of similar technology. All these occupation use traditional manual tools but are similarly also exposed to the use of some labour-saving machinery. Another similarity is that all these groups have also secured considerable de facto control over the organisation and pace of their work. These similar features allow us to home in on, and to consider analytically, the effects of exposure to different kinds of dirt and to compare the different effects it has. It will be argued that exposure to dirt is an important factor – possibly the most important factor – in shaping responses of workers to these different kinds of work. There are, of course, some other differences between these occupations which are important, among them the fact that only two of them have developed a supportive local community. Where it existed, community had the effect of insulating members of occupations from the force of any adverse judgements from the wider society and mitigated the effects of dealing with dirt. Table 1 sets out the main similarities and differences I think important between the occupations that are singled out for consideration.

Yet, on closer examination, it seems that the social stigma of working with dirt is the decisive factor in shaping responses to these different types of work. Although all these occupations are readily identifiable as involving exposure to dirt, they actually entail both different amounts of dirt and, perhaps more importantly, dirt of different degrees of potency. It is only by handling large amounts of dirt and/or potent pollutants that a sense of indignity in work arises. Gross pollution produces a sense of defilement that is very difficult to assuage or even defray.

Traditional agricultural labouring did indeed involve handling dirt. But a number of factors limit the impact of this. Among these is the

Table 1 Features of work in three manual occupations

	Agricultural labourers (late nineteenth century)	Coal miners (early to mid-twentieth century)	Slaughterhouse workers (late twentieth century)
Working with hand tools + limited labour-saving machinery	+	+	+
Self-organisation of work	+	+	+
Supportive community	+	+	−
Exposure to dirt	+	++	+++
Perception of indignity	−	+	++

fact that the amounts of dirt involved were often not very great, nor was the dirt involved (typically earth itself) thought particularly polluting. Mining, by contrast, whether it was mechanised or not, involved exposure to massive amounts of dirt as a by-product of its main task of hewing and removing coal. Though a matter of diminishing importance as the century progressed, the dirt of mining was an important factor in the evaluation of miners through much of the twentieth century. Exposure to dirt certainly did shape the responses of miners to their work. Finally, slaughterhouse workers are not only exposed to dirt in abundance, but the matter concerned comprises some potent pollutants – animal products and fluids such as urine and ordure and blood. Here it is argued that the anthropological record suggests that slaughterhouse workers are strongly polluted by the work they do. Even today, to a considerable extent, they cannot avoid or sidestep the social discredit which arises from their exposure to the potent dirtiness they handle every day.

To develop the argument further, a more detailed consideration of some of the literature relating to these three occupations will now be undertaken.

Agricultural labouring: delving the earth

In its original form – in an agricultural setting – labouring work involves digging or delving to clear or to tidy and to cultivate areas of ground. Today, a common name for what is dug is in fact simply 'dirt'. Because of this, it is no doubt a common assumption that agricultural labouring was inherently dirty. Historically, however, earth has not always been regarded as polluting as it now tends to be in an age that has some knowledge of microbiology.[2] Traditionally, indeed, the word dirt was reserved for worthless elements of soil – it was waste from which good earth or other useful matter was sharply distinguished. This is a usage that is preserved today in mining in which the coal or ore (which is sought and valued) is understood as different from the 'dirt' or 'spoil' (which is discarded). But, in agricultural communities, even the worthless dirt was not itself regarded as dangerous. The traditional saying: 'we all eat a peck of dirt before we die', which is still widely quoted, is indicative of the attitude. A peck, incidentally, was no small amount, being a little more than two imperial gallons (Leith, 1996).

Agricultural labouring was work undertaken with traditional hand tools, and the contribution of human effort to the accomplishment of the work was, fairly obviously, relatively great. Labouring typically involved hard labour. In this work, care of the tools, and the acquisition of skill in their use, was left to the workers themselves. However, in the traditional setting of agriculture, and the assumptions of the gentry to one side, this work was not experienced as degrading. Those who laboured and or knew what it truly entailed were free from any prejudice that it was or could be degrading. Obviously, it was socially necessary work, without which few could eat.

There are numerous ethnographic studies of rural villages in the British Isles beginning in the 1920s (Frankenberg, 1966), but they concentrate on land ownership, kinship networks and community relationships. There is remarkably little consideration in these studies of content and nature of agricultural work itself, and how it was done. There is certainly nothing to parallel the detailed participative studies of industrial work which came later. The writing which best approximates the ethnographic study of agricultural work itself is not in the anthropological record so much as in the diaries and letters of contemporary observers, such as George Bourne (1984) and Flora Thompson (1947). Thompson, for example, dutifully recorded her observations of farming and the behaviour of labourers as she knew them at the turn into the twentieth century. She is one of only very few writers who have left an account of the work habits of the agricultural labourer. Among other things, she notes the pride of labourers in the exercise of their skills:

> 'The labourers worked hard and well when they considered the occasion demanded it and kept up a good steady pace at other times. . . the majority took pride in their craft and were fond of explaining to an outsider that field work was not the fool's job that

some townsmen considered it to be. Things had to be done just so and at the exact moment, they said; there were ins and outs in good land work which took a man's lifetime to learn. . . ' (Thompson, 1947, p. 42).

A number of positive themes are found again and again from descriptions of manual work with hand tools such as spades and picks. One of the recurrent points of note, which is unexpected by those who have never tried using traditional tools, is the pleasure that comes from working with them. This point is made repeatedly by writers from the nineteenth century onwards. In the twentieth century, John Steinbeck, an unusually acute observer of people working, wrote in the *The Grapes of Wrath* (1957, p. 272) the following description of digging a ditch with a pickaxe:

'Tom hefted the pick. "Jumpin' Jesus! If she don't feel good!". . . .'

'Tom took off his coat and dropped it on the dirt pile. He pushed up his cap and stepped into the ditch. Then he spat on his hands. The pick rose into the air and flashed down. Tom grunted softly. The pick rose and fell and the grunt came at the moment it sank into the ground and loosened the soil'.

'Wilkie said: "Yes, sir, Pa, we got here a first grade muck-stick man. This here boy has been married to that there little digger."'

'Tom said: "I put in time (umph). Yes, sir, I sure did (umph). Put in my years (umph). Kinda like the feel (umph)."'

We find a similar note of enjoyment in the use of tools for labouring work in a surprising range of sources. The recent writing of the doyen of contemporary middle-class leisure gardeners, Monty Don, is one. Thus:

'Good tools do not make a good gardener, but they do add enormously to the pleasure of gardening. Every single time I use my spade I enjoy the experience. . . . It introduces a pure aesthetic element to a task above and beyond its success. Digging a rich loam becomes one of life's great sensual pleasures. Good soil plus good spade equals good time' (Don, 2003).

But it is not only the physical and aesthetic pleasures of labouring work that is referred to by commentators, though it is clearly an attribute that can dignify it. The effective use of hand tools depends on the physical strength and dexterity of the user, and, for this very reason, precisely because the work is not augmented by mechanical assistance, labouring is a context for heroic acts of courage and endurance. Flora Thompson notes that although the agricultural labourers she observed had developed some effort limitation practices, they also put forth prodigious efforts if the needs of the task required them. She writes of the agricultural labourers she knew that:

> 'Their favourite virtue was endurance. A man would say, ". . . that field o' oo-ats has to come in afore night, for there's rain a-comin''. But we did not flinch, not we! Got the last loo-ad under cover by midnight. A'most too fagged out to walk home; but we didn't flinch. We done it' (Thompson, 1947, p. 38).

A recent book which also indicates that work of heroic proportions can dignify labouring work is the story of Calum Macleod (Hutchinson, 2006). When the bureaucrats in Inverness decided that the expense involved did not justify connecting his croft to the outside world with a metalled road, Macleod single-handedly built a 2-mile long road of standard design across a wilderness of rock to his home on the island of Raasay in the Hebrides. In the hours not spent working his land, Macleod cleared the route for – and then built – a motorable road with only the work of his hands and the tools of the labourer. It took him 20 years of work. In the course of construction, he wore out six picks and six shovels, five sledge hammers, four spades, three wheel barrows and one crowbar. His chronicler, Roger Hutchinson, suggests that by the time his work was done, and the road was finished and tarred (1982), there was no community left for it to serve. Hutchinson also sardonically notes that when the crofter died (1987), at least the undertaker's hearse could collect him from his door. Although this feat of labouring was, in an obvious way, futile, it is impossible to regard it as anything other than dignified.

In the above accounts of dignified labouring, there are some common threads: these are the element of voluntariness, self-organisation and commitment. When these important features of work are absent, and discipline is externally imposed, and undertaking the work is primarily motivated by money, the possibility of dignified work comes into question. We should not forget that several of Fredrick Taylor's examples of successful 'scientific management' relate to the reorganisation of labouring work, albeit in factory settings. Despite the impressive figures of increased productivity that accompany Taylor's account of the reorganisation of the work of the labourer, Schmidt, for example, we do not tend to regard him as heroic, merely a dupe. It seems that once labouring work passes out of the control of the labourer, its dignity and value are under threat.

Perhaps the most notorious example of labouring that lacks dignity is that of the navvies who constructed first the canals and then the railways that contributed to the industrialisation of Britain. Accounts of the heroic efforts of work performance that navvies put forth as a matter of routine are of course to be found (Brooke, 1963; Coleman, 1983). But feats of work and endurance did not and could not dignify them. Here it was not only that the work was undertaken mainly for the wages it paid, that was the only problem. It was also that these workers were detached from any local community, and this made their existence threatening in the receiving society. The invasion of large numbers of men of alien speech and lawless habits understandably aroused fear. Partly the undignified status afforded the navvies is attributable to racism, as, in the early stages, many navvies in England were Irish and Scottish. But the facts that they were motivated and disciplined mainly by their need to earn, and often accepted very little regulation outside of that, were key factors determining their lack of social standing.

To conclude this discussion, the following points are noted. First, the dirt to which agricultural labourers were routinely exposed was not, at the time, held to be particularly dirtying. The capacity for the development of skill, the autonomy afforded the workers and the value of the results of the work undertaken all help to account for the fact that this work was not experienced as being at all polluting. The secure location of the workers in long-established communities also located the worker socially and insulated them from any alternative evaluations of the work they did.

Mining: dirt on an industrial scale

For much of its history since its beginnings, mining was a version of labouring. In its original forms, mining simply involved labouring using the same kinds of hand tools as were used in farming. In many areas, where there was coal-bearing land, for example, mining began by working surface outcrops of coal, and farmers sometimes pursued mining as an additional activity alongside agriculture. However, mining as an activity acquired a stigma that by and large farming did not. In Britain, coal mining with hand tools persisted a very long time, well into the twentieth century. Hall (1981) suggests that British mines were very slow in modernising; by 1934 only about 40 per cent of British coal was cut by machine, compared with nearly 100 per cent cutting and handling in the Rhur. Writing about a semi-mechanised mine in 1956, Dennis et al. (1956) emphasise the amount of manual work involved in mining at that date.

Mechanised mining involves a series of considerable engineering challenges, but the problem of overcoming these was not the main reason that mechanised mining made slow headway in Britain. Hand working of coal persisted well into the twentieth century because of the particular system of mine ownership and mine-working that had emerged in this country. Because of peculiarities of history and law, even the owner of 'freehold' land could not claim rights to what was below the subsoil. Subsurface minerals were claimed by the crown or the aristocracy – which had granted the title of 'freehold' in the land in the first place. For this reason, a particular kind of division in the capitalisation of mines emerged, called the 'butty system'. From the late eighteenth century onwards, the owners of the minerals below the surface would raise the main capital required for constructing a mine, and especially making the shafts down to the deposits. They would also often own the other costly capital such as winding gear and the railways for transporting mined material. However, in coal mining, it was another group (this time petty capitalists) who would provide the working capital for actual mining activities: they provided the tools, the tubs and corves that were used to hew and to bring out the coal.

The butty system allowed the aristocratic owners of mines to draw an income from mining activity, and even, if they were active, to control such things as the rate of extraction, without actually dirtying their hands. But it also contributed to the perpetuation of the undercapitalised system of mine-working found in Britain. Partly as a result, until well into the twentieth century, in most places coal getting largely relied on using traditional tools and labour. The predominant technique of mining was labour intensive well into the twentieth century. What was called the 'stall and pillar method' predominated. This involved simply dividing the coal seam into a number of small pitches or 'stalls'. Each of these stalls provided enough coal face to be worked by small teams of miners (typically multiples of 2 or 3) working as partners or 'marras'. Each stall was divided off from the next by a substantial pillar of coal, which was left to support the roof. The well-known sociotechnical systems studies in British mines, undertaken following the nationalisation of the mines in 1947 (published in collected form as Trist et al., 1963) found that, even after the Second World War, the stall and pillar method of mining was still in use in many British mines. The legendary solidarity of the miners is held to derive ultimately from the teamwork engendered by the need for miners to work co-operatively in small teams as required by stall and pillar methods of extraction.

Thus, the work of the miner, for a long period of British history, had many of the features of traditional labouring. Here too we see working with hand tools. Here too there was the development of skill and dexterity in doing the work that was considered with agricultural labouring, as well as the pride in the mastery of the task. Writing after the Second World War, Dennis et al. report that the tools of the collier are 'pick, hammer and shovel' (1956, p. 47) and that 'Pride in work is a very important part of a miner's life. Old men delight in stories of their strength and skill in youth... Men over 60, still working on heavy contracts, are visibly proud of themselves and resent any preferential treatment' (1956, p. 73). There are some clear parallels here with points made by Flora Thompson about the pride in the work taken by the agricultural labourer.

Writing in the early 1950s, just before Dennis et al., Zweig suggests that the miner and other working-class groups resisted mechanisation and the introduction of labour-saving capital equipment (Zweig, 1952, p. 82). This assertion is not supported by evidence or references; however, it is true that this sort of inclination may be a by-product of the miners' motivation to preserve their control of their own work performance, which they did assiduously. Typically they would not allow employers or their deputies even to watch them at work. This was despite the fact that, from the late nineteenth century, employers had duties to see that miners observed safe working practices. Miners typically stopped work when any deputy approached them. Because of highly variable working conditions in each stall, the stall and pillar method of mining encouraged the negotiation of contracts by groups of miners for the completion of particular work. Until a late stage, even after stall and pillar mining had largely been replaced by the much more mechanised 'long-wall method' of mining, groups working a particular coal face continued to negotiate contracts and were paid on a collective pay note. By this means, miners retained collective control of their pay and output and hence also over the intensity of their work. De facto then, miners achieved much the same kind of autonomy from supervision found in agricultural labouring.

Indeed, as with the agricultural workers, the degree of autonomy from supervision achieved did not lead to reduced working effort. Miners would almost invariably work fast and hard. Thus, although their work was often not effectively supervised by managers, teams of miners would discipline themselves and work hard in pursuit of high wages. Their aim would be to achieve relatively high earnings from fulfilling a local contract expeditiously. For these reasons, miners in British mines usually worked very fast and sustained high levels of effort, despite the fact that they were usually working using hand tools. Thus Dennis et al. write: 'From the start to the finish of a shift the collier keeps up a hammer and tongs rhythm, broken only by 15 or 20 minutes for snap (i.e., eating a sandwich or two and drinking some water)' (1956, p. 40).

As miners themselves were aware, however, there was a problem about the status and dignity of mining not present in other types of work. Dennis et al. comment specifically that:

'No drinking water is provided underground. . . and there are no washing facilities, so that every man is obliged to consume a certain amount of coal dust at best, grease and oil at worst, with his 'snap'. Lavatories are to all intents and purposes non-existent. All these conditions must change before the miner can really feel a complete change in his status. . . ' (1956, p. 72).

Commenting more generally on the matter of the status of miners, these authors say:

'For long, and they know this, mine-working has been looked down on; this is felt strongly, and a man's assertion of pride in being a miner is an attempted self-assurance that he does not care what non-miners think of him' (1956, p. 73).

Here we have a version of the move which sociologists have identified as 'counter coup' (Hughes, 1985). This is something which will be considered in more detail when we examine the behaviour of slaughterhouse workers in the next section. Briefly, however, what happens is that a workgroup counters the adverse judgement of external groups, by asserting and emphasising a more general and alternative set of values and beliefs running counter to those of the surrounding society. Counter coup narratives subvert, and sometimes attempt to invert, the estimation of the surrounding community concerning one's occupational status.

The reason for the low status of the miners, and the need for them to mount a counter coup, is no very great mystery. An important contribution to their low status was the dirtiness of mining and their problems in keeping clean. Historians (Griffin, 1977; Nef, 1932) have drawn attention to the dirtiness of mining – and inevitably therefore of miners – and the impact of this. Before the nineteenth century, a miner might be a serf, or perhaps have a semi-servile condition. This serfdom persisted in British mining (especially in Scotland) much longer than the system did in agriculture, and the legacy of this also affected the status of miners – even after wage labour predominated in the industry. Griffin (1977, p. 20) writes:

'Whatever the pitman's formal status [as serf or free labourer], he seems to have been regarded with distaste or worse in every district. This may have been due in part to the reality of his servitude. Again, even when personal cleanliness was not esteemed very highly, the homes, clothes and skin of miners were permanently discoloured. In new mining districts, the invasion of dark-skinned strangers, housed in mean hovels, was inevitably unpopular, and miners were regarded with hostility by the original inhabitants'.

D.H. Lawrence, famously beginning his novel *Sons and Lovers* with an account of the experience of a mining family around the turn of the twentieth century, briefly describes the manual labour involved in the stall and pillar method of mining. He sketches not only the physical demands of mining, but also suggests some of its consequences for the domestic life of the miner, hinting at the dirt and indignity. Though clearly Lawrence in some ways is attracted to the physicality of mining, the dirt repulses him. In some passages, indeed, Lawrence rubs his reader's nose in the dirt. In one scene, he writes of an encounter between the pitman, Morel, and his wife in their bedroom after the birth of the main character of the novel. In this description of the miner at home Lawrence writes:

> 'His face was black, and smeared with sweat. His singlet had dried again, soaking the dirt in. He had a dirty woollen scarf around his throat. So he stood at the foot of the bed' (Lawrence, 1913/1948, p. 45).

Even if we recognise that it is part of Lawrence's literary purpose to blacken the miner, emphasising in particular the difference in the manners and sensibility of the miner and those of his wife, the emphasis on the way that the dirt arising from mining work is brought into the domestic sphere is extraordinary.

Against the kind of view implicit in the passage quoted from Lawrence cited above, in which the miner at times disregards the need for cleanliness, there is little evidence to think celebration of dirt was an important element in any miners' counter coup. Stories alleging that miners were so backward they would store coal in the baths provided in new housing provided by local authorities are almost certainly apocryphal. Writing in 1952, however, Zweig suggests that miners have at times voted against proposals for the installation of pithead baths. However, none of the circumstances of any such decisions were reported nor details given of when and where such votes were supposedly taken. Against this sort of view, George Orwell (1937) argues strongly for the scrupulous cleanliness of the miner in his home, observing closely and reporting on the personal cleaning rituals of some of the miners he visited. Orwell at least had taken the trouble go amongst miners and to stay in their homes, as well as visiting mines. Orwell also argues for the immorality of making the miner endure unnecessary dirtiness. At the time he wrote *The Road to Wigan Pier*, the idea that mine owners might provide bathing facilities at the pithead seemed hopelessly utopian. More than 20 years after Orwell reported, however, Dennis et al. (1956) suggest that pithead baths would be greatly welcomed by miners. Against the opinions of Zweig, Dennis et al. suggest that public display of the dirt, 'going home in his muck' (1956, p. 82), was the worst consequence of working with dirt.

From this consideration of the reports of coal mining, then, the dirt associated with mining did pose a problem for the status and dignity of the miner. But just how far the dirt encountered in mining was experienced by miners as matter of shame and regret, and what effects this may have had, have not been analysed. By the time Dennis et al. (1956) were writing, many mining areas, including the one studied by these authors, had established supportive communities in the locality of the mine, in which the conditions under which mining work was typically undertaken would be well understood. But such communities could not entirely insulate miners from all perception of the adverse evaluation of mining in the wider society. It is thus a very intriguing question to ask how far the adverse reactions of the wider society, which were undoubtedly made in the 1950s, were experienced by miners as degradation. Moreover, did this sort of thing add fuel to their industrial militancy? It is certain that miners were for many years the militant elite of the working class, and coal-face workers, that is, those most exposed to the dust and dirt produced in the coal-extraction processes, were typically the leaders of the occupation itself.

Questions concerning the contribution of the dirt involved in mining to the miners' sense of disgruntlement and alienation have not been identified let alone seriously discussed by the social scientists. It is nonetheless a puzzle why this particular occupation, which had secured local control over the pace of work and its level of earnings, added so importantly to the figures on the incidence of strikes for much of the twentieth century (Cronin, 1979, pp. 159–162). The dirtiness of mining is often overlooked by the few social scientists who have studied the occupation, in favour of emphasising its arduousness, danger and, by extension, the heroism of miners. (See for example Fitzpatrick, 1980; Salaman, 1981; though see also Vaught and Smith, 1980, for a study of an American deep coal mine that does touch on some of these important themes.)

Slaughterhouse work: handling powerful pollutants

Slaughterhouse work is in some ways similar to labouring or mining: it is routine manual work that is extremely dirty. It can be highly mechanised, and this kind of slaughtering operation has often been described by social scientists and journalists (Inkson, 1977; Sinclair, 1985). Chinoy (1955) argues that a mechanised Cincinnati slaughterhouse was a model for Henry Ford I in his invention of the assembly line. For the most part, slaughterhouses continue to be organised as production (or, to be more accurate, reduction) lines. In Britain, however, slaughterhouses are often not very large and are not highly mechanised workplaces such as are found in the USA. (For a recent account of developments in the industry in the USA, see Schlosser, 2002, chapters 7 and 8.) In the present account of slaughtering work, information collected in an ethnographic study of a small English slaughterhouse directed by the author in the 1980s will be the main source of observations and insights (see Ackroyd and Crowdy, 1990).

What makes slaughterhouses of interest in this context is that the work undertaken in many English examples exhibits features that are similar to labouring and mining, as discussed above. This work also requires the use of hand tools and the use of considerable skill and dexterity in the use of them. Here also there was remote and mostly ineffective external supervision, and a great deal of control over the organisation of work routinely exercised by the workers themselves. In many ways, the workplace behaviour of slaughterhouse workers is very similar to those observed in mining. When there were animals to be killed and dressed, the slaughtermen worked fast and hard. Much as the miners observed by Dennis et al. (1956), these employees also took pride in being capable of doing all aspects of their physically demanding work: they habitually aimed at finishing the available batches of animals in the minimum time. Furthermore, the reasons for this hard work were the same as were operative in mining: maximising earnings from a specific contract that had been negotiated locally. There was a piecework bonus system paid in the slaughterhouse to the gang as a whole on the basis of the numbers of animals slaughtered and dressed in the week, and this constituted a high proportion of the wage. Unlike the miners, in pursuit of 'bonus', slaughtering gangs would work through a shift without a break until there was no more work to be done. Competition between gangs for the available work, motivated by desire for maximising the piecework bonus, guaranteed that high levels of effort were sustained and removed the need for close supervision.

Two points stand out when comparing the reports of miners and what was found amongst the slaughtering gangs. The first concerns the extent and the manner in which hierarchy was imposed in slaughtering gangs; the second concerns the vigour with which they mounted their counter coup against the perceived indignity of their occupation, which was very much stronger than anything reported for mining. To deal with the first of these briefly, it was very noticeable how strong the impulse of a group to control its own members actually was in the abattoir. There was an atmosphere of imperfectly concealed antagonism in the slaughtering gangs; and aggression would periodically break out in apparently gratuitous demonstrative acts. They key observation was, however, that most of the aggression was aimed at other members of the work group, especially at the most junior. Aggression against workmates was commonly aimed at those workers judged to be tardy, and so holding back the earnings of group. The slow ones were invariably beginners. In many of these events, sexual imagery and ideas were often present, but the most compelling feature was the use of the available dirt in the workplace to attack and degrade fellow workers. It was common not only for a worker to be harassed by verbal comments encouraging him to keep up, but also for him to become the target of missiles. Thus, a carcass would be pushed violently along the overhead rails into the path of a worker falling behind with his work, or entrails would be flung across the workplace aimed at him, and so on.

There were collective harassments that were particularly degrading. In such events, not only is the dignity of the worker at stake, but the threat to it is so severe that their continued membership of the group is also at stake. In an early article, Garfinkel (1956) has analysed the formal properties of degradation ceremonies. The aim of such events often seems to be to test the loyalty and work capacity of a worker to the limit, to see if they can survive. Although there were other kinds of events involving the use of dirt in the slaughterhouse, and pressure was not always one way, it was usually targeted on particular individuals as a way of imposing discipline, and setting in place or reinforcing an informal hierarchy (see also, Ackroyd and Crowdy, 1990). In one series of events observed in the slaughterhouse, for example, a new worker was pressured by work being piled up at his workstation, and on a daily basis he was attacked by missiles. Events culminated in the man being 'baptized': he was summarily grabbed and held upside down by the gang with his head in a tub of blood. Interestingly, this was after he had passed the test of absorbing much of the pressure that had been exerted on him. Similar events have been reported in a large number of industrial settings, where degradations by dirt are widely reported as 'rites de passage'. (For a summary of some of the evidence revealed by research, see Ackroyd and Thompson, 1999, pp. 61–65.)

Slaughterhouse workers are generally aware that unflattering accounts of their job are common, nor are they in much doubt about why this is. As Meara (1974) suggests in a cross-national study of meat workers, work with meat tends to be dirty. For slaughterhouse workers, direct contamination by blood, other bodily fluids and animal excreta is difficult to avoid. Dirt of this kind, of course, is widely held to be particularly repugnant. It is dirty in more than a physical sense. Killing animals certainly often evokes revulsion. The emergence of urban society, involving the separation of the majority of the population from any familiarity with farming and the rearing of animals for food, has fostered an 'arcadian' view of the countryside (Newby, 1979) in which all things rural – and especially animals – tend to be sentimentally idealised. In short, animals are seen to be a uniquely 'raw' material for factory production. In recent years, public revulsion has, if anything, intensified. Developments in moral philosophy and the emergence of new animal rights pressure groups have put the welfare of animals on the agenda of local and national politics.

The work of the slaughterman is so centrally concerned with blood, entrails and death that it is impossible to deny these even to the superficially informed. But the idea that slaughtering is necessary if meat is wanted for food actually does little to reconcile the squeamish. In the face of adverse reactions, like the miner, the slaughterhouse worker chooses to mount a counter coup. The slaughtermen in our study typically rejected the adverse valuation of their work when they encountered it very strongly. Far from denying or hiding their occupation, they acknowledged it and asserted its value. For the younger men in particular, there was a conspicuous tendency to draw attention to their work. In general, they gave up the attempt, both inside and outside the workplace, to 'pass as normal', that is, be accepted as ordinary workers. They challenged and sought to invert the public view of the matter. By emphasising what they suggested was the heroic manliness needed to undertake slaughtering, these workers sought to turn their association with blood into a source of status. Meara (1974, p. 263) also refers to a similar attempt on the part of the American meat cutters, according to which, they are '. . . able to overturn common definitions. . . of the work as dirty. . . and so confer honour on themselves'.

Thus, opposition to the common or typical assessment of slaughtering was mounted with a counter-narrative which emphasised the importance of slaughtering. Both the demand for meat in society and the personal toughness required to obtain it were emphasised. Additionally, the hypocrisy of regarding animals with sentimental endearment and yet eating meat was emphasised. In pursuing this sort of robust line, the slaughterhouse workers, according to their own testimony, eschewed any attempt to avoid being identified as what they were.

The ways the men mounted their counter coup were many and various. Clearly too, they pressed their counter-coup much further than the miners typically did. Though showers must be provided by law in British slaughterhouses, as nowadays they are in mines, they were seldom used in the slaughterhouse reported on here. During a 3-month period in which work was continuously observed in the plant, not one instance of the use of showers was recorded. The slaughterhouse workers left the workplace with blood still visibly covering their wrists and neck. Younger men were sometimes observed deliberately splashing the visible parts of their chests with blood before leaving the plant for the day. It is a legal requirement that food workers change their clothing every day and more frequently when they are heavily soiled. But the slaughterhouse workers did not observe the regulations at all scrupulously. They wore their bloodstained overalls with pride. Yet despite all this overt assertion of alternative values, it seems clear that the slaughterhouse workers mounted their coup in the knowledge that the attempt would mostly fail: that they would, almost invariably, encounter distaste from the general public. In practice, and contrary to what they said, this meant that situations in which there might be encounters with strangers (and likely rejections) were avoided.

There are several points that can be made about the extreme responses of the slaughtermen. First, although they had achieved collective control of their work in a similar way to the miners and agricultural labourers, this did not contribute to a positive self-image on their part. In reality, it was extremely difficult for them to escape the stigma arising from handling such potent dirt. The lack of a supportive community was an additional handicap not experienced by the other groups in this respect also. Slaughtermen stuck together, consigned to their own company, in the absence of a wider community supporting their values. Sustained observation indicated that slaughtermen in our study spent a great deal of their non-work time with other slaughtermen, and it is difficult to avoid the conclusion that they did so specifically to avoid exchanging background information with strangers. Like being a policeman, being a slaughterman is not an occupation with which you can expect to achieve easy social acceptance. Though they may deny the possibility that they care very much whether they achieve social acceptance or not, it seems more than plausible that the feelings of rejection and distaste they routinely encounter feeds into and helps to fuel the aggression that characterises much of their work behaviour. Unlike the miners, whose aggression could be legitimately channelled outwards into industrial militancy, the aggression of the slaughtermen is directed inwards and is expiated in the enactment of the ritualised degradations of fellow workers that have already been described.

Conclusions

If policy makers and intellectuals are serious about the need to understand when work is undignified, then considering the impact of dirt and feelings of pollution is instructive. Even though all three of the occupations considered here achieved many of the features of work organisation which are widely regarded as conducive to achieving dignified work – such as high levels of autonomy from close supervision and the collective control of levels of work intensity (see also Sayer, Coats, Bolton and Wibberley, this volume) – it is a surprise to find that it is still possible for two of them to be experienced as undignified and sometimes degrading. It has been argued here that exposure to pollution explains these differences of experience.

The foregoing survey of some of the social scientific and literary record concerning the three occupations considered here suggests that it was and still is possible for work that is physically dirty to threaten the status and the dignity of workers, despite many other positive features. Table 2 summarises the findings of this discussion. Agricultural labourers in the nineteenth century clearly did not experience their work as undignified, despite the fact that their work was much concerned with the soil. In general, however, we tend not to make the assumption, which early nineteenth-century novelists like Jane Austen did, that manual work is necessarily and intrinsically undignified. Indeed, the onset of modernity is associated with the progressive de-materialisation of dirt. In our age, matter is more and more considered to be simply matter, and if it is not in its right place, then this is not necessarily a subject for concern. To a remarkable extent in

Table 2   Dirt and dignity in three manual occupations

	Agricultural labourers (late nineteenth century)	Coal miners (early to mid-twentieth century)	Slaughterhouse workers (late twentieth century)
Exposure to dirt	+	++	+++
Degree of pollution attributed by others	+	++	+++
Existence of a supportive community	+	+	–
Counter-coup mounted	– (none)	+ (some)	+++ [highly developed (but ineffective)]
Threat to dignity	–	++	+++

modern life, moral considerations are mostly stripped away from the assessment of things.

However, as this study shows, the modern world clearly has not entirely dispensed with a connection between dirt and discredit. It is not clear that the miner in the early part of the nineteenth century or the contemporary worker in an abattoir escape social distaste, even though the pollutants they deal with, considered as material, are acknowledged to be not particularly polluting. Coal dust on the face and body of the miner today, is, morally speaking neither here nor there; it might be considered as much a mark of heroism as a source of stigma. On the other hand, the blood on the hands and bodies of the slaughterhouse workers is not likely to be seen as mere matter out of place and are likely to be responded to by shock and anger. The rights of animals have become more rather than less salient in the last 20 years since the research in the slaughterhouse discussed above was completed. Exposure to this type of dirt is probably experienced as even more deeply polluting that it was in the past. Even two decades ago, despite taking some extraordinary steps to avoid the consequences of their pollution, the slaughterhouse workers were deeply compromised by their exposure to blood and other animal fluids they necessarily misplaced in the course of their work. In some circumstances, then, it is very clear that exposure to dirt may still threaten both status and perceived dignity. Indeed, contemporary accounts of work indicate that dirt is an important factor in how work is individually experienced and socially perceived, not only in the low-status McJobs where workers complain that a strong (and lingering) smell of fried food on their hair and clothes attracts distaste from family, friends and even passers by, or paid care and domestic work that is automatically associated with the dirty work of body care and other people's dirt, but also higher status occupations such as veterinary surgeons or nurses where the necessary handling of dirt as part of their skilled labour undermines their social standing (Bolton, 2003; Lindsay and McQuaid, 2004; Stacey, 2005; The Work Foundation, 2005; Toynbee, 2003). The symbolic aspects of things clearly can at times dramatically subvert the expectations of our materialistic culture.

References

Ackroyd, S. and Crowdy, P. (1990) 'Can Culture be Managed? Working with Raw Material: The Case of the English Slaughterhouse Workers', *Personnel Review*, **19**, 5, 3–14.

Ackroyd, S. and Thompson, P. (1999) *Organisational Misbehaviour*, London: Sage.

Bauman, Z. (1989) *Modernity and the Holocaust*, Cambridge: Polity.

Bolton, S. C. (2003) 'Women's Work, Dirty Work: The Gynaecology Nurse as "Other" ', *Gender, Work and Organisations*, **19**, 2, 5–23.

Bourne, G. (1984) *Change in the Village*, Harmonsworth: Penguin (First published in 1912).

Brooke, D. (1963) *The Railway Navvy*, London: David and Charles.

Chinoy, E. (1955) *The Automobile Worker and the American Dream*, New York: Doubleday.

Coleman, T. (1983) *The Railway Navvies*, London: William Hutchinson.

Cronin, J. E. (1979) *Industrial Conflict in Modern Britain*, London: Croom Helm.

Davis, M. (1983) *Smut: Erotic Reality/Obscene Ideology*, Chicago: University Press.

Dennis, N., Henriques, F. and Slaughter, C. (1956) *Coal is Our Life*, London: Eyre and Spottiswoode.

Don, M. (2003) *The Complete Gardener*, London: Doring Kindersley.

Douglas, M. (1966) *Purity and Danger: An Analysis of the Concepts of Pollution and Taboo*, London: Routledge.

Fitzpatrick, J. (1980) 'Adapting to Danger: A Participant Observation Study of an Underground Mine', *Sociology of Work and Occupations*, **7**, 2, 131–158.

Frankenberg, R. (1966) *Communities in Britain: Social life in Town and Country*, Harmondsworth: Penguin.

Garfinkel, H. (1956) 'Conditions of Successful Degradation Ceremonies', *American Journal of Sociology*, **61**, 2, 420–424.

Griffin, A. R. (1977) *The British Coalmining Industry: Retrospect and Prospect*, Buxton: Moorland.

Hall, T. (1981) *King Coal: Miners, Coal and Britain's Industrial Future*, Harmondsworth: Penguin.

Hughes, E. C. (1985) 'Work and the Self', in *The Sociological Eye*, Somerset, NJ: Transaction Publications.

Hutchinson, R. (2006) *Calum's Road*, London: Birlinn.

Inkson, K. (1977) 'The Man on the Dis-Assembly Line: New Zealand Freezing Workers', *Australia and New Zealand Journal of Sociology*, **13**, 1, 2–11.

Lawrence, D. H. (1948) *Sons and Lovers*, Harmonsworth: Penguin (First published in 1913 by Heinemann).

Leith, P. (1996) 'Peck of Dirt', *Royal Society of Arts Journal*, **144**, 25–31.

Lindsay, C. and McQuaid, R. W. (2004) 'Avoiding the "McJobs": Unemployed Job Seekers and Attitudes to Service Work', *Work, Employment and Society*, **18**, 2, 297–319.

Meara, H. (1974) 'Honor in Dirty Work: The Cases of American Meat Cutters and Turkish Butchers', *Sociology of Work and Occupations*, **1**, 259–283.

Nef, J. U. (1932) *The Rise of the British Coal Industry*, London: Frank Cass.

Newby, H. (1979) *Green and Pleasant Land?* London: Hutchinson.

Orwell, G. (1937) *The Road to Wigan Pier*, London: Victor Gollancz.

Reeves, R. (2001) *Happy Mondays. Putting the Pleasure back into Work*, London: Pearson Education Limited.

Salaman, G. (1981) *Community and Occupation*, Cambridge: Cambridge University Press.

Schlosser, E. (2002) *Fast Food Nation*, London: Penguin.

Sinclair, U. (1985) *The Jungle*, Harmondsworth: Penguin (First published in 1906 by Doubleday, Page and Co.).

Stacey, C. (2005) 'Finding Dignity in Dirty Work: The Constraints and Rewards of Low-Wage Home Care Labour', *Sociology of Health & Illness*, **27**, 6, 831–854.

Steinbeck, J. (1957) *The Grapes of Wrath*, Harmondsworth: Penguin (First published in 1939 by Heinemann).

Thompson, F. (1947) *Lark Rise to Candleford*, Oxford: Oxford University Press (First published as Lark Rise in 1939).

Toynbee, P. (2003) *Hard Work. Life in Low Pay Britain*, London: Bloomsbury.

Trist, E., Higgin, G., Murray, H. and Pollock, A. (1963) *Organizational Choice: Capabilities of Groups at the Coal Face under Changing Technologies*, London: Tavistock.

Vaught, C. and Smith D. L. (1980) 'Incorporation and Mechanical Solidarity in an Underground Coal Mine', *Sociology of Work and Occupations*, **7**, 159–187.

The Work Foundation (2005) Domestics: UK Domestic Workers and their Reluctant Employers. http://www.theworkfoundation.com/pdf/Domestics.pdf

Zweig, F. (1952) *The British Worker*, Harmondsworth: Penguin.

Part Two: Dignity, Work and the Political Economy

4

Respect at work: just how good are British workplaces?

David Coats

The false promise of HRM

The notion of 'respect at work' may sound like a departure from conventional thinking about the employment relationship, but a moment's reflection will show that it is an idea with a venerable pedigree. We can follow our story back to the nineteenth century with writers as diverse as Marx, John Ruskin and William Morris identifying alienation, subordination and control as central features of the employment relationship. In their view, work in the factory system reduced employees to cogs in a machine rather than people who took pride in their craft and the products that they made. Charlie Chaplin's *Modern Times*, released in 1936, created high comedy out of Taylorist mass production – and suggested that the application of sophisticated technology was not necessarily an unqualified benefit for workers. At the same time as he entertains us, Chaplin uses slapstick to make a rather more profound point. From the employer's perspective, the production system is self-evidently efficient, but workers can only view their experience as dehumanising.

Of course, it is now argued that these are matters of historical interest only. The world of work has been revolutionised. We have said farewell to Mr Gradgrind and welcomed a new generation of employers who understand or at least profess to believe that our employees are our greatest assets. Expressed in more measured terms, it is now widely asserted that the application of 'enlightened' Human

Resource Management (HRM) policies can create a virtuous circle of high productivity and high levels of employee satisfaction. Conflict has disappeared from the workplace, and work is now an unqualified source of pleasure and enjoyment rather than a necessary evil. In other words, we have reached the sunlit uplands where 'work is more fun than fun'.

Whether this statement of Panglossian optimism is an accurate picture or not will be explored further in this chapter. But perhaps we ought to record as a preliminary point that there is compelling evidence to the contrary, suggesting that conflict is still present in the world of work, that workers lack autonomy, control and task discretion and that for many people work can and should be better. Nevertheless, there is something in the aspiration of HRM to create 'good' workplaces, with contented and productive employees, which takes us close to the core of respect at work. In principle at least, there is a concern with the quality of work and a wish to ensure that employees find fulfilment in their jobs. Yet despite this apparent desire to take account of the human factor, it is a genuine weakness in the HRM approach that employees are generally seen as a means to the achievement of organisational goals. At the heart of many HR strategies is the quest for alignment between an individual's desires and the organisational mission. To that extent HRM is 'unitarist' in believing that conflict can be removed completely from the employment relationship. Where conflict does arise, it is the result of either incompatible personalities producing personal friction; inadequate communication; 'stupidity', manifested as the inability of some individuals to understand what is in their own best interests; or, the work of agitators stirring up the apathetic majority who would otherwise be content (Fox, 1966).

Expressed in slightly different terms, what is missing from the HRM account is any sense that the employment relationship is characterised by an imbalance of power between worker and employer (Kahn-Freund, 1983). To begin with, the worker is an individual, but the employer is a collective of shareholders and professional managers with a considerable volume of physical capital behind them. The freedom to hire and fire lies at the heart of the employer's power and creates what economists would describe as an 'information asymmetry'. For example, the employer will possess a good deal of labour market intelligence, will have a fair idea of where to find a replacement employee and will, other things being equal, have little difficulty in accommodating the costs of recruitment and training. The employee on the other hand will not necessarily be aware of all the employment opportunities available, may have to risk a spell of unemployment and may find that their skills are no longer in demand.

As one commentator suggested in the 1960s, the differences of interest between employer and employee are unavoidable:

'There are two sides to industry, whatever the pattern of ownership and management... These are harsh facts that cannot be spirited away by moral-rearmament touring troupes, or luncheons of progressive businessmen or syndicalist castles in the air' (Crosland, 1962, p. 219).

Some might say that this is a rather old-fashioned view, but the case I want to make here is that the fundamental inequality inscribed in the employment relationship has not been changed by any of the innovations introduced by the HR profession over the last 30 years. Of course, the world of work is very different, not least because the stereotype of the full-time male breadwinner has disappeared from the scene, and the world of work is more diverse. Similarly, we have witnessed the increasing use of more rigorous procedures for recruitment and selection – psychometric testing, the use of assessment centres, equality and diversity programmes, flexible working, performance management systems and performance pay. But none of this has shifted the fundamental imbalance of power between employer and employee. Indeed, the decline of trade unions means that employers have relatively more freedom today to manage their organisations as they wish than at any time in the recent past.

However, this decisive shift in the balance of power has not necessarily led to an improvement in productivity and organisational performance. The UK still has a wide productivity gap with our major trading partners and in the medium term our relative prosperity will decline if nothing is done. Yet this persistent productivity weakness is hard to explain if we believe the arguments advanced by the HR profession. They say that not only does the application of 'enlightened' HRM lead to happier and more fulfilled employees but that the introduction of high-performance work systems (HPWS), reinforced by HRM policies and practices, leads to higher productivity.

At best, this case remains unproven, and an accumulating body of evidence points only to an association between HPWS and productivity. As Toby Wall and Stephen Wood (2005) have pointed out, much of the 'evidence' is based on methodologies that are not as robust as they should be. There is a reliance on 'single source' measures, like the reports of CEOs or HR directors, small samples with low response rates and qualitative rather than longitudinal studies; in other words, we have no sound idea about the effects of these practices over time, and most analyses simply give a 'snap-shot' of performance that may fail to explain what is really going on. Moreover, it sometimes seems that researchers, by characterising these systems as 'high performance', are presupposing the very effects that they claim to be researching. A better approach of course would be to advance a series of hypotheses that can be tested over time to produce rather more robust and compelling findings.

Rethinking the employment relationship

What I want to offer here is a different lens for viewing the experience of work. The core principle underpinning the argument is that we must see work as a fully human activity that engages all our skills, talents, capabilities and emotions. It is founded on the belief that in a democratic society we have certain rights as citizens that apply whether we are at home, in public or at work. Work is where we spend a high proportion of our adult lives, and it ought to be the case that many aspects of our humanity that we value outside work should be equally valuable at work. In other words, we cannot view the employment relationship as a merely economic transaction. Work is unavoidably a social act.

John Kay has captured this line of argument by suggesting that our society is characterised by the 'disciplined pluralism' of 'embedded markets', by which he means that markets have their place but cannot dominate and operate in a network of intermediate institutions (between the individual and the state), which ensure that people can be counted on to keep their promises and deal fairly with others. In his view, trust is a necessary condition for the efficient operation of markets that cannot be generated by markets themselves (Kay, 2003):

> 'The economic world is complex. Self-interest is an important motivation, but it is not the exclusive motivation. Our other concerns influence our work and business lives as well as our personal lives. We need the approbation of our friends, the trust of our colleagues, the satisfaction of performing activities that are worthwhile in themselves and give others pleasure. These motives are not materialistic, but that does not mean that they are not economic. They are an essential part of the mechanisms through which successful business operates. Without them business and economic systems would be impoverished – in material as well as in other terms' (Kay, 2003, p. 337).

This is a very useful corrective to the widespread view that work is like any other commercial contract, where workers surrender their liberty (and most of their rights) in return for a wage or salary. The alleged rationale is that 'businesses are not democracies' because directors are accountable to shareholders and should not therefore 'be burdened, distracted and delayed by any manifestations of... industrial democracy' (Lea, 2003, p. 35). At least this opinion has the merit of clarity, although it would be hard to find an employer today who was honest (or perhaps foolish) enough to adopt it as an operational principle, if only because they might find it hard to recruit employees willing to subject themselves to an autocracy where managers decide and workers do as they are told.

Moreover, this account offers only a partial understanding of how the labour market works and is based on a very crude model of human psychology. Homo economicus, as a rational wealth maximiser, would be willing to submit to this kind of authoritarianism, but we know that most market participants are motivated by rather more than the desire to maximise utility (Lane, 1991). Equally, the market fundamentalist model ignores the notion of 'embeddedness' completely and fails to understand that markets cannot work at all unless those involved are motivated by rather more than the desire for private gain. Indeed, it fails to recognise that the labour market is a market in people rather than things and that it is simply wrong to believe that this is a market like any other. Workers do not surrender their rights as citizens when they cross their employer's threshold.

Our task therefore is to rethink our approach to the employment relationship in a way that reflects John Kay's critique of market fundamentalism and seeks to recover the idea that work does not necessarily have to be an alienating experience. Once we have completed this task, we can then develop a notion of 'good work' to test against the reality of British workplaces. To what extent can we be confident that employees are being treated with respect? Or, to put the question slightly differently, how much 'good work' is there in Britain today, where are the problems and how might we go about constructing some workable solutions?

The first part of our enterprise can be assisted by the work of the American scholar John Budd, who has suggested that we should redefine the objectives of the employment relationship as efficiency, equity and voice, giving equal weight to each principle (Budd, 2004). Efficiency is self-evidently important to employers, who would otherwise find it difficult to run their organisations successfully. It embraces the idea that organisations in competitive markets are driven to seek higher productivity and higher quality products and services. Furthermore, the quest for efficiency carries within it the notion that employees must be managed in a particular way to secure high productivity and product quality. In other words, it is difficult to see how these objectives can be achieved if workers are disaffected, alienated and willing to adopt the sabotage of the productive process as their mission. Of course, it is possible, as the market fundamentalist model suggests, to achieve a reasonable level of performance through coercion; sometimes employers can secure an advantage by being nastier to employees than their competitors. But this strategy carries with it certain hazards, not the least of which is that consumers may be less inclined to buy a company's products if they believe that the workers have been treated badly. Reputational risk is now widely recognised as a real risk, with a potentially adverse impact on business performance.

Equity matters for two reasons. First, in western democracies the idea of 'fairness' is deeply embedded in our culture. Despite an apparently growing tolerance of income inequality (at least in Anglo-Saxon countries), there is a widespread sense that the effort we make at work should be reflected in the rewards that we receive. Interpersonal comparisons remain important and employees' motivation is affected if they can see others in the same situation are in receipt of higher pay or superior conditions of employment. But more profoundly, we care about equity because this is a fundamental principle of citizenship. As members of a political community, we have claims of rights that give rise to certain expectations about how we should be treated. For example, we have a legitimate expectation that we will not experience discrimination on the grounds of gender, sexuality, race, disability or age. Applying this principle to the world of work again reflects the notion that work is a fully human activity and that our rights as citizens are just as applicable at work as elsewhere. Furthermore, all of these factors are simply features of who we are, we cannot change them (without taking some rather drastic measures) or choose them and our fellow citizens are ignoring an important aspect of our humanity if they use these characteristics as a reason for discrimination. In other words, our fellows are failing to recognise the principle that we are all, as citizens, entitled to equal concern and respect.

Finally, voice is important to us because freedom of speech and freedom of association are important to us. Allowing citizens to come together in organisations of their choosing is not simply a hedge against dictatorship, but an important source of social capital and, in itself, an activity that enables us to grow as human beings (Putnam, 2001). The possibility of social interaction of this kind allows us to acquire the capacity for democratic engagement and develop a sense of civic responsibility. Citizenship is something that we learn through experience and cannot simply be conjured out of thin air.

Democracy at national level is remote from the lives of most of us, and our engagement with these processes can be distant and episodic – often consisting of no more than voting in general elections. But understanding how these processes work and appreciating why they are important is sustained by direct experience of similar processes at a community level. Trade unions, works councils and other 'employee voice' institutions can be academies of citizenship, encouraging 'civic virtue' and democratic participation.

Equally, voice is important because we value the right to free speech. The liberty to express our opinions is once again seen as constitutive of our notion of human flourishing, it is rooted in the view that we make progress as a society by allowing a multiplicity of opinions to flourish, which permits in turn a degree of social experimentation and differentiation. In other words, developed democracies are characterised by 'reasonable pluralism' (Rawls, 2001). Citizens will disagree, express different preferences and adopt different religious and philosophical systems – and we value these differences as expressions of our common humanity. The challenge of course is to find instruments to manage the 'incommensurability of human ends'. How can we sustain a high degree of social cohesion and stability in a society where people often want different things and this fact of diversity is celebrated as one of the advantages of democracy? In this context, freedom of association and free speech are connected, because these rights enable those with similar views and preferences to express themselves in an organised way and reach understandings with those who do not necessarily share their views.

Of course, some employers take the view that 'voice' should only be valued if it 'adds value' to a business, in other words if it has a productivity-enhancing effect (CBI, 2003). It should be clear from all that has been said so far that this is inconsistent with the case that work is a fully human activity. Sometimes we act in a particular way because it is the right thing to do, not because that course of action increases productivity. The basic principle has been well expressed by Joseph Stiglitz, formerly chief economist at the World Bank:

'We care about the society we live in. We believe in democracy, regardless of whether it increases economic efficiency or not . . . Democratic processes must entail open dialogue and broadly active civic engagement, and require that individuals have a voice in the decisions that affect them, including economic decisions . . . Economic democracy is an essential part of a democratic society' (Stiglitz, 2001, p. 304).

Defining good work

Now that we have a clear understanding of how the employment relationship should be viewed from the perspective of work as a fully human activity, we can move on to define what we mean by 'good work'. A useful way of proceeding is to identify those aspects of the workplace environment that generate adverse effects, particularly adverse health effects, for employees (Marmot, 2004). This is important because the capacity for purposive action is severely limited if we experience poor health and well-being. Our life chances are diminished along with our life expectancy. There is strong evidence of course that work is better than worklessness, but there is little doubt that work can be bad for you too (Layard, 2004, 2005).

The features of 'bad jobs' might therefore be described as follows:

- Employment insecurity.
- A lack of control over the pace of work and the key decisions that affect the workplace.
- Limited task discretion and monotonous or repetitive work.
- Inadequate levels of skill, which means that employees are unable to cope with periods of intense pressure.
- An imbalance between the effort that the worker makes and the rewards that they receive – this is not simply about pay, but includes praise for good performance.
- Limited social capital – whether informal friendship networks or formal associations like trade unions, which make workers more resilient in the face of the vicissitudes of their working lives.

This gives us a series of negative benchmarks to be used to assess whether the UK has genuinely reached the happy position where most jobs are good jobs. But it might also be useful to offer a positive description so that we have a more developed idea of what 'good work' really means. Inevitably this will give rise to contested conceptions and the following is offered in the expectation that it will be challenged. Nevertheless, it is important to make the effort, if only to provoke a discussion and I would therefore suggest that 'good work' must embrace the following:

- Full employment – defined as the availability of jobs for all those who wish to work.
- Fair pay (including equal pay for work of equal value).
- The absence of discrimination on the grounds of race, gender, sexuality and disability or age.
- Secure and interesting jobs that employees find fulfilling, which contribute to the achievement of high performance and sustainable business success.

- A style and ethos of management that is based on high levels of trust and recognises that managing people fairly and effectively is crucial to skilled work and high performance.
- Choice, flexibility and control over working hours.
- Autonomy and control over the pace of work and the working environment.
- Statutory minimum standards to protect the most vulnerable workers against exploitation.
- Voice for workers in the critical employer decisions that affect their futures.

These objectives may look ambitious, but we might also reasonably say that they are a modest statement of the conditions that need to be met before we can argue with conviction that work is being treated as a fully human activity. Quite coincidentally they are, in large measure, consistent with Maslow's hierarchy of needs, and therefore derived from relatively recent psychological insights into the nature of fundamental human wants and desires (Maslow, 1954). Maslow's argument is that humans seek to satisfy basic needs first, for food and physical security for example, before going on to satisfy higher needs like the desire for love, self-esteem and respect and ultimately 'self-actualisation' – which essentially means the development of one's capabilities so that one can become 'more and more what one is, to become everything that one is capable of becoming'. Obviously work may not be the only arena for people to achieve their full potential – life outside work is important too – but it must surely be the case that people can find self-esteem and respect in their experience of work. This view is consistent with John Kay's observation referred to earlier that economic life is impossible without 'the approbation of our friends, the trust of our colleagues and the satisfaction of activities that are worthwhile in themselves'. We might reasonably conclude, contrary to the nostrums of market fundamentalists, that trust, respect and voice, far from being impediments to productive efficiency, are indispensable elements of an effective employment relationship.

An audit of good work in the UK

Nevertheless, there is ample evidence to show that there has been a decline in job satisfaction over the last decade, despite the widespread rhetoric that 'employees are the greatest assets of a business'. Robert Taylor (2002) argues persuasively that employee satisfaction since 1992 has declined on almost every dimension, with significant falls in happiness with pay, job prospects and training – and this seems to affect all groups in the labour market. Perhaps the most striking phenomenon is the decline in satisfaction with working time and an increase in the intensity of work. People say that they have more work to do and that they have to work harder to do it.

Throughout the 1990s, there was an increase in perceived employment insecurity, despite the fact that job tenures (the length of time that people spend in a job) have scarcely changed in the last 15 years. A survey commissioned by the Organisation for Economic Co-operation and Development (OECD) in 2001 showed that the UK had the second highest level of perceived employment insecurity in the developed world – lying just behind South Korea, which at least had the excuse of the Asian crisis, job losses and macroeconomic instability (OECD, 2001). The findings for the UK are surprising, not least because economic conditions were benign, the labour market was expanding, unemployment was falling and long-term unemployment had virtually disappeared. However, the position seems to have been ameliorated somewhat in recent years, with the 2004 Workplace Employment Relations Survey (WERS) showing that only one in six now feel insecure about their jobs (Kersley et al., 2006).

To some extent, this is a consequence of full employment, with workers feeling less anxious about their futures. But we are still left with a substantial minority who do feel insecure, even though experience suggests that they have little reason for this belief. Perhaps we can best explain this phenomenon as a consequence of intensifying competition, which accelerates the pace of change inside organisations, with shorter product cycles, just in time production systems and the 'permanent revolution' of endless reorganisation and restructuring. Of course, there is a strong argument that this process should not be resisted and that, other things being equal, it leads to higher productivity, higher levels of output, more economic growth and more prosperity. On the other hand, one might say that all these positive outcomes have been achieved at the cost of a 'dehumanisation' of the workplace over the last decade, with fewer opportunities for workers to express their views and exercise some influence over those events that affect their working lives most directly.

This manifests itself in a paradox. Even though a cumulative body of research shows that giving employees more autonomy and control leads to productivity growth, the trend in the last decade has been in the opposite direction. Duncan Gallie and his colleagues find strong evidence of declining task discretion and a significant reduction in autonomy (Gallie, 2004). Michael White and Stephen Hill suggest that while employees may have more freedom to decide how they deliver their targets, employers now operate more rigorous regimes of accountability through sophisticated performance management systems and extensive surveillance: 'we don't care how you get the job done, but you have to get it done or suffer the consequences' (White and Hill, 2004). Both studies show workers have less effective control than was the case a decade ago.

Even so, it would be wrong to be relentlessly gloomy about changing levels of job satisfaction; work remains the proverbial curate's egg – good in parts. For example, WERS 2004 reveals a reasonable degree of overall happiness, with almost three in four workers saying that they are satisfied or very satisfied with 'work itself'. But on some measures (pay and involvement in decision making), around two-thirds of workers are neutral, dissatisfied or very dissatisfied with their experience of work (Kersley et al., 2006). In this context, perhaps the most important result is that only 38 per cent of employees are satisfied with their level of involvement in decision making in the workplace. These findings confirm the argument advanced by the TUC and others that there is a representation gap in many British workplaces; people want collective voice but at present have no means of expressing their views effectively (Coats, 2004; Towers, 1997; TUC, 2003). Equally, while 57 per cent of employees say that they are happy with their level of job influence, this means that 43 per cent are not, with 14 per cent either dissatisfied or very dissatisfied. These results suggest in turn that the decline of task discretion and autonomy have been combined with a loss of 'voice' and are reinforced by the WERS finding that joint consultation has declined even though the government has been ostensibly promoting the beneficial effects of collective consultation (Kersley et al., 2006). One might infer too that there has been a decline in social capital in many workplaces that could make employees less resilient when confronted with crises in their working lives.

We have already noted that there is a high level of dissatisfaction with pay. Of course, one could argue that employees will always say that they should earn more, but this is to dispose of the argument too easily. There is an equally strong case that this finding reflects widespread effort-reward imbalances in many British workplaces. This cumulative body of evidence goes a long way towards explaining why many employees have reported deterioration in the quality of working life (Bunting, 2004; Taylor, 2002). WERS also explored a range of job-related well-being measures, which produced a similar picture of general satisfaction combined with some very disturbing findings. For example, one in five employees reports that their job makes them feel tense all or most of the time and 47 per cent say that their job makes them worried all, most or some of the time. On the other hand,

38 per cent say that their job makes them feel content all or most of the time and 26 per cent that their job makes them feel relaxed. Even if these findings fail to give a picture of unmitigated misery, they do suggest that there are serious problems that both government and employers would be foolish to ignore.

Michael White has explored the impact of the so-called HPWS on the implementation of family-friendly policies and finds evidence of both work intensification and declining flexibility (White, 2003). In some ways, this is surprising because it has often been assumed that HPWS are in their very nature better for employees. It is said that multiskilling, multitasking, flatter hierarchies, more team working and more joint problem solving are all associated with better health and higher levels of job satisfaction. 'High-performance jobs' are by definition richer and more fulfilling jobs, and the quality of employment will inevitably improve as the knowledge economy develops and as market forces push more jobs up the value chain. Certainly, this is the view implicit in the Department of Trade and Industry's narrative about high-performance workplaces, but it neglects both our earlier argument that the performance effects of these practices are ambiguous and the emerging research that, for employees, these practices are often associated with work intensification rather than higher quality employment (Godard, 2004).

These studies are important because they make clear that new forms of work organisation can be associated with a deterioration of the working environment as well as improvement. Confirming Taylor's argument, Francis Green has suggested that rising skill levels have also been matched by a process of work intensification, with an increasing number of workers saying that they are 'working under a great deal of tension' and agreeing strongly with the statement that 'my job requires me to work very hard'. However, he notes that the phenomenon seems to have peaked in 1997 and there has been no deterioration since that time (Green, 2005). Green has located some of the rising dissatisfaction with work in a mismatch between employee skill and the nature of the jobs they are doing. While employers' skill requirements may have risen, workers' levels of formal qualification have risen faster so that an increasing proportion of employees are overqualified for the jobs that they do. Inevitably, this feeds through into lower levels of job satisfaction. Employees get frustrated that they are unable fully to deploy their skills (Green, 2003). Boredom is of course one of the factors that produces adverse health effects, and it is reasonable to suggest that employees who are both overqualified and underutilised will have a profound sense of their status.

This raises some interesting questions about the ability of employers to make the best use of a highly skilled workforce. In other words, Green's phenomenon of skills mismatching could intensify as levels of formal education rise and employers continue to offer routine and rather unrewarding jobs. Ewart Keep and Ken Mayhew have suggested that little will change until regulation forces employers to adopt 'high road' rather than 'low road' product market strategies (Keep and Mayhew, 2001). In other words, only government intervention can require employers to think innovatively about how they unlock the talents of all their employees. If nothing is done, then employers will be able to continue to make the otherwise rational choice that good profits can be made from low-quality, undifferentiated, mass-market products, produced by a low-productivity workforce – and such organisations will by definition be unable to offer anything other than 'bad jobs'. These are important considerations as we examine the role of public policy in creating an environment that enables employers in their turn to create and sustain more 'good jobs'.

A practical agenda for the future

So what then should be done? Who is responsible for addressing these problems? How much can be done by government and how much by employers, trade unions and other stakeholders? Perhaps we should start by articulating the simple principle that government cannot create high-quality employment by legislative fiat. Obviously, government can establish minimum statutory standards, but it cannot require employers to offer interesting, secure and well-rewarded jobs. On the other hand, there can be no doubt that government has a 'bully pulpit' and can influence the overall climate of the debate. Issues on the government's agenda in the world of work will unavoidably demand a response for employers and trade unions.

Government therefore has a role in at least the following areas:

- Improving the supply of and demand for skills
- Using regulation as a driver of performance improvement
- Providing effective support to businesses which might otherwise struggle with compliance with regulation
- Acting as a repository of best practice on work organisation, job design and management standards
- Enthusiastically implementing the regulations on information and consultation to ensure that workers have the 'voice' that they want and need

Furthermore, we have already noted that dissatisfaction with working time is an important cause of wider dissatisfaction with work. Despite their unwillingness to implement the EU directive with any real enthusiasm, the government are likely to find that they cannot address the UK's long-hour culture unless they adopt a more interventionist stance. A useful first step would be to adopt a phased approach to the removal of the so-called opt-out from the 48-hour week, with a limit on the length of the average working week (measured over a 12-month reference period) that progressively reduces over (say) five years to the limit specified in the EU Directive. This approach was successfully adopted in the Republic of Ireland and has had no adverse impact on economic growth or employment.

Much has already been done to improve the skills supply but rather less to improve the quality of employer demand. The risk of course is that the skills institutions do no more than attempt to meet the existing pattern of demand, which will do little to solve the UK's productivity conundrum. Sector Skills Councils (SSCs) could play an important role here by making clear the extent to which a sector must 'raise its game' to have a sustainable future. However, these are new institutions, which are just beginning to build their legitimacy. Unless they are integrated into a comprehensive government policy for the improvement of organisational performance they will fail to achieve their potential, or have any impact on overall job quality.

The scale of the challenge is clear. As Ewart Keep has persuasively argued, if some British employers had a workforce trained to German or Nordic standards, they would not know what to do with them (Keep, 2000). Even if the SSCs are improving supply to meet what should be a clear demand, there is no guarantee that all or even a majority of employers will understand the nature of this challenge. This is where well-crafted and proportionate regulation can play an important role in changing employer behaviour and encouraging innovation. For many employers of course regulation is simply a 'burden on business', yet another cost that reduces 'competitiveness'. No government would ever regulate anything at all if they really feared that business was unable to cope. Yet the evidence of the last eight years suggests that a substantial re-regulation of the UK labour market has, through the minimum wage, tighter dismissal rules, the social chapter measures and new rights for working parents, produced no adverse effects on the economy.

Indeed, a more positive case can be made. Those firms that are operating at the margins of the law will have little choice but to improve their performance or run the risk of failure. Having to pay the minimum wage has been accommodated by many employers so far through reductions in profits or increases in prices – there is no evidence of any job loss effect – but eventually these strategies will run their course, and these businesses will have little alternative but to look for performance and productivity improvements to manage the increased wage costs (Low Pay Commission, 2003). A very similar point might be made about health and safety regulation, where the need to comply has led organisations to rethink their processes, reorganise work or redesign jobs. Contrary to many employers' expectations, the effect has been an improvement in productivity. Furthermore, reputable employers can be confident that regulation insulates them against unfair competition from the unscrupulous. As Winston Churchill said when introducing the wages boards legislation in 1909, in the absence of minimum wages the good employer will be undercut by the bad, and the bad employer will be undercut by the worst.

Few employers have been willing to embrace such a pro-regulation argument with enthusiasm, but this is precisely the case that needs to be made to establish a clear link between state intervention and improved productivity and performance. Otherwise, advocates of pro-portionate regulation will always be on the defensive, constantly fending off attacks from those who believe that any regulation is a brake on entrepreneurial dynamism. Government has an obligation to ensure that businesses can comply with regulation and should offer support to small medium enterprises (SMEs) in particular to enable them to respond innovatively. Otherwise, SMEs are likely to complain quite legitimately that they lack the capacity to comply or rethink their business processes to improve performance. This means that high priority must be given to the range of services offered by Business Links and to the role of the Small Business Service. There should also be investment in other services that small businesses access voluntarily – such as ACAS – to ensure that they are in a position either to give advice or to ensure businesses are put in touch with someone who can. Furthermore, the DTI should see itself as the repository of good practice and should disseminate this information to employers in collaboration with the social partners.

This best practice function is particularly important in the realm of work organisation and job design where, as we have seen, many employers struggle to 'let go', trust their workers and create an environment where managers are mentors and facilitators rather than supervisors or auditors. Once again some progress has already been made, the government has recognised that quality of work is a public health issue and the Department of Health and the Department of Work and Pensions (2005) have developed a joint strategy for the promotion of health and well-being in the workplace. All of this is welcome, but many employers and trade unions still have a rather traditional attitude to the promotion of workplace health and safety – it is all about risk assessment, risk management and the rehabilitation of employees with medical conditions. Yet a more radical agenda would look at the nature of employment to identify the root causes of work-related ill health. This is not to suggest that the current approach to health and safety should be abandoned, but that more should be done to ensure that the factors driving ill health (insecurity, effort-reward imbalances, monotony and repetition) are removed from as many workplaces as possible.

Of course, this agenda does not lend itself to a simple regulatory solution. These are complex issues, and progress largely depends on the willingness of employers to rethink their processes and management structures to design out the negative factors. What is needed is a much clearer articulation of the role of regulation (establishing minimum standards and framework conditions) and the role of voluntary action to apply good practice. Government can go so far, but the best guarantee that progress will be made is the presence of dynamic voice institutions in the workplace (whether trade unions or works councils) pressing employers to improve their performance.

Government has a role to play of course in creating the conditions in which these institutions can thrive. Even if it is a step too far to reinstate, the notion that collective bargaining is a collective good for both employers and employees, current policy, at least in principle, places a high value on workplace information and consultation. One might say that this is a test of the government's seriousness of purpose and their commitment to a particular conception of human flourishing in the world of work. The argument presented here suggests that the information and consultation regulations should be promoted (and enforced) with rather more enthusiasm than has been evinced so far. In practical terms, this means that government must tell a more compelling story about the linkages between productivity, voice and the quality of employment that does not depend on the limited range of 'high-performance practices' that we have already discussed. They should adopt an explicitly pluralist frame of reference, recognising that conflict is inevitable in the workplace but that public policy should foster relationships focused on making the cake bigger rather than on deciding on the size of the slices for each party (Freeman and Medoff, 1984).

None of these measures can guarantee that we will see more good jobs in the UK, but experience in the Nordic countries, Austria and the Netherlands suggests that robust institutions reinforced by meaningful dialogue between employers, workers and their representatives can achieve a rather better tradeoff between justice and efficiency than we have managed so far in the UK. British workplaces may not be awful, but many of them can and should be significantly better. Accepting this reality is the first step towards developing a programme for government, employers and trade unions founded on the understanding that work is a social act, a fully human activity and an arena where we continue to enjoy all our rights as citizens. Our task then is to revive the notion of 'industrial citizenship' more than 50 years after the British sociologist T.H. Marshall coined the phrase (Marshall, 1950, 1991). Living up to our values demands nothing less.

References

Budd, J. W. (2004) *Employment with a Human Face*, Cornell: Cornell University Press.

Bunting, M. (2004) *Willing Slaves*, London: HarperCollins.

CBI (2003) High Performance Workplaces: The Role of Employee Involvement in a Modern Economy – CBI Response, Confederation of British Industry. http://www.cbi.org.uk

Coats, D. (2004) Speaking Up! Voice, Industrial Democracy and Organisational Performance. TWF. http://www.theworkfoundation.com

Crosland, C. A. R. (1962) *The Conservative Enemy*, New York: Jonathan Cape.

Department of Health and Department of Work and Pensions (2005) *Health, Work and Well-Being: A Strategy for the Employment of Working Age People*, TSO.

Fox, A. (1966) 'Industrial Sociology and Industrial Relations', Research Paper 3, Royal Commission on Trade Unions and Employers' Associations, London: HMSO.

Freeman, R. B. and Medoff, J. L. (1984) *What Do Unions Do?* Oxford: Basic Books.

Gallie, D. (2004) 'Changing Patterns of Task Discretion in Britain', *Work Employment and Society*, **18**, 243–266.

Godard, J. (2004) 'A Critical Assessment of the High Performance Paradigm', *British Journal Industrial Relations*, **42**, 348–378.

Green, F. (2003) 'The Demands of Work', in *The Labour Market Under New Labour* (Dickens, R., ed.), Basingstoke: Palgrave.

Green, F. (2005) *Demanding Work*, Princeton: Princeton University Press.

Kahn-Freund, O. (1983) *Labour and the Law*, London: Stevens and Sons.

Kay, J. (2003) *The Truth About Markets*, London: Penguin-Allen Lane.

Keep, E. (2000) *Creating a Knowledge Driven Economy – Definitions, Challenges and Opportunities*. SKOPE. http://www.skope.ox.ac.uk

Keep, E. and Mayhew, K. (2001) *Globalisation, Models of Competitive Advantage and Skills*. SKOPE. http://www.skope.ox.ac.uk

Kersley, B., Alpin, C., Forth, J., Bryson, A., Bewley, H., Dix, G. and Oxenbridge, S. (2006) *Inside the Workplace: Findings from the 2004 Workplace Employment Relations Survey*, Oxon: Routledge.

Lane, R. E. (1991) *The Market Experience*, Cambridge: Cambridge University Press.

Layard, R. (2004) *Good Jobs and Bad Jobs*. CEP Occasional Paper No 19. http://cep.lse.ac.uk

Layard, R. (2005) *Happiness: Lessons From a New Science*, London: Allen Lane.

Lea, R. (2003) *Red Tape in the Workplace*, Institute of Directors. http://www.iod.co.uk

Low Pay Commission (2003) *The National Minimum Wage: Building on Success*, TSO.

Marmot, M. (2004) *Status Syndrome*, London: Bloomsbury.

Marshall T. H. (1991 [1950]) *Citizenship and Social Class*, London: Pluto Press.

Maslow, A. (1954) *Motivation and Personality*, Harlow: Longmans.

OECD (2001) *Employment Outlook*, OECD.

Putnam, R. D. (2001) *Bowling Alone*, New York: Simon and Schuster Ltd.

Rawls, J. (2001) *Justice as Fairness: A Restatement*, Boston: Harvard University Press.

Stiglitz, J. E. (2001) 'Democratic Development as the Fruits of Labour', in *The Rebel Within: Joseph Stiglitz and the World Bank*, (Chang, H.-J., ed.) Wimbledon: Anthem Press.

Taylor, R. (2002) *Britain's World of Work – Myths and Realities*, Economic and Social Research Council. http://www.esrcsocietytoday.esrc.ac.uk

Towers, B. (1997) *The Representation Gap: Change and Reform in the British and American Workplace*, Oxford: Oxford University Press.

TUC (2003) *A Perfect Union*, London: Trade Union Congress.

Wall, T. and Wood, S. (2005) 'The Romance of Human Resource Management and Business Performance, and the Case for Big Science', *Human Relations*, **58**, 4, 429–462.

White, M. (2003) 'High Performance Work Practices, Working Hours and Work Life Balance', *British Journal of Industrial Relations*, **41**, 175–195.

White, M. and Hill, S. (2004) *Managing to Change? British Workplaces and the Future of Work*, Basingstoke: Palgrave.

5

Is good work productive work?

John Philpott

Introduction

The nature of the link between the way people are managed, labour productivity and how well organisations perform is a matter of keen debate. Intertwined with this is the relationship between management practice and the quality of people's working lives. The provision of 'good', 'dignified' (or simply 'better') work is at times posited as an essential prerequisite to higher productivity and organisational performance and at others as no more than a cost, either borne voluntarily by benevolent employers or imposed by state regulation and absorbed as lower profits (or more commonly) passed on to workers in the form of lower pay rises. The business case for the adoption of various worker-friendly management practices, or the general economic efficiency case for statutory employment rights that require their adoption, thus usually rests on some form of cost-benefit assessment of their impact.

The tendency of the traditional political right is to view such practices as a cost if they are imposed in the absence of a clear business case. The traditional political left meanwhile tend to view them as socially desirable, regardless of whether a cost or a benefit to business or the economy as a whole. The latter view also chimes with the ethical or theological case for dignified work such as that espoused by the late Pope John Paul II in his famous 1981 Encyclical on human work (Laborem Exercens) which states that 'work is for man, not man for work'. In other words, people are not human resources simply to be used at the whim of employers but human beings for whom the availability of dignified work is essential to the fulfilment of their humanity.

Increasingly, however, under the influence of the dominant centre left/centre right political consensus, policy-makers seek to either promote the business case for worker-friendly management practices and/or argue that improved employment regulation can if sensibly implemented also be employer friendly as well as ethically good. This latter stance is exemplified in the UK by the Blair government's fairness at work agenda which purports to combine economic efficiency and social justice in the workplace.

There is nonetheless considerable scepticism of the scope for genuine positive sum (or so called 'win-win') outcomes in the field of employment practice and policy, with continued emphasis on the need to assess the extent of tradeoffs between efficiency and equity outcomes. Moreover, at the level of popular perception, any assertion that productive work from the employers' viewpoint can also mean better work for employees challenges a deeply ingrained belief within UK society that there is an inevitable adverse tradeoff between anything that improves labour productivity and the social condition of labour. As a result, talk of 'modernised work practices' is often treated with suspicion rather than welcomed as a sign of progress. This is in part a legacy of the low-trust industrial relations of the twentieth century and in part also to the predominance of left leaning capitalist critique in much academic analysis of the workplace.

Yet despite this, it can be argued that the underlying economics of work is at present altering the productivity/working conditions equation in developed economies like that of the UK, at the very least reducing any adverse tradeoff and opening up opportunities for win-win outcomes. As high-quality customised products and services become more important to competitive success and profitability so does the treatment of people at work. Organisations that want to succeed thus need to switch from business models that manage workers simply as costs to be minimised to models that instead manage workers as valuable assets that must be well treated. Whatever the merit of the power (or class) inequality view of employment relations in the past or present, modes of production in developed economies are gradually shifting in favour of some form of shared-interest capitalism. In other words, productive work really can be good work and vice versa.

However, although the positive impact of the shift towards shared interest is evident in many indicators of job quality, the shift is neither smooth nor universal across or within industrial sectors, with operation of simple cost-based business models still widespread. This explains some less positive developments in working life and the continued existence of many poor-quality jobs. And it also raises important public policy issues.

People management and working conditions in British historical perspective

Fear of the consequences of change in the pace or pattern of work, whether due to new technology, improved management techniques or greater competitive pressure, has been a constant source of social anxiety and insecurity ever since the first industrial revolution. The term 'Luddite', still hurled pejoratively at those who express unease in the face of change, derives from that period. Paternalist capitalism – exemplified first by Robert Owen and later the Quaker industrialist families such as Cadbury and Rowntree – demonstrated the commercial benefits of providing good working conditions. But despite this, the negative social connotations attached to talk of improvements in productivity or modernised work practices was reinforced with the emergence of the Taylorist-style scientific people management that was to remain dominant throughout much of the twentieth century, especially in the more prevalent mega manufacturing corporations.

Taylorism was a remarkably successful engine of productivity growth and profit generation during the 'pile it high, sell it cheap' era of standardised mass manufacturing production. And in terms of financial reward, it was good for workers too. Unfortunately, the routine, specialised work required by organisations whose end game is high volume at low cost can be boring, if not soul destroying, while people employed by such organisations come to associate efforts to raise productivity with longer working hours and greater pressure to get things done.

Trade unions were the most significant institutional response to Taylorism. Unions offered a means of extracting a greater share of whatever profit was made – even if not always securing improved working conditions – their cooperation with management in turn determining productivity and the potential for profit generation. But while in principle the mutual benefit gained from cooperation created scope for shared-interest employment relations, this was more often than not undermined by mutual distrust inherent in the Taylorised workplace. Scientific management renders workers little more than cogs in the organisational machine. Management simply involves making sure these human cogs keep turning as long and as fast as possible, by way of regimented top-down command and control techniques, and ideally finding ways of reducing the total number of cogs required in order to cut costs. For organisations that operate in this way, people management is a matter of process rather than strategy, necessary only to ensure that enough workers walk in through the door when required, that they are equipped with the specialist skills they need, that they are paid on time, that they do not become so unhappy as to cause unrest and that enough are shipped out the door with as little fuss as possible when the demand for their effort dries up.

Although in everyday practice the depersonalised nature of management of this kind is mitigated by the injection into employment relations of human personality – tales of the benefits of 'good' as opposed to 'bad' managers are manifold – it is not normally conducive to high trust. And when operating within a British tradition of class hostility, it is not surprising that unrest rather than cooperation was the order of the day for much of the twentieth century. The result was what was once known as 'the British disease'; low productivity and often rampant wage and price inflation as organised workers used their power to gain higher pay from profit squeezed organisations which in turn passed cost hikes onto consumers.

The progressive response to such mutual distrust and its consequences was the emergence of welfare work, itself strongly influenced by the thinking of the Quaker capitalists. The Welfare Workers' Association (WWA, founded in 1913 with much effort from Seebohm Rowntree, and initial forerunner of today's Chartered Institute of Personnel and Development) provided a focus for individuals and firms pioneering improvement in the general condition and well-being of people at work. The Association's stated objectives also included that of fostering good industrial relations. To achieve this, welfare workers cooperated with employers and workers, including trade unions, the latter recognised by the WWA as the 'chosen means of self-expression' of working people. But in contrast to advocates of either unfettered management or socialist state control of industry and commerce, the WWA saw workers and managers not as class enemies but partners with a shared interest in success. By the late twentieth century, however, what started out as welfare work had metamorphosed into a distinct managerial function, first as personnel management and latter human resource management (HRM). And though the focus on shared interest and improved working conditions remained, HR practitioners sought to develop a harder business focus to counter the common accusation that the HR function, whilst necessary to perform routine administrative tasks, adds no more than a soft veneer to organisational performance.

The conjunction of this change in the HR focus with the emergence of more intense global competition and domestic competitive pressures, plus effective abandonment of full employment as a key public policy goal, altered the relationship between the HR function and employees. Competition and mass unemployment demolished the job security once associated with Taylorism in advanced western economies – especially in the manufacturing sectors – as organisations struggled to match the bargain-basement prices offered by low-cost competitors based in developing countries. In this context, HR was increasingly seen as the deliverer of the P45, echoing the general management rhetoric of cost efficiency, greater work effort and employment flexibility, rather than some kind of 'employee champion' seeking to enhance the quality of working life. Moreover, with smaller organisations accounting for a growing share of total employment as larger organisations downsized, many employees found themselves bereft of any meaningful professional HR support at all.

The new people management

Late twentieth-century economic and labour market conditions therefore militated against the notion of dignified work. Indeed, there was a tendency at the time to posit the return of a harsher mode of capitalism akin to that of the nineteenth century, structural change and liberal policy reforms having emasculated organised labour (particularly in the private sector) and reduced individual employment rights. Yet though there are still many exponents of one or other version of this kind of depressing scenario, a variety of developments suggest a more positive outlook for the future of work, leastways in the early part of the current century. Amongst these positive developments are greater economic stability, the return to full employment and gradual enhancement of employment rights, including adherence to provisions of the European Social Chapter. But above all is an appreciation of the limits, in today's knowledge-based and service-based economy, of business models based solely on cost efficiency.

With increasingly sophisticated consumers demanding high quality and efficient service rather than just low-priced standardised goods, the challenge to all organisations – not just global players but also commercial and public-sector organisations serving purely domestic markets – is to compete on the basis of quality, design, personalised service and efficiency of delivery. This means being responsive to customer demand and innovative in both product and service development to keep ahead of the game. Moreover, increasing competition, continual advances in technology and changing consumer tastes also mean that organisations must be prepared for change and able to constantly adapt and reorganise.

The corollary is that because high-quality customised products and services are rich in inputs of knowledge and 'the personal touch', people assets (or 'human capital') become vital to raising the value of goods and services. This implies a radically different approach to people management. People are assets with feet; organisations therefore need to do everything they can to become employers of choice in order to attract, motivate and retain staff. Organisations also have to equip workers to be adaptable, to operate in teams and to engage in ongoing learning, rather than train people in highly specialised skills to perform routine, unchanging tasks.

Most fundamental of all, successful organisations need to make people management integral to everything they do rather than treat it as a specialist function left to those with an interest in 'the soft stuff'. Consequently, all managers have to transform their relations with those they manage: out-go command, control and the passing down of instructions, in-come autonomy, discretion and the sharing of information. This is vital, not only in order to ensure effective performance, but also, and crucially, to maintain the trust necessary to enable organisations to constantly reorganise, either in response to or in anticipation of changes in the environments in which they operate. Managers thus need to be able to lead people rather than simply manage them; qualities of leadership become as important as management per se. The result is not, as sometimes mistakenly assumed, less management but a different kind of management. While there is less room in organisations for middle managers – the lieutenants of traditional command and control, whose ranks have indeed dwindled in the past two decades – the cadre of 'leader managers' able to motivate teams and networks is growing.

Depictions of the new people management and work organisation come in a variety of forms. It is commonly referred to as 'high-performance working' or 'smarter working' [Chartered Institute of Personnel and Development and the Engineering Employers' Federation (CIPD and EEF), 2003]. The corresponding management practices consist of things like creative job design, continuous appraisal, autonomous or semiautonomous team working, ongoing learning, performance-related pay and flexible hours (Purcell et al., 2003). But in whatever guise it requires a marked degree of shared-interest engagement between management – senior, line and HR – and employees. And although it is organisational effectiveness rather than simply concern for the welfare of workers that provides the driving force, the new people management practices needed to make the most of human assets also score highest on all the indicators that are found by economists and psychologists to make workers happy. These are autonomy and scope for discretion, control over the pace of work, a supportive climate, mutual trust, a dynamic atmosphere and participation in decision making. This suggests that the quality of working life has to be good if work is to be effective. If not, organisations find it difficult to secure the motivation and commitment they need from those they employ in order to 'go the extra mile' at work.

It is of course arguable that the need of organisations to foster shared interest with employees is no more than a cosmetic gloss on the fundamental power inequality that always exists within capitalism. Indeed, some critical depictions of objectively 'good workplaces' – such as those in lists of 'best companies to work for' – portray these as little more than a con designed to seduce employees into committing their discretionary effort to the organisation. The popularly received assertion that the workplace is increasingly full of overworked 'willing slaves' falls into this category (Bunting, 2004). Yet even if true – the empirical basis for this assertion itself being questionable – this view has to acknowledge that in a competitive labour market organisations are having to promise good work on one or other dimensions to persuade employees to commit and engage their energies.

Anti-capitalist critics meanwhile highlight the poor pay and conditions of workers in developing countries as being inextricably linked to ostensibly high-value business models pursued by many global corporations. This fact is used to call into question the ethical position of such organisations and said to potentially undermine the pay and job security of workers in developed economies who constantly face the threat that their jobs will be 'offshored' to lower cost locations. But though this is beyond dispute in a global economy, it is no more than a statement of the blindingly obvious. The operation of profit-seeking organisations in dynamic open market economies will always result in winners and losers, and there is never a guarantee that economic conditions in any country conducive to more worker-friendly modes of production will not at some point give way to those conducive to a harsher work environment. Yet accepting change as a fact of economic life does not mean that the quality of working life must always and everywhere be under pressure – and, at present, conditions conducive to better quality work are prevalent in the UK and other developed economies.

The dimensions of good work

If this conclusion is true, one might expect to see evidence of improving conditions of work. But when examining available indicators, it is important to be clear about the pitfalls involved in measuring change in the quality of work. This not only needs to account for various identifiable monetary and non-monetary attributes of work but also for the subjective weightings individuals give to the type of work they do. Most analysts focus on tangible quality indicators like pay, job security, hours of work, working environment and safety. Sometimes added to these are institutional support provisions for workers such as employment protection laws, trade union recognition and health and safety regulation. However, it is generally recognised that job quality also encompasses a range of less tangible aspects such as job content and challenge, autonomy and scope for discretion, control over the pace of work, a supportive climate, mutual trust, a dynamic atmosphere, opportunities for training and career progression and participation in decision making.

Tangible and intangible aspects of work are clearly evident in taxonomies of dignity of work and dignity in work. But using this kind of taxonomy to assess the quality of work risks imposing analysts' own subjective value judgements on employees' actual experience of work and can fail to adjust for the extent to which individuals may make voluntary tradeoffs between different aspects of jobs. For example, the long-standing theory of compensating differentials uses differences in the non-monetary attributes of jobs to help explain why workers may accept lower pay in a particular occupation or with a particular employer even though higher reward may be on offer elsewhere. Likewise, while some people value scope for autonomy at work others will consider this daunting or stressful and prefer jobs with clearly defined and limited roles. What is drudgery to some can be personally rewarding, or at least less demanding, to others.

This kind of complexity renders somewhat pointless rather stale debates, evident since the 1980s, over whether, say, manufacturing jobs are 'better' than service sector jobs, or full-time jobs better than part-time. While full-time jobs still generally offer better terms and conditions, most part-timers prefer the other advantages that flow from shorter hours. Similarly, many less-well-paid jobs are entry-level positions that reflect either the low general skills individuals bring to the market or their need to acquire on-the-job work experience. Whether individuals view such work positively or negatively will reflect the choices and constraints they face in moving up the job ladder and/or their personal aspirations.

Are working conditions improving?

To account for this complexity, measurement of the quality of work usually requires large opinion surveys that ask people what aspects of work they find most or least appealing and, as a proxy for perceived job quality, how satisfied they are with the various aspects of their own jobs and how satisfied they are with their jobs overall. There are numerous published studies of this kind, including regular CIPD surveys of employee attitudes that are analysed in the framework of the so-called Psychological Contract (e.g., Guest and Conway, 2004). The latter term refers to the tacit deal between employer/manager and employee which underpins their relationship by establishing what each party expects from the other.

In simple terms, the various aspects of job quality can be said to comprise what the employer offers as his/her part of the deal. The employee's rating of the quality of the offer will affect his/her willingness to accept the job, how satisfied he/she is in the job and the likelihood of him/her quitting the job. Job satisfaction will in turn be affected by underlying shifts in the contours of the deal. These might include changing expectations on the part of the employee, or a change in what the employer offers or expects from the employee. These might be individual changes or seismic shifts in either employer practice (e.g., 'global market pressures') or social attitudes (e.g., post-9/11 life values angst).

Available survey evidence typically finds a very high overall level of job satisfaction in the UK (usually at least two-thirds of employees say they are satisfied with their work) though with some groups of people more satisfied than others (other characteristics being equal): women more than men; the less educated more than the highly educated; managers more than other employees; non-union members more than union members; public-sector employees more than private-sector employees (though these sectoral differences exhibit fluctuations over time); people in smaller workplaces more than people in large workplaces; self-employed people more than employees (Gardner and Oswald, 1999). The overall trend in the past decade has been for the level of job satisfaction to remain broadly flat with a slight tendency to a decrease (having controlled for factors like changes in the types of jobs people do). This is significant since most objective measures of job quality would suggest that this has improved (Fitzner, 2006).

Tight labour markets and a record number of people in work have resulted in greater overall job security, with the redundancy rate falling to a historical low in 2005. Real (i.e., price inflation adjusted) wages have increased at all points in the pay distribution and across all major industrial sectors. Between 1995 and 2005, real wage growth averaged around 2.75 per cent per annum in the private sector and 2.5 per cent in the public sector. Average working hours meanwhile have fallen significantly to a record low, as has the proportion of people working very long hours, while there has been an increase in the incidence of various forms of flexible working. The proportion of men working more than 48 hours fell by a fifth between 1998 and 2005.

Shorter hours and more flexible work patterns are in part due to improvements in basic employment rights, most notably regulations to implement the European Union Working Time Directive which took effect in 1998. Even more significant is the National Minimum Wage introduced in 1999 which, although low relative to average earnings, has increased faster than average pay. This has enabled less skilled employees to at least hold their own in the pay distribution. In the process, while the proportion of jobs in the highest decile of the distribution has grown, there has been a sharp fall in the proportion of jobs in the lowest decile, the proportion of jobs offering median pay remaining relatively unchanged.

In other words, insofar as one can describe jobs as 'good' or 'bad' on the basis of pay, conditions and minimum standards, the UK has experienced a clear shift in the direction of good jobs. What has happened is that improvement in tangible job quality has been offset by increased dissatisfaction with the pressure of work and the degree of autonomy or task discretion on offer (Clark, 2005; Green and Tsitsianis, 2005). This gives rise to a specific work-related form of the now widely commented on happiness-economic growth paradox whereby in recent decades measured social happiness has not risen despite considerable growth in national income (Layard, 2005). Improvements in the material conditions of work do not seem to be making workers happier because at the same time pressure of work adds to stress and related observable phenomenon such as mounting psychological ill health and high levels of sickness-related absence from work. Indeed, this can even cause workers to express dissatisfaction with the degree of improvement they experience in tangible things like pay and hours of work.

Why no improvement in job satisfaction?

On the face of things stable overall job satisfaction casts doubt on the earlier optimistic conclusion that current economic and policy developments are favourable to improved job quality. But closer examination suggests that observed lack of improvement results not from an absence of positive drivers but rather from a combination of failure to adopt new high-performance people management practices quickly enough and difficulties encountered in introducing such practices, especially in a context of traditional low-trust employment relations.

At most, only one in five UK organisations are implementing high-performance people management practices in a consistent way. Around two in five apply more than 20 such practices, but take-up of specific practices varies considerably. For example, according to a Department of Trade and Industry funded study of high-performance working, while over 90 per cent of organisations operate annual appraisals, only two-thirds offer staff flexible working options, only one-third offer performance-related pay to all employees and only a quarter organise staff into autonomous self-directed work teams (Sung and Ashton, 2005). Moreover, there is little to suggest that UK organisations are making rapid progress in implementation.

The 2004 Workplace Employment Relations Survey (WERS, part-sponsored by the DTI) found that both the incidence and operation of teamworking and the proportion of staff equipped to be multiskilled (or functionally flexible) have changed little since 1998 (the year of the previous WERS) (Kersley et al., 2006). Only in 6 per cent of workplaces are teams given autonomy to appoint their own leaders. There was an increase of 6 percentage points between 1998 and 2004 in the proportion of workplaces organising non-managerial staff in problem-solving groups, although, even in the latter year, the overall incidence of workplaces where this occurred was small (21 per cent).

The consequences of this are most commonly discussed in the context of the UK's relatively poor productivity performance (the well-known 'productivity gap'). But if, as argued earlier, there is an inherent link between high-performance management practices and worker satisfaction, low or slow take-up of such practices will stymie improvements in job quality too. This of course begs the question why, if high-performance management is so good, are not organisations rushing to introduce it? Surely there must be a strong business case for doing so regardless of any associated considerations of the quality of work? The answer lies in what might be called the 'three I's': organisational ignorance, inertia and inadequacy.

While heads of organisations talk constantly about 'making the most of our people', some are remarkably ignorant of what this actually entails. A multisector survey of chief executives of 462 UK organisations found that only 1 in 10 considered people management a top priority ahead of financial or marketing issues, despite the fact that two-thirds reckoned they relied on their people as a significant source of competitive advantage (Guest et al., 2002). Inertia, by contrast, results in organisations explicitly rejecting high-performance management. Sometimes, the necessary change is thought too costly or too difficult, or the benefits uncertain when compared with tried and trusted ways of working, even though these may not be delivering spectacular results.

This problem is identifiable in a variety of other features of the UK economy closely allied to low take-up of high-performance people management, such as deficient investment in research and development and skills. These deficiencies limit the ability of organisations to improve the quality of products and services leaving some with little alternative but to compete downmarket on the basis of low cost using low-skilled workers – giving rise to the well-known notion that the UK economy is trapped in a 'low-quality, low-skills equilibrium'. This helps explain certain features of the UK labour market, such as the still wide pay gap and substantial pockets of unskilled joblessness, and increased use of migrant workers, which in turn compacts a depressed strata of society on low incomes unable to demand high-quality goods and services. Consequently, organisations may continue to operate in low-cost market niches to meet this demand unless or until faced with severe competition or market difficulties.

Alongside the ignorant and inert are organisations that, whilst aware of the potential advantages of high-performance people management, are simply inadequate to respond. This may stem from lack of information on what might be done or lack of advice on how to do it. But it can also reflect inept or misguided implementation. Ineptitude is sometimes rooted in outdated organisational cultures which limit the ability of managers to achieve necessary reorganisation (for example, where a history of mutual mistrust creates resistance to change or where there is reluctance to dismantle corporate cultures built around command and control). New ways of working are sometimes introduced without workers being properly consulted or line managers themselves being adequately equipped for the task. Particular difficulties can arise from the introduction of new technologies which may involve not just new working practices but impose entirely new (and often unforeseen) pressures on staff, as often evidenced in the rapid advance of information technology in the workplace during the past decade which has both created opportunities for greater employee autonomy and flexible work patterns and increased scope for monitoring and surveillance of employees.

Inept efforts at managerial reform can indeed at times be more harmful to perceived job quality than no reform at all, by either threatening to disrupt the psychological contract or making promises of improvement that do not materialise. Similarly, for some workers and managers, the greater autonomy and discretion required by new management practices will often result in a greater burden of responsibility and effort than they have been used to. Some will be more comfortable with giving and receiving instruction than sharing knowledge and working in teams. Identifying the best fit between organisational requirements and employee orientations thus requires considerable managerial skill. However, such ineptitude should not necessarily be portrayed as being symptomatic of the inevitable existence of inadequate managers (such as the fictional David Brent). Just as detrimental to a healthy psychological contract are perfectly adequate managers in thrall of misguided or outdated management speak. A good example of this is continued emphasis on the merit of 'labour market flexibility' with use of rhetoric more suited to the 1980s than the twenty-first century. Although certain flexible work practices (notably those related to working time and reward) are integral to most high-performance management settings, the rhetoric of flexibility usually conveys the impression that the primary objective of management is to improve cost efficiency or cost-based competitiveness rather than to enhance the quality of goods and services. Given the associated connotations with downsizing, offshoring and increased work intensity, it is not surprising that this creates unease within the workplace, weakens the psychological contract and diminishes job satisfaction regardless of any objective improvement in more tangible conditions of work.

Tension also arises from the fashion for ever more rigorous forms of measurement systems to be introduced to monitor the effectiveness of management practices. The principal purpose of measurement in high-performance work settings is benign – to encourage organisations to treat people as assets rather than costs. This in turn is a bulwark against crude cost-cutting in the face of short-run financial pressures and thus helps sustain trust. But over wielding measurement systems can themselves sometimes be a vice rather than a virtue. They can take on a Taylorist hue and give rise to staff dissatisfaction; especially if linked to simplistic performance targets or introduced low-trust organisational cultures and thus seen as a means of reinforcing managerial command and control. This has been a particular problem in the public sector in recent years where the culture of centralised target setting, in still strongly unionised workplaces, has caused staff unease despite relatively rapid improvement in pay, conditions and the adoption of high-performance management practices.

Public policy and the common good at work

The apparent failure of many UK organisations to respond rapidly or adequately enough to the underlying factors driving an improvement in working conditions raises a variety of public policy issues. The long prevailing British tradition is that government should intervene as little as possible since organisations are better judges of how best to manage people than politicians or bureaucrats. While high-performance people management practices form the body through which the human lifeblood of organisations flows, what breathes life into successful organisations is their spirit or culture – the crucial aspects of which are a sense of shared vision, a common purpose and mutual trust. The efforts of policy-makers to encourage organisations to modernise working practices are thus unlikely to prove successful without a step change in organisational culture. But changing the culture of organisations is difficult. Culture change cannot be imposed quickly from outside but has to be brought about gradually from within.

According to this view, policy-makers should thus aspire to do no more than persuade or exhort organisations to raise their game, with the assistance of bodies equipped to help provide technical support, guidance or voluntary codes of practice. The CIPD, for example, as the professional body for HR practitioners, assists the policy process through its active participation on government working groups and task forces, regular submissions to policy consultations and Parliamentary committees and frequent comment in learned journals and the media. Nonetheless, public policy measures can exert pressure on organisations to move in the direction of shared-interest cultures.

Indirect measures include those that put market pressure on organisations and/or alter the conditions or incentives they face. By far, the best spur to higher performance, for example, is increased competition, which government can influence in a variety of ways by combating monopoly power in markets and encouraging more business start-ups. Similarly, government policies for education and training can make a big difference. Increasing the supply of basic and technical skills in the workforce makes it easier for organisations to adopt high-performance work strategies while at the same time limiting the supply of less skilled labour. And improving the quality of management education and training makes it more likely that organisations will develop the leadership capacity needed to deliver high performance. More direct measures include those that aim to improve the governance and accountability of organisations and, in particular, encourage organisations (and, where relevant, their shareholders) to place greater emphasis on the contribution people make to performance in the hope that this will spur take-up of state-of-the-art people management practices.

Yet while the doctrine of 'let managers manage' might be sound in principle, the existence of market failures, poor practice or downright bad practice and continued prevalence of poor working environments sometimes provides a justification for stronger forms of government intervention, such as financial sticks and carrots or regulation and compulsion. Moreover, even where there are no discernible economic grounds for intervening to alter management practice, there may be instances where moral or ethical considerations take precedent over the business case. Indeed, the Papal positing, as mentioned earlier, of work being for man not man for work makes a moral case for policies, with the explicit objective of enhancing the quality of work. As evidence of illegal practice demonstrates, it can be profitable to employ children or to operate without due regard to the health and safety of staff, but society, and the vast majority of organisations, rightly find this unacceptable. For example, health and safety regulations introduced over recent decades have added greatly to the common good. While there is still undoubted room for improvement, it is unlikely that the transformation in the quality of the factory and office environment experienced in the past generation would have occurred to anything like the same extent without tough regulation.

The convener of the inaugural 1913 meeting of the WWA, Seebohm Rowntree, acknowledged long ago the limits of voluntarism. Although it was the duty of enlightened employers and bodies like the WWA to promote the case for good people management, there was no guarantee that the message would be heeded. His book *The Human Needs of Labour* (1918) therefore strongly advocated the need for a statutory minimum wage, while his later work, *The Human Factor in Business* (1921), railed against autocratic management and recommended the spread of work councils to provide workers with a voice.

However, recognition of the limits of voluntarism does not provide justification for unlimited intervention by government. Most organisations act in the best interests of those they employ. And while the law can be an appropriate instrument for dealing with specific failings of organisational or management practice, it is normally too blunt to cope with the complexity of organisational life (giving rise to the drawbacks of the 'one-size-fits all' nature of much employment regulation). Government intervention must therefore be both proportionate and appropriate – which in practice means that the role of public policy in improving the quality of work needs to be considered in the context of the principle of subsidiarity. The latter is most frequently referred to in relation to the workings of the European Union but is actually a general principle (derived, incidentally, from the governing principles of the Catholic Church) which states that a higher authority – in the context discussed here 'government' or 'the law' – should not interfere in the workings of a lower authority – here the 'organisation' or 'the employer' – unless failure to do so were to diminish the common good. This in turn implies that government intervention in the affairs of organisations is neither inherently 'good' nor 'bad' – as might be implied by traditional ideological disputes between the political right and left – but needs to be assessed in relation to specific policy issues.

In any particular instance, it is first essential that policy-makers demonstrate the degree of divergence between what economists call the private and social rate of return to a management practice – how much society gains over and above the gain to an employer or organisation. In addition, the economic and social costs and benefits of any policy intervention – including those to consumers and taxpayers resulting from any effects on prices or taxation – must be made clear. This is especially true in the case of interventions where there is no obvious market failure to be addressed and where a policy is deemed to serve the common good even though it overrides purely business-case considerations. Policies that do not clearly result in win-win outcomes for both organisations and societies will involve tradeoffs and hence winners and losers. For example, it can be argued that restrictions on unskilled immigration would, other things being equal, encourage organisations dependent on low-paid migrant labour to alter terms and conditions of employment in order to attract more home-grown staff that might otherwise reject such work. But doing so might in turn raise the price to consumers of certain goods and services, in the process reducing real incomes with particularly adverse consequences for those on low incomes.

In such situations, an assessment of the overall effect on the common good is possible only if the potential costs to the losers are made as explicit as the potential benefits to the winners and some calculation made of the ratio of benefits to costs. Such situations may also require a more complex ethical assessment of what best advances the common good, for example where measures ostensibly designed to enhance the dignity of people in work increases the risk that some people might as a direct consequence suffer the pain and indignity of unemployment. This suggests that the best course is to adopt a gradualist approach to employment policy, combining the introduction of sensibly implemented minimum legal standards with efforts to encourage organisations to voluntarily adopt management practices best suited to their specific needs and those they employ. By contrast, most of the quick fixes commonly proposed, such as a big hike in the national minimum wage, much tougher legal limits on hours of work or far greater collective employment rights, simply do not address the underlying causes of dissatisfaction with work, convey significant costs relative to benefits and ultimately provide ammunition to opponents of progressive employment policy.

This conclusion inevitably rankles with those of us frustrated by the painfully slow progress in the direction of better work. But sensible and rational policy-making is always preferable to responding to the populist quick fix or ideas derived from narrow ideology or vested interest. For ultimately, only work that is consistent with the wider common good can be truly considered good work.

References

Bunting, M. (2004) *Willing Slaves: How the Overwork Culture is Ruling Our Lives*, London: Harper Collins.

Chartered Institute of Personnel and Development and the Engineering Employers' Federation (2003) *Maximising Employee Potential and Business Performance: The Role of High-performance Working*, London: Chartered Institute of Personnel and Development and the Engineering Employers' Federation.

Clark, A. (2005) 'Your Money or Your Life: Changing Job Quality in OECD Countries', *British Journal of Industrial Relations,* **43**, 3, 377–400.

Fitzner, G. (2006) *How Have Employees Fared? Recent UK Trends*, DTI Employment Relations Research Series No. 56, London: Department of Trade and Industry.

Gardner, J. A. and Oswald, A. J. (1999) *The Determinants of Job Satisfaction in Britain*, University of Warwick Research Paper, March.

Green, F. and Tsitsianis, N. (2005) 'An Investigation of National Trends in Job Satisfaction in Britain and Germany', *British Journal of Industrial Relations*, **43**, 3, 401–429.

Guest, D. and Conway, N. (2004) *Employee Well Being and the Psychological Contract*, London: Chartered Institute of Personnel and Development.

Guest, D., King, Z., Conway, N., Michie, J. and Sheehan-Quinn, M. (2002) *Voices from the Boardroom*, London: Chartered Institute of Personnel and Development.

Kersley, B., Alpin, C., Forth, J., Bryson, A., Bewley, H., Dix, G. and Oxenbridge, S. (2006) *Inside the Workplace: Findings from the 2004 Workplace Employment Relations Survey*, Oxon: Routledge.

Layard, P. R. G. (2005) *Happiness: Lessons from a New Science,* London: Penguin.

Purcell, J., Kinnie, N., Hutchinson, S., Rayton, B., and Stuart, J. (2003) *Understanding the People and Performance Link: Unlocking the Black Box*, London: Chartered Institute of Personnel and Development.

Sung, J. and Ashton, D. (2005) *High-performance Work Practices: Linking Strategy and Skills to Performance Outcomes*, London: Department of Trade and Industry.

6

The informal economy and dignified work

Niall Cooper and Catherine May

Can Cinderella ever achieve dignity?

The informal economy is in many ways the Cinderella subject of the 'dignity at work' debate: the badly dressed poor relation who toils away cleaning up other people's mess with no status, and who rarely sees the light of day. In the absence of a Prince Charming to transform their prospects, what chance do those working in the informal economy have of enjoying 'dignified' work? As the 2002 International Labour Conference concluded (using the term of 'decent' in place of 'dignified'):

> 'Contrary to earlier predictions, the informal economy has been growing rapidly in almost every corner of the globe, including industrialized countries – it can no longer be considered a temporary or residual phenomenon... But work in the informal economy cannot be termed "decent" compared to recognized, protected, secure, formal employment' (International Labour Conference, 90th Session, 2002).

For significant numbers of people in the UK, as elsewhere, the informal economy – with all the risks, vulnerabilities and lack of employment rights – is a daily reality. Whilst for some this is a rational choice, for many, in the absence of other options, it is essentially part of their 'survival strategy'. Nevertheless, the existence of the informal sector presents policy makers with a dilemma. Should they respond pragmatically to its existence as a provider of employment and incomes or seek to extend regulation and social protection to it and thereby possibly reduce its capacity to provide jobs and incomes for an ever expanding labour force? Whilst the UK policy response is overwhelmingly characterised by negative and punitive attitudes towards those working in the informal economy, it can be argued that by stigmatising those found working informally it serves to decrease their own sense of dignity and worth.

This chapter explores the problem of defining, researching and quantifying the scale of the informal economy, and its inter-relationship with issues of gender and discrimination. It draws on research carried out by Oxfam's UK Poverty Programme and Church Action on Poverty (CAP) during 2005, which documented the differing experiences, risks and motives of those working in the informal economy – cash-in-hand, migrant workers with and without documents, and asylum seekers. The research found that for many people, the work was seen as a top-up to low benefits and a more lucrative choice than low-wage formal equivalents and, although precarious and risky, for some it was the only opportunity they had to secure a livelihood. The chapter concludes that it was a struggle for people to access dignity while working in the informal economy due to the low quantity and quality of alternatives and the stigma attached.

What is the informal economy?

Employment within the informal economy has many names: 'on the black, cash-in-hand, moonlighters, ghosts, under the table, off the books'. By its very nature, informal work is hard to describe and harder to research. There is no universally accurate or accepted description or definition; the 2002 International Labour Conference on decent work and the informal economy noted that there is a broad understanding that the term 'informal economy' refers to 'all economic activities by workers and economic units that are – in law or in practice – not covered or insufficiently covered by formal arrangements... operating outside the formal reach of the law' (International Labour Conference, 90th Session 2002a). Within the UK, the Small Business Council has arrived at a much more straightforward definition: informal paid work is that which

'involves the paid production and sale of goods or services which are unregistered, or hidden from the state for tax, benefit and/or labour law purposes, but which are legal in all other respects' (Small Business Council, 2004).

To undertake informal work within the UK involves not paying employment-related tax or national insurance, continuing to claim state benefits or working without the legally required visa. It also signifies being beyond the mainstream of UK employment legislation such as the National Minimum Wage, maternity and paternity leave, sick leave and holiday leave. It means workers in the informal economy are open to exploitation, with no recourse to legal protection from the state, instead being reliant on employers to keep their activities clandestine so that they can avoid detection.

Much of the international literature on the informal economy includes those who work in small unregistered enterprises, both employers and employees, as well as self-employed persons who work in their own or family businesses (WIEGO, 2005). Discussion within a UK context is mostly focused more narrowly on people on low incomes, doing informal or undeclared paid work, cash-in-hand, whilst claiming benefits or otherwise not entitled to work (e.g., by reason of their immigration status). Even this term encompasses such a diverse range of activities and types of work that it is questionable whether the informal economy can be adequately conceived of as a cohesive 'sector'. The contrast between the way in which the term is used in international and domestic debates has consequences for public attitudes and policy responses to the informal economy, which will be explored later in the chapter.

How big is the informal sector?

The frequently 'hidden' nature of informal work, its diversity and the wide range of activities it encompasses make the task of collecting accurate statistics on the scale and numbers involved exceedingly difficult. It has been estimated that the informal economy accounts for between three and seven per cent of British GDP. In 2004, the Small Business Service estimated that the informal economy accounted for 6.8 per cent of GDP, roughly equivalent to £75 billion, mostly involving small businesses and 'one-man-bands' (sic) (Small Business Council, 2004b). In areas such as Merseyside, industrial decline in the early 1980s led to a sudden contraction in the formal economy; a big cash economy arose in its place, covering everything from plumbing and building to drugs and organised crime.

Although more people are working in formal employment than ever before, the low wages of many jobs means some people choose to continue claiming state benefits while working, either by not declaring earnings, avoiding tax, smuggling or credit card fraud. The Northern Economic Research Unit, based at the University of Northumbria, estimated the value of the informal economy in the North East in 2000 at £246 million, but with the high level of regional unemployment (9.1 per cent compared to a national average of 5.9 per cent) it was suggested that the figure could be much higher (Tees Valley Joint Strategy Unit, 2000). Given the difficulties of data collection, official statistics probably underestimate its size and economic contribution. At an international level, there is evidence that the informal economy has expanded and become more diverse in recent years. With enhanced global competition, lengthened supply chains and weakening of states' abilities to enforce labour standards, the informal economy and the formal economy have become increasingly linked.

Gender and incomes in the informal economy

Gender also plays a key role both in informal working and in its links to the formal economy (WIEGO, 2005). The incomes of both men and women are lower in the informal sector than in the formal sector. The gender gap in income/wages appears higher in the informal sector than in the formal sector, and the relatively large gap in income/wages is mainly due to two inter-related factors:

- Informal incomes worldwide tend to decline as one moves across the following types of employment: employer, self-employed, casual wage worker, sub-contract worker.
- Women worldwide are under-represented in high-income activities and over-represented in low-income activities (notably, sub-contract work) (ibid.).

In the UK, research over the last 20 years shows that participation in the labour market is significantly influenced by gender inequalities in the work place and women being segregated in certain types of jobs. The care of children and other domestic responsibilities leads to women more often working part-time because it enables them to combine work and childcare once maternity leave is over (de Schampheleire et al., 1998). Women make up the largest number of lone parent households in the UK, meaning the demand for decent and affordable childcare is particularly crucial for this group. In addition, women from ethnic minority groups are more likely to work in the family and in the informal economy than their white counterparts. Whilst participation rates in the formal economy amongst Pakistani and Bangladeshi women in particular are as low as 20 per cent, this may well reflect the fact that they are more likely to engage in homeworking or other forms of informal working (1990 Trust, 2002).

The UK approach: coercion and criminalisation

Within the UK, attitudes to the informal economy are largely characterised as being negative, coercive and punitive. The Grabiner enquiry
into the informal economy, commissioned by the Treasury in 1999,
concluded that the informal economy was a 'problem' to be addressed
only through punishment and deterrence:

> 'As long as people can profit by not declaring their work, it will
> be impossible entirely to eradicate the hidden economy. There-
> fore, the most effective way of tackling the problem is significantly
> to improve the likelihood of detecting and penalizing offenders.
> What is needed is a strong environment of deterrence' (Grabiner in
> Williams, 2004, p. 227).

Speaking as Chancellor of the Exchequer in 2000, Gordon Brown
described the informal economy as something apart from the 'real'
economy and any activity in the informal sector as somehow
being 'lost'.

> 'For years, billions of pounds have been lost to the informal
> economy every year, leaving honest, hard-working taxpayers foot-
> ing the bill for those who either don't pay the taxes they owe or
> claim benefit while they are working. Defrauding the benefit system
> means defrauding the poor and preventing us getting the resources
> to those in need. We're giving people every opportunity, helping
> them with training, helping them with child care, we are helping
> people with the transitional costs of getting back into work. But we
> have also got to provide people with the incentives to get back into
> the real economy' (Brown, 2000).

This punitive approach is best demonstrated by the Department for
Work and Pensons' national publicity campaign to 'catch a benefit cheat',
encouraging friends and neighbours to report people working informally, with the aim of recovering some of the £2 billion that it estimates
is lost through social security fraud each year. Around 60 per cent
comes from claims for Income Support, Jobseeker's Allowance and
Housing Benefit. The example below, from the Department's own
website, shows a typical situation where benefit fraud is committed.

> 'Mr Smith was unemployed and claiming Jobseeker's Allowance
> when he was offered some temporary building work paying cash
> in hand. He didn't report this extra income and he was earning
> over the allowable amount for the period that he was working.

This meant that he was getting benefits that he was not entitled to and was committing benefit fraud' (Department for Work and Pensions, 2006).

The reality of working in the informal economy

So, what is it like to work in the informal economy, and to what extent can the actual reality be described as dignified? Given all the inherent risks involved, why do people choose to work in the 'Cinderella' economy?

In November 2005, Oxfam's UK Poverty Programme and CAP undertook a piece of research into the reality of the conditions for people working in the informal economy. The aim was to explore the reasons why people work in the informal economy, and their experiences. In particular, it was decided to focus on four groups of workers, first those carrying out cash-in-hand work while receiving benefits, including homeworkers. The second and third groups were migrant workers, both those with and those without the documents to work in the UK. The final group we spoke to were asylum seekers. The findings concluded that people were aware of the risks, yet chose to take this route as result of the low number of options within their lives and livelihood opportunities.

This section briefly examines each of these groups of workers in the informal economy, what drives them to 'choose' this form of work and the risks they encounter in doing so. It will also explore the kinds of work done and the similarities and differences between the groups. Many of the quotes are taken directly from the research undertaken by the two organisations, based on interviews from participants met in the time scale identified above (May, 2005). Other quotes are from research undertaken in 2005 and 2006 by Community Links (Katungi et al., 2006) and the Centre for Economic and Social Inclusion (Centre for Economic and Social Inclusion, 2005).

Cash-in-hand

Many of the people we met during the research were working cash-in-hand while also claiming job-seeking state benefits. The reason most often given for doing this was because they found the benefits system complicated and inflexible. For them, the world of employment had changed to consist of short-term, low-pay contracts, with a need for high flexibility on the part of the worker. Susan and Miriam's examples demonstrate the difficulties of trying to find appropriate employment whilst juggling childcare responsibilities. In both these cases, the respondents chose to continue claiming benefits while working cash-in-hand. The interview with Susan reveals a common theme for lone parents (in particular mothers) struggling to get by with young children: 'my initial reason was survival with 2 young children' (Susan,[1] mid-40s). As a result of relying on welfare benefits for shelter and sustenance such as housing allowance, council tax rebates and job seekers allowance, Susan felt unable to take the step into formal employment. Instead, she preferred to remain with the security of welfare benefits, and the added cash brought in from her informal work in the village, ironing and cleaning in several local houses. Susan had calculated her weekly budget very closely and estimated that the money brought in from the cash-in-hand work paid for school uniforms, school trips and presents at Christmas and birthdays. Susan knew the risk she took doing this work, and felt she had been 'fighting to get off benefits since day one', but went on to cite the lack of opportunities in a rural area and fear of leaving the security that welfare benefits supplied as key reasons to continue claiming and working cash-in-hand. Miriam, a resident of East London, found similar issues living in the city, maintaining

> 'Those with no qualifications, never had a decent job, single mothers with childcare issues, like me, those who are in debt, like me, . . . it's very difficult to get out of that situation and find formal work because so many barriers are in your way' (cited in Katungi et al., 2006, p. 13).

The benefits system provides an essential safety net for many people on low or no income, yet also creates a bind with the inbuilt infrastructure and bureaucracy. The complex form-filling and the delay involved in recouping welfare benefits were mentioned by people as a key reason to keep claiming benefits and for not declaring their work. For a family or individual in debt, the fear of coming off benefits would be exacerbated by the need to make repayments, particularly to loans sharks.

In addition to the need for the security of welfare benefits is the need for decent, affordable childcare, without which options outside the home are limited. For some people, caring is one of the reasons they chose to take work in manufacturing or production within the home, for example packing Christmas crackers or tights. Ninety per cent of the estimated one million UK homeworkers are women and 50 per cent are from black and minority ethnic communities; they are particularly invisible to mainstream society despite the direct contribution that their production makes to the economy. Often homeworkers are paid less than the minimum wage, and the denial of their employment status means they are rarely able to access workplace benefits such as sick leave, maternity leave or holiday pay. They also struggle to get any redundancy pay, meaning many are left with no money after years of service when production moves or ends. While working from home may fit with the needs of the household, such as caring for children or other dependents, as described by Linda Devereux, Director of the National Group on Homeworking, it is also true that 'This is not the kind of flexibility that any woman worker is hoping for' (Devereux in Oxfam, 2004, p. 20).

The bind of responsibilities, particularly for care, combined with the need for an income means working informally is seen as the only option for many people. While working in the informal economy does provide an avenue to some financial assurance, it is in fact a risk due to the lack of ability to claim any protection. This is illustrated in Chris's example:

> 'I had a bad experience as an informal employee in a garage. I was paid less than the minimum wage, worked long hours and got the sack when I took a week off work due to my son's illness. The most frustrating thing was that I could not complain anywhere because I was on benefits' (cited in Katungi et al., 2006, p. 21).

This situation is widespread, with employers able to use to their advantage the power they have over those in their workforce who are claiming benefits while taking informal work.

For people working cash-in-hand, it is clear that the lack of flexibility in the current benefits system combined with the lack of employment opportunities means the risk of working informally is calculated and still taken. The current attitude of the UK Government of 'detecting and penalising' completely ignores the reality for many people, with the suggestion that working cash-in-hand is the selfish choice of those sponging off the system rather than being a strategic financial necessity. For many of these workers, in particular for women bringing up children single-handedly, the cash-in-hand informal economy is their means of accessing a livelihood and is a genuine way of making a contribution to their family in a way they feel cannot be achieved through benefits or low-waged work alone. This is especially the case for homeworkers whose desire to work from home on a low-waged, low-skilled basis is often exploited by manufacturers in this poorly regulated area. However, the punishment approach is reflected in the continuing negative portrayal of people working cash-in-hand in a great deal of mainstream consideration.

There is no official statistic for how many people work or businesses operate in this way. However, it is clear that there is a need to improve both how it is portrayed and regulated. There are many advantages for formalising the workplace (e.g., easier inspection of workplaces for health and safety), yet the current attitude is to punish those most at risk. The Government should consider other, more supportive, ways of bringing people into the formal sphere, instead of portraying the cash-in-hand worker as a destructive member of society. Aside from the nature of the work itself, the risks of being 'found out' and the social stigma that accompany the punitive approach are themselves major contributors to undermining the dignity of working in the cash-in-hand economy.

Documented migrant workers

'We know we are not treated right by the agency, but we are too afraid of being sacked, or losing our jobs to complain. We don't understand enough English so don't know what rights we have, and would not know how to get another job. We don't tell people about the conditions because we are so afraid of losing our jobs' (Germano, male, late-20s).

For centuries, people have travelled to the UK in order to access economic opportunities. In 2004, the UK opened its labour markets for access to people from the eight Eastern European countries that had joined the European Union to be able to enter the UK and seek work. There are also many people from all over the world entering to seek both high-skilled and low-skilled work. For many, this is an opportunity to escape the poverty of their home country and to build both financial security and experience. For many migrant workers themselves, considerations of 'dignity' may be secondary, given the economics of necessity. But such 'push' factors mean that even migrant workers with a legal right to work in the UK easily fall prey to unscrupulous employment practices on the margins of the formal economy. Many migrant workers also face stigmatisation and even harassment while working in the UK.

'Germano' had the right to work in the UK and was paid the National Minimum Wage; however the agency who have employed him were able to exploit him through very high charges for rent, for travel to work and not paying him for all the hours he had worked. He was terrified of leaving his employer (the agency) as he relied on them for interpretation and owed them money for the journey from his country of origin. The employer sent him to workplaces all over England, never staying in one place long enough to get to know the factories in which he worked, or seek alternative employment. Anderson and Rogaly (2005) describe this relationship as one of patron/client or master/servant, with the agency benefiting directly from the lack of knowledge of the worker as to the English language, or the rights and benefits to which they are due (Anderson and Rogaly, 2005).

There are still many people migrating to the UK in order to take low-paid and insecure work. Citizens Advice believe as many as 200,000 workers enter the UK every year (Citizens Advice, 2004). Research in London amongst a random sample of people working in hospitality, hospitals and the underground found that of those in low-income jobs over 90 per cent were migrants, half of whom had been born in Sub-Saharan Africa (Evans et al., 2005). This work is typically paid at the National Minimum Wage, and without sick, holiday or redundancy pay. By using employment agencies in sub-contracting chains, the large hotels, transport agencies and hospitals are able to minimise their responsibility for the workforce within their organisations. These chains lead to the detachment of the worker from the employer – allowing for less dependency and responsibility both up and down the supply chain. The willingness of middlemen or agencies to exploit migrant workers further worsen the situation. In particular, the common deductions from wages allow the agencies to control the migrant workers through their weakened financial security.

Examples of mistreatment of migrant workers are widespread, including evidence of existence within the agricultural and packaging supply chains for large UK supermarket chains. The Ethical Trade Initiative (ETI), a body made up of businesses, trade unions and non-governmental organisations organising to improve the working conditions within retail supply chains, investigated the conditions within the workplaces in South Lincolnshire where fruit, vegetables, flowers and meals are prepared for supermarkets. The investigation found 107 points of improvement at the workplaces who volunteered to be inspected. The ETI director announced:

'I think the industry was surprised, not by the horror stories, but by the extent to which it goes on... you would expect to get the better ones as volunteers. When you find problems here, you think, God, what's down the line' (Lawrence, 2004a, p. 12).

For migrant workers, these experiences of exploitation are then combined with sometimes shocking levels of bigotry. As with people working cash-in-hand, migrant workers also face considerable intolerance, particularly in the form of prejudice and suspicion that they entered the UK in order to 'help themselves to our free health service, education system and . . . state benefits' (Trade Union Congress, 2004, p. 8). This type of sentiment has boiled over to direct racist attacks in areas such as Northern Ireland, where at an extreme, petrol bombs have been used in racist attacks against migrant workers from Eastern Europe (Trade Union Congress, 2004, p. 26).

For a migrant worker, the prospect of encountering dignity at work is damaged by the forms of exploitation that mean they work on the margins of formal UK employment, far detached from the employer at the top of the supply chain. As demonstrated in this section, these employers include supermarkets, hospitality and the London Underground, all of whom use supply chains and are then so distant from the worker as to be able to deny responsibility. Further to this is the disapproval migrant workers meet from parts of the UK population. Clearly, there is a demand for low-skilled, casual and flexible labour within the UK. And yet the migrant workers are rarely supported by organisations or the state, and for many their lack of English language and knowledge about their rights means they find themselves trapped. If Cinderella came to the UK looking for work today, the prospects of securing dignified work in the informal economy would be extremely slim.

Undocumented migrant workers

It is not known how many people in the UK are working without the necessary papers to do so. Estimates produce a varied number, including those who have entered the UK through unlawful means (e.g., stowaways on the back of lorries) and those who have entered the country lawfully (e.g., on tourist or student visas) but have broken the conditions of their visas by taking work while in the UK. The latter group may be the most common, as is the switching between 'legal and illegal', through access to another visa or through seeking asylum. Undocumented migrant workers are notoriously transient, their lack of interaction with UK mainstream services means that they are able to move without trace, but also that they are vulnerable to exploitative and dangerous conditions. At a tragic extreme, 25 Chinese cockle pickers in Morecombe Bay in the North West of England lost their lives when they were swept out to sea as the tides came in.

None had received any training or realised the danger of the incoming waves which swept them away, yet Morecombe Bay continues to be a popular area for those without the documents to seek employment in the UK (Murphy, 2005, p. 6).

Being dependent upon an employer not just for work, but also for secrecy, puts the worker under great pressure. As a group, undocumented migrant workers are not considered sympathetically by the media and are unlikely to receive support during their time in the UK. The only support they do receive is from informal friendship and family networks, or institutions such as churches. More distinctly, they are also a hidden and unrecognised force – often working in private households as cleaners or carers, or on transient sites in construction or agriculture. The nature of their illegality also means they are reluctant to approach authorities or support agencies with a complaint, realising the likely result will be their own deportation. The focus of media and government will be upon the visa status of the worker, as opposed to the contribution of their work or the exploitation they face. This makes it very common for undocumented migrant workers to be working in conditions which are far removed from dignified, with little opportunity for changing their situation.

A particularly vulnerable group are women migrant workers without documents, many of whom take up employment in order to support their families in their country of origin. This remittance dependency means a need for regular and predictable income, forcing women into an even greater dependent relationship with their employer. The sacrifices taken by migrant women are recounted below:

> 'We did not see our mother for 15 years. She chose to live in Belgium and work in bad conditions as an undocumented migrant worker to send me and my brothers to school in the Philippines. When I came here I realised how much she had sacrificed to leave her home and children for 15 years in order to look after someone else's home and children. She told me even the nicer employers treated her like garbage – when they did not need her anymore, they chucked her away' (Marlene, woman, 22).

At an extreme, women become victims of sexual exploitation at the hands of their employer in return for employment and secrecy. Lawrence (2004b, p. 47) cites the example of a worker recounting how 'one of the gangmasters would boast that he could take any woman to bed. He'd say the women had no choice because they were illegal'.

This powerfully demonstrates the control the employer wields over a worker in such situations. This is true not only of sex work, but also in other forms of employment (e.g., domestic or construction work).

The conditions in which some undocumented migrants are working have been found to be so appalling as to be described as slavery or forced labour (Anti-Slavery International, 2003; Anderson and Rogaly, 2005).

For many undocumented migrant workers, employment in the UK provides an alternative to the poverty experienced within their country of origin. As long as the supply of labour is present through different forms of entry into the UK and the demand continues, it is likely that there will be migratory trends to take work in the UK. The illegality of the worker leaves them vulnerable to exploitation and dangerous conditions. Yet, too often, debate focuses on people's immigration status rather than the employment conditions they face. The situation of undocumented migrant workers must be understood in the context of where they have come from – the poverty that is then relatively heightened through their financial and social exclusion within the UK. Once in the UK, the degrees of exploitation are such that dignity is far from achievable, with employers able to wield control over workers including through sexual abuse and slavery-like conditions.

Asylum seekers

'I'm serving people who don't want to do these jobs... but I'd rather go to work than take money from others' (Hussein, mid-30s).

The people who were interviewed for our research had arrived in the UK in order to seek asylum, and when their claims had been refused were told by the Home Office that they were unable to legally access paid employment and should await deportation. Hussein and others knew the risks they were taking, but none were prepared to return to their countries of origin (Afghanistan, Iraq and Iran) because of their belief in the inherent dangers. For these asylum seekers, their jobs were a route to safety should the direction for deportation come through.

Those interviewed were earning less than the minimum wage and had no workplace benefits such as holiday or sick leave. The illegitimacy of their work meant they could not access any form of trade union or legal support.

'One day in an accident I got burnt all down my back by a spilt hot drink, I was taken to hospital but could not tell them what had happened as I was working illegally. My employer did take me to hospital but only after I insisted as he was worried he would be implied for employing someone off the books. I was working every night 6pm–5am for £3 an hour, for a year' (Nadia, late-20s).

On top of the financial exclusion is the political and media rhetoric stigmatising asylum seekers, who are often accused of taking advantage of the UK's public services. The widespread prejudice is clearly portrayed in Valentine and McDonald's report (2004) which found asylum seekers are:

'the group towards whom the most open and blatant prejudice was directed, often expressed in terms of anger. It is generally socially acceptable to express such views, and there appears to be little social sanction against this form of prejudice' (Valentine and McDonald, 2004, p. 11).

Among the asylum seekers met during the research, it was acknowledged that they were considered to be an unpopular group, as one man admitted: 'people hate me outside, without even knowing me' (Tom, mid-20s). Most commonly, this prejudice is directed towards male asylum seekers; however this does not mean that women are in a better, or safer position, but that the 'invisibility of minority women reflects the wider marginalisation of women in society' (Valentine and McDonald, 2004, p. 12). Women do not face the overt hostility experienced by men because they are relatively invisible within wider UK society. For women, the inability to gain legal employment combined with their invisibility decreases the dignity with which they are viewed. The double impact of being a marginalised gender within a marginalised group is reflected in the conditions some female asylum seekers face in their illegal workplace.

As with people working cash-in-hand, and some migrant workers, asylum seekers who are working rely on the complicity of their employers not to report them to the authorities. For many, they therefore have to accept conditions with which they are acutely unhappy in order to keep the job.

'Although I am happy to have this work, I feel pressure to take any hours offered, no holiday, no sick leave due to fear of losing my job. I need the security of the job, if Iraq is seen as safe again and deportation becomes likely, I want to know I could "disappear" and survive' (Tom, mid-20s).

For these asylum seekers, the illegality of accessing work merely increased their vulnerability and dependency on the employer and colleagues. Despite this, they all found employment, even if in dangerous and exploitative conditions as a means of ensuring survival. Further to their inability to access formal employment, asylum seekers also face some of the highest levels of stigmatisation and dehumanisation in the UK. Women, who are considered to be more 'invisible', experience the greater risk. The types of risk and stigma faced by all asylum seekers means dignity is difficult to achieve, yet for many this is considered preferable to a return to their country of origin.

Can the informal economy lead to dignified work?

All of the people described in the above section were working in some way in the informal economy. For all of them, this seemed the most effective way of providing for themselves and their families in a life where they felt they had limited choices, either because of their caring responsibilities or their immigration status. These limited choices combined with the stigma they face means they are all struggling to access dignity within their work, often because they are exploited by employers aware of their powerful position over someone working informally.

The analysis so far leads back to the question: Can the informal economy provide dignified work? The response to this question varies sharply, depending on one's underlying ideas and beliefs about informal working. Within the UK, workers in the informal economy are not only criminalised but also miss out on rights to pensions, sick pay and other statutory employment rights. In contrast to the punitive approach, campaigners argue that in order to persuade workers and the self-employed to join the formal economy, government needs to cut back non-essential regulation of micro-business and allow people to claim benefits while earning (Turner, 2003).

Arguably, the Labour government's welfare-to-work programme and New Deal for Lone Parents are aimed not just at enlarging labour market participation, but at shifting activities from the informal to the formal economy, through increasing the incentives and support to enter the formal labour market. The problem is that those at present engaged in the informal economy (and especially in undeclared cash work while claiming) do not have strong incentives to cooperate with the new schemes. However, recent research in East London has found that supportive approaches to the informal sector can have success where poverty drives the decision to work informally. The researchers concluded that Government needs to understand and include the informal economy in its strategies if it is to reach its anti-poverty targets (Katungi et al., 2006).

In contrast to the UK approach, participation in the informal economy is viewed in much more positive terms in many countries of the South, particularly where there are much higher levels of informal economic activity. In Zimbabwe, 'the figure was 60 per cent. In Brazil and Turkey, around half of non-farm workers are in the informal sector' (*Economist*, 2004). Working in the informal economy is recognised as part of a survival strategy for people to increase their current income, and to combat financial exclusion. While the existence of a developed welfare state distinguishes the UK from many other countries, there could still be rich learning from the skills and strategies of organisations built to support workers in the informal economy in some of those countries.

Unemployed and/or people who experience poverty are sometimes able to develop informal strategies to counter exclusion and stimulate their inclusion and participation in society; awareness of this should encourage social policies aiming at inclusion to recognise and support these strategies. These informal strategies are often neglected or counter-acted, because they are considered fraudulent or because they are seen as diminishing people's labour-market availability. Thus, a paradoxical situation may be created in which 'active' social policies are making people passive, or in which people see themselves forced to hide their activities from officials. This official attitude towards informal inclusion strategies may be understandable from the point of view of social policies aiming at labour-market participation only, but from a broader perspective on social inclusion and tackling poverty, there is enough reason to investigate the degree to which these informal strategies do actually meet people's needs and how their inclusionary potential can be improved (van Berkel, 1999).

This has also been recognised in a Department for Work and Pensions (DWP) research report on worklessness

"In reality, it may not be rational for individuals to choose to work in the formal economy for a number of (often inter-related) reasons: a lack of opportunities in the formal labour market; a lack of information about the financial rewards from formal employment (e.g., tax credits); higher financial gains from working the in the informal economy than the formal one; and being motivated by things other than just financial gain (e.g., peer group respect or wanting to stay at home to bring up children)' (Ritchie et al., 2005, p. 2).

The International Labour Organisation (ILO) recognises that 'continued progress towards recognized, protected decent work will only be possible by identifying and addressing the underlying causes of informality' (International Labour Conference, 90th Session 2002a, p. 4). Much work still needs to be done before we can say that we fully understand the range of causal factors behind the growth of the informal economy within the UK – not least the complex interaction between the informal and formal economies and wider social policies. This presents a challenge which researchers and policy makers need to address more adequately if Cinderella is to have any realistic hope of going to the ball of 'dignified work' into the future.

References

Anderson, B. and Rogaly, B. (2005) *Forced Labour and Migration to the UK*, TUC paper, TUC, London.

Anti-Slavery International (2003) *The Migration-Trafficking Nexus. Combating Trafficking through the Protection of Migrant's Human Rights.* http://www.antislavery.org/homepage/resources/the%20migration%20trafficking%20nexus%202003.pdf. Accessed 30/09/2006.

Brown, G. (2000) *Speaking on Radio 4 Today Programme*, 9 March.

Centre for Economic and Social Inclusion (2005) *The Informal Economy in Merseyside, A Report for the Merseyside Entrepreneurship Commission*, London: CESI.

Citizens Advice (2004) *Nowhere to Turn*, London: Citizens Advice.

Department for Work and Pensions (2006) http://www.targetingfraud.gov.uk/cost.html. Accessed 11/01/2006.

de Schampheleire, J., Garcia, S. and Gomez, A. (eds) (1998) *A Comparative Review of Research on Work and Social Inclusion*, TSER Research Project, p. 6 Targeted Socio-economic Research (TSER) Programme, Brussels.

Evans, Y., Herbert, J., Datta, K., May, J., McIlwaine, C. and Wills, J. (2005) *Making the City Work: Low Paid Employment in London*, London: Queen Mary University of London.

International Labour Conference, 90th Session (2002) *Report VI, Decent Work and the Informal Economy.* http://www.ilo.org/public/english/standards/relm/ilc/ilc90/pdf/rep-vi.pdf. Accessed 16/10/2006.

International Labour Conference, 90th Session (2002a) *Conclusions Concerning Decent Work and the Informal Economy*, Record of Proceedings, vol. II, p. 25/53, para. 3. http://www.ilo.org/public/english/standards/relm/ilc/ilc90/pdf/pr-25res.pdf. Accessed 16/10/2006.

Katungi, D., Neale, E. and Barber, A. (2006) *People in Low-Paid Informal Work: 'Need Not Greed'*, Bristol: Policy Press.

Lawrence, F. (2004a) 'Labour Laws Breached, Study Finds', *The Guardian*, 17 November, p. 12.

Lawrence, F. (2004b) *Not on the Label*, London: Penguin Books.

May, C. (2005) *A Snapshot of the Informal Economy in England and Scotland*, Unpublished Report, Oxfam.

Murphy, A. (2005) 'One Year on and They Still Gamble with their Lives', *Daily Post*. http://icccheshireonline.icnetwork.co.uk/0100news/0100regionalnews.tm_objectid=15152284. Accessed 04/02/2005.

Oxfam (2004) *Trading Away Our Rights*, Oxford: Oxfam International.

Ritchie, H., Casebourne, J. and Rick, J. (2005) 'Understanding Workless People and Communities: A Literature Review', DWP Research Report 255. http://www.employment-studies.co.uk/summary/summary.php?id=dwp255. Accessed 30/09/2006.

Small Business Council (2004a) *People in Low-Paid Informal Work*, in Joseph Rowntree Foundation (2006) JRF Findings, York: Joseph Rowntree Foundation.

Small Business Council (2004b) *Small Businesses in the Informal Economy Making the Transition to the Formal Economy Evidence and Key Stakeholder Opinion*, London: HMSO.

Tees Valley Joint Strategy Unit (2000) *The Tees Valley Economy*, Issue 48. http://www.teesvalley-jsu.gov.uk/reports/tv_economy/mar2000a.pdf. Accessed 04/02/2005.

Trade Union Congress (2004) *Propping up Rural and Small Town Britain: Migrant Workers From the New Europe*, London: TUC.

1990 Trust (2002) Some Facts about Ethnic Minority Women in the UK. http://www.blink.org.uk/pdescription.asp?key=952&grp=11&cat=268. Accessed 16/10/2006.

Turner, D. (2003) 'Benefits Trap "boosts black economy"', *Financial Times*, 29 August, p. 5.

Valentine, G. and McDonald, I. (2004) *Understanding Prejudice: Attitudes Towards Minorities*, London: Stone wall. http://www.stonewall.org.uk. Accessed 16/10/2006.

Van Berkel, R. (1999) *Final Report of the Inclusion through Participation Project*, Political Economy Research Centre, University of Sheffield, November.

WIEGO Factsheet (2005) *The Informal Economy*. http://www.wiego.org/main/fact1.shtml. Accessed 30/09/2006.

Williams, C. (2004) 'Tackling the Underground Economy in Deprived Populations: A Critical Evaluation of the Deterrence Approach', *Public Administration and Management: An Interactive Journal* **9**, 3, 224–239.

Part Three: Dignity in Workplace Practice

7

The consequences of management competence for working with dignity: a cross-methods validation[1]

Randy Hodson

The provision of work with dignity provides important advantages to organisations as they operate in increasingly competitive environments. Accordingly, the study of dignity at work should occupy a central place in studies of management practice (Pfeffer, 1998; Podsakoff et al., 2000). Management competence is a potentially core foundation for work with dignity. Competent managerial behaviour is being increasingly discussed in the organisational literature under a variety of rubrics, including trust and trustworthiness, perceived organisational support and leadership (see Bass, 1985; Tyler, 2001).

Certain limitations have hampered the study of management competence and working with dignity. In particular, most studies of management competence, working with dignity and related topics have relied on case studies of single organisations collected through surveys (see Anderson and Pearson, 1999; Cropanzano et al., 2002). Surveys may elicit only surface responses and meanings, leaving deeper causes and consequences concealed (Bolton and Boyd, 2003). And case studies limit organisational variation in the causes and consequences of working with dignity, thus making its organisational foundations difficult to discover.

The current chapter seeks to advance the study of management competence and employee dignity through addressing these limitations. I measure management competence and working with dignity using not only survey data, but also data systematically coded from organisational ethnographies. This strategy both introduces significant organisational variation and allows cross-methods checks on prior findings that have relied primarily on survey data (see Hackman, 2003). *Employee dignity* includes having the opportunity to take pride in one's work and being spared from excessive vertical or horizontal conflict (see also Lamont, 2000). *Management competence* includes the provision and maintenance of a coherent organisation of production as well as support and recognition for employees' rights and interests (Whitener et al., 1998).

I first discuss the concepts of working with dignity and managerial competence as umbrella concepts summarising a range of insights from organisational ethnographies. I then operationalise these concepts in a model of working with dignity and evaluate that model across both ethnographic and survey data.

Working with dignity

Working with dignity is a complex phenomenon with diverse facets. Organisational ethnographies are rich with discussions of the role of dignity in providing motivation and meaning at work (Applebaum, 1992; Hodson, 2001; Nord et al., 1990). An analysis of these ethnographies suggests at least three major facets of working with dignity: (1) the opportunity to take pride and initiative in work as evidenced by organisational citizenship behaviours (OCBs), (2) the absence of excessive conflict with bosses and supervisors, and (3) the absence of excessive conflict with peers and co-workers. These three aspects of the experience of working with dignity are discussed below.

Organisational citizenship behaviour

Organisational ethnographies abound with contextually rich accounts of employees' feelings of *pride in their accomplishments* – a core component of organisational citizenship (e.g., 'Joe possessed pride in his work and boasted of a year's worth of coils without a single rejection' [Seider, 1984, p. 26]). Pride in work is also exemplified in an ethnography of ironworkers. The worker responsible for maintaining the large crane used to lift the steel girders, for instance, evidences great pride in attending to his daily chores:

> 'Most oilers are nearly invisible, fuelling and lubricating their rigs before the day begins for the rest of us, vanishing to God knows where during the bulk of the day, reappearing at 4:00 to preside over putting the rig to bed. Beane, however, was not of that stripe. He fussed over the crane like a stage mother, constantly wiping away puddles of oil or grease, touching up scratches with fresh paint, agonizing loudly whenever a load banged into the stick' (Cherry, 1974, p. 166).

OCB is commonly defined as positive actions on the part of workers to improve productivity and cohesion in the workplace that are above and beyond organisational requirements (Organ, 1988). Studies that highlight employee citizenship build on a model of organisational effectiveness in which technical factors of production must be supplemented by worker initiative and enthusiasm in order to reach optimal levels (Drucker, 1993). Pride in work, extra effort, increased cooperation, peer training and commitment to organisational goals have all been identified as components of employee citizenship behaviour (Podsakoff et al., 2000; Smith et al., 1983). Such behaviours underwrite dignity at work because employees are able to experience pride and meaning in their daily tasks.

Conflict in organisations

Peaceful, cooperative and supportive relations between actors in the workplace are essential for organisational effectiveness and for the experience of dignity at work. Conflict, however, is a common occurrence both vertically between workers and managers and horizontally among co-workers (Kolb and Bartunek, 1992). The study of workplace conflict is thus an important component of the study of working with dignity.

Conflict with management

A certain degree of conflict between supervisors and employees is endemic to the workplace (Ackroyd and Thompson, 1999; Edwards and Wajcman, 2005; Prasad and Prasad, 2000; Pratt, 2000). Such vertical conflict, however, can be expected to be more common and more severe in situations where managers fail to respect workers and their concerns (Mouly and Sankaran, 1997). An example of employee–management conflict in a setting typified by chronic management incompetence and disrespect is provided by an ethnography of a poorly run wiring harness factory (Juravich, 1985). Workers are yelled at by supervisors in front of other workers (p. 136); they are fired without warning (p. 143); machinery is not kept in working order (p. 39); and new parts are not ordered (p. 75). As a consequence, workers intentionally break machinery, undercut the floor manager and retreat into ritual behaviour to achieve at least minimal meaning at work (p. 56). In this setting, management competence is clearly missing and worker dignity is undermined.

An example of *conflict with supervisors* is provided by an ethnography of a cigarette-manufacturing plant in the UK. During summer, the employees are provided with a lemonade break in the afternoon. On a particularly stifling summer afternoon, the lemonade is delayed. A personnel manager makes the mistake of walking into the production room at this time, where he is met with a barrage of 'Where's our lemonade?' A senior worker continues the assault:

> IVY: Where are you going for your holidays this year, Mr. Dowling?
> MR. DOWLING: I'm not going anywhere. I can't afford it. I bought the wife a car and I've spent our money. Honestly.
> IVY: Have you? Ah! What a shame. Can't you sell some of your shares then?
> MR. DOWLING: No, can't do that.
> IVY: Come on, just a few.

This produced laughter all round, the manager and his attempt at being 'just one of the workers' exposed to ridicule, and at the same time exploited for a laugh (Pollert, 1981, pp. 152–153).

Co-worker infighting

Co-worker relations constitute an important part of the 'social climate' at work and define central aspects of the work settings in which workers experience meaning, identity and dignity (Selznick, 1969). Negative co-worker relations can be a chronic source of frustration and dissatisfaction (Anderson and Pearson, 1999; Jehn, 1995) and can have serious negative effects on productivity (Dunlop and Lee, 2004). Conversely, supportive behaviours among co-workers can encourage meaning and fulfilment in work (Bommer et al., 2003). Harmonious co-worker relations can be an important casualty in situations in which competent and supportive management is weak, absent or inconsistent (Pfeffer, 1998). Infighting among employees is thus also an important form of conflict in the workplace that can undermine working with dignity. A corrosive pattern of chronic *gossip and backbiting* is evidenced in an ethnography of temporary clerical workers:

'Not only were individual temps the butt of contemptuous and often bitchy remarks made by the permanents, but the whole group of us were sometimes subject to generalised insults and cool behavior. Temps were often discussed by the permanent staff. This usually happened when all the temps had left at 4.30 p.m' (McNally, 1979, p. 169).

Management competence

Management competence is increasingly identified as a key precondition for working with dignity (Kunda, 1992; Shore and Coyle-Shapiro, 2003; Tekleab and Taylor, 2003; Tsui et al., 1997). The umbrella concept of management competence provides a useful organising device for a wide domain of themes related to management practice. These themes include trust (Adler, 2001), reciprocity (Fox, 1974), organisational justice (Bies, 1987; Selznick, 1969), legitimacy (Barley and Kunda, 1992; Knights and McCabe, 1999), integrity (Becker, 1998), trustworthiness (Whitener et al., 1998) and leadership (Bass, 1985). Over time, the study of these themes has moved from a focus on attitudes of trust towards management to a focus on managerial behaviours that are, in fact, trustworthy. In so doing, researchers have attempted to bridge the difficult divide between attitudes and behaviours. The use of ethnographic data in the current chapter allows us to explore competent managerial behaviour in greater depth and to utilise direct observational measures of managerial behaviour rather than self-reports.

A contradictory (and disrespectful) managerial style is illustrated in the following episode from a meat packing plant in the American Midwest in which a worker is caught between an authoritarian general manger and an abusive line supervisor:

'The general. . . came to look at my work and raised hell with me. "Only skin in this barrel! I don't want to see no fat in there and I don't want to see no meat!" He picked out scraps from my tub and said I was throwing too much meat into the fat tub. The only way we could trim closer was to slow down. That seemed as though it might also save my hand, so I was all for it. I reasoned that Clyde (the line supervisor) could not badger me or Owen about speed after the general had told us to trim closer. . . (But) Clyde blew up. . . he stood over me throwing meat and yelling, "Speed! Speed! You can't stand here all day!"... I started to work again, but Clyde pushed the rest of the meat onto the floor in disgust and ordered me to get on my blue frock and clean the floor' (Fink, 1998, p. 28).

Social and technical foundations of management competence

Organisational ethnographies suggest a core set of behavioural norms for management. These norms involve two distinct realms: (1) ensuring the technical viability and smooth functioning of production, and (2) developing organisational social capital and respecting workers and their interests (Barnard, 1950; Drucker, 1993). These realms parallel the technical and social aspects of work as first conceptualised by Roethlisberger and Dickson (1939). Abiding by such norms creates an organisational climate in which employees can work with confidence and good faith (Nahapiet and Ghoshal, 1998).

The latter theme concerning managerial support and respect for workers is illustrated in the following excerpt from an ethnography of a newly opened Toyota plant in the southern United States:

'Ruddlehouse described a situation with a team member in her area who had a drinking problem. She said Toyota could have fired him. He repeatedly violated the rules regarding attendance and performance. Instead, his supervisor and the HR rep worked with him, force him to join AA and see a counselor. In Ruddlehouse's words, "Toyota really stepped on him and helped him straighten up his act. That helped me respect them. They really are here to try to help people. I think there are a lot of ways where they really do have the people in mind." Several interviewees told me about a particular team member who was injured on the job. Lemming gave this account of the story: "Toyota could have kicked him out the door and there is nothing he could have done about it. Instead they retrained him and now he is working in another area."... (Employees trust) that Toyota, if made aware of the problem and if given enough time, will correct the oversight, mistake, or injustice. This implies an extension of the tacit agreement referred to previously that if Toyota is reasonable, flexible, and humane in its treatment of employees, the employees will reciprocate by viewing Toyota mistakes as benign oversights that will be rectified when Toyota is made aware of the problem' (Besser, 1996, pp. 101–104).

A model of dignity and respect

The model I propose for cross-methods validation is thus one that includes a central role for management competence as a potentially key influence on various facets of working with dignity. It is important, however, when evaluating this model to also consider other possible determinants of employee dignity (Podsakoff et al., 2000). Core organisational determinants that are both theoretically relevant and available in both the ethnographic and survey data include establishment size, local ownership and unionisation (Cornfield and McCammon, 2003; Cummings, 1993; Heath and Sitkin, 2001; Whitener et al., 1998). In addition, I also include skill level, and the gender and racial composition of the work group as important job and labour force controls (Lincoln and Kalleberg, 1990; Schnake, 1991). For the ethnographic data, I also include the year the study was completed as a control.

Hypotheses

Our expectations for the analysis can be summarised in the following set of hypotheses:

Hypothesis 1: Management competence will have significant and large effects on working with dignity relative to other determinants.

Hypothesis 2: The effects of the various determinants of working with dignity will be reproduced across survey and ethnographic data, thus providing cross-methods validation of these effects.

Methods

A multi-method approach is particularly important for the study of working with dignity at this point in the development of the field. Organisational studies are all too frequently divided into nonoverlapping domains of surveys and ethnographic observation. The lack of systematic cross-referencing of findings between methods has resulted in few findings being confirmed across methods. In the current chapter, I thus utilise both survey data and data from a systematic content coding of ethnographic accounts to evaluate our model of management competence and working with dignity. Both data sets utilised include detailed measures of management competence and working with dignity as well as measures of organisational and job characteristics. In addition, both data sets contain information from a variety of organisations, thus allowing the introduction of considerable organisational variation into the analysis.

The ethnographic data

The analysis presented in this chapter utilises content-coded data generated by systematically coding information from the full population of book-length organisational ethnographies ($n = 204$). Organisational ethnographies cover a wider range of topics than most surveys, including in-depth investigations of employee behaviour, management behaviour and workplace conflict. The utilisation of the full population of organisational ethnographies allows us to gather information across a wide range of organisational contexts. The systematic analysis of data from a comprehensive set of organisation ethnographies thus takes advantage of the depth of observation offered by ethnographies (Hodson, 1999; Mouly and Sankaran, 1997, p. 181) while avoiding the limits posed by analysis of a single case or a limited set of case studies. The goals of the coding project included ascertaining the leading questions pursued by organisational ethnographers, summarising the knowledge they have gained on these issues and comparing these findings to those of survey-based research. This strategy addresses the repeated call from organisational researchers to develop methods that combine quantitative and qualitative techniques of data collection and analysis (see Hammersley, 1997; Leana and Van Buren, 1999, p. 552; Wood, 2000).

Organisational ethnographies are grounded on sustained observation of workplaces and workplace relations – a depth of observation considered by ethnographers to be essential for getting sufficiently behind the scenes to perceive workplace relations accurately (Lee, 1999; Prasad, 2002). In-depth observation is particularly important for observing the nature and consequences of such nuanced phenomena as management competence and working with dignity. The coding of information from these ethnographies allows the development of multifaceted measures of managerial and employee behaviour, as well as measures of the contexts in which these behaviours occur and the consequences of these behaviours.

Selecting the cases

The data collection part of the ethnographic content analysis project proceeded in two waves. The first occurred in the early 1990s with the assistance of a graduate practicum. The second occurred in the early 2000s with support from the National Science Foundation. The second wave both extended the number of cases coded and added additional measures. Because no comprehensive list of organisational ethnographies was available, I utilised a bottom-up approach in locating suitable cases. In this process, thousands of published case studies were examined to locate and evaluate appropriate ethnographies. Likely titles were generated by computer-assisted searches of archives, perusal of the bibliographies of ethnographies already located, extensive use of interlibrary loan and searching the library shelves in the immediate area of previously identified ethnographies. We also utilised an advisory board of 22 experts in organisational ethnography to review our list and recommend other books to consider. Iteratively applying these search procedures resulted in an exhaustive search – eventually our pursuit of new leads produced only titles already considered.

We subsequently examined each book in detail. The criteria for inclusion in the final pool to be coded were: (1) the use of direct ethnographic methods of observation over a period of at least six months; (2) a focus on a single organisational setting; and (3) a focus on at least one clearly identified group of workers – an assembly line, a typing pool, a task group or some other identifiable work group. The requirements of direct ethnographic observation and a focus on a specific organisation and work group are necessary in order to obtain the depth of observation and understanding needed to ascertain and measure subtle aspects of worker and management behaviour that are often cloaked behind easily proffered categories and explanations (Van Maanen, 1998).

The selection process generated 204 ethnographic cases. These cases were derived from 156 separate books because the observations reported in some books allowed the coding of multiple cases. For example, two cases were coded from a book by Lee (1998) reporting on two Litton Electronics factories, one in Hong Kong and one in Shenzhen. These ethnographies constitute the population of published book-length English-language ethnographies that focus on an identifiable work group in a single organisation and that provide relatively complete information on the organisation, the nature of the work taking place there and managers' and employees' behaviours at work.[2]

From narratives to numbers

A team of four researchers – the author and three advanced graduate students – developed the coding instrument for the ethnographies. First, we developed a preliminary list of relevant concepts and response categories. Second, over a period of six months, eight representative ethnographies were read and coded by each of the four team members. After each ethnography was coded, we discussed our respective codings to decide on the retention, removal or addition of items and to develop new response categories and coding protocols. Our goal was to create an instrument with relatively complete coverage of content that could be completed for every ethnography with high reliability by trained coders. During this process, we were repeatedly taken with how frequently workers perceived management as incompetent, how frequently workers were mistreated by management and how profoundly disturbing incompetence and mistreatment were to employees. The current chapter follows up on these initial observations and attempts to examine the consequences of management competence relative to other organisational characteristics that may also contribute to employee dignity and well-being.

The ethnographies were read and coded by the same team of four researchers, by eight members of a graduate research practicum and by additional graduate research assistants supported through a National Science Foundation grant. Coders recorded all page numbers identifying the passages used for coding each variable. If multiple instances of a behaviour were found, the coder was instructed to review all previous passages cited, reconcile inconsistencies between the passages and record the best answer, along with all relevant page numbers. Coders were instructed to look for behavioural indicators or specific descriptions for each variable coded and not to rely on ethnographers' summary statements or evaluations (Weber, 1990).

As an example of the coding process, conflictual co-worker relations, which is an important outcome measure in the analysis, was coded from an ethnography of bank employees in the following manner. The ethnographer describes a social world of invidious comparison and backbiting:

> 'Individuals try to fashion... personal identifications by criticising others, thus indirectly asserting their own individual worth and even superiority.... Each individual knows that she herself may become an object of criticism. This creates an enervating apprehensiveness of others' judgements' (Jackall, 1978, pp. 121–122).

A records clerk at the bank, when asked if she is staying for a holiday party, expresses a widely felt anxiety: 'I stay because if I don't, they'll talk about me' (p. 121). Another worker reports: 'They're a bunch of phoneys... They are snotty. I feel awful if I'm around any of them' (p. 121). A third reports: 'Everyone is two-faced, and you have to watch out for yourself' (p. 122). The negative social atmosphere in the bank results in significant personal antagonisms between employees:

> 'There is a division between us and (another group of workers)... They go around with their noses in the air... (They're)

female, very female. Like when a male walks in the office, they're like a bunch of high school girls. They're always giggling... There's one who drives me crazy the way she walks. She is shaped like a seahorse and the way she walks is like she's saying, "I'm beautiful." (Jackall, 1978, pp. 121–122; emphasis in original).

We coded these episodes as representing frequent co-worker conflict in the workplace. This coding is further supported by the absence of any reports by the ethnographer of positive or supportive co-worker relations in this setting.

The research team met twice weekly to discuss coding problems and questions. At these meetings, the codings for each ethnography completed were reviewed in detail, and all coding questions were debated and resolved as a group. A 13 per cent sample of the cases was recoded as a reliability check. The correlations between these codings and the original codings indicate a relatively high degree of reliability (average inter-correlation = 0.79). Validity checks indicate that the ethnographies evidence no distinct patterns of findings based on ethnographer characteristics, such as theoretical orientation or gender (Hodson, 1999).[3]

The survey data

A telephone survey of a random sample of 371 employed adults living in the Midwestern United States provides data parallel to that collected from the ethnographies. The survey was implemented in the spring of 1992 – simultaneous with the completion of the first wave of ethnographic data collection. The collection of parallel variables in the ethnographic data and the telephone survey allows the evaluation of common models of management competence and working with dignity across two very different methods of observation but at a similar time frame. The telephone interviews were approximately 35 minutes in length and included both open-ended and closed questions. Systematic overlap between the questions included in the survey and the organisational ethnography data was planned into the research design, and a principal goal of the survey was to serve as a cross-methods check on conclusions derived from the ethnographic data.

Because survey methodology uses standardised and widely understood procedures, only a brief description of these procedures is provided. The survey design, implemented through computer-assisted random digit dialling, sampled telephone exchanges throughout the state and included cities, small towns and rural areas. Screening was conducted at each household contacted to determine whether any household member was at least 18 years of age and currently working for pay (excluding individuals who were self-employed or who worked without pay in a family farm or business). If more than one adult member of the household was working for pay, the appropriate respondent was computer selected. Supervisors regularly monitored the interviewing with each interviewer being monitored at least twice during each four-hour shift. The response rate for the survey was 70.0 per cent.

Variables

Similar concepts for our analysis of working with dignity and management competence are measured in the two data sets. For scaled concepts, however, the number of items in the scales sometimes varies between data sources because of data availability. The number of response categories for variables also sometimes differs between the two data sets. Most of the survey questions use a four-point Likert scale, as is standard practice in survey instruments. The ethnographic questions use more customised response categories. These response categories were developed through the reading and coding of the ethnographies as described in the *Methods* section. The response categories were selected to most accurately and reliably portray the characterisations typically made in the ethnographic accounts, and these characterisations do not necessarily fit neatly into four-point Likert scales designed for individual survey respondents. Accordingly, although concepts are identical between data sources, the exact items and the number of response categories sometimes vary according to the dictates of each method. In the *Results* section, standardised coefficients are utilised to remove differences in scale between variables from the two data sets.

The meanings of the survey questions are revealed by their wordings. Many of the ethnographic variables are also self-explanatory. Examples of the ethnographic material behind the coding of other concepts, such as employee dignity, can help illuminate their content and meaning. Low levels of *cooperation* (a component of OCB), for example, are revealed in Alvin Gouldner's classic study contrasting underground miners and the more closely supervised workers in the associated above ground gypsum board factory:

'On the surface, though, even when an emergency occurred many workers showed but little motivation. . . There was a break-down at the wet-end today . . . The younger men *relax* and *make jokes*. They lean across the board machine and *talk with each other* in clusters.

The foremen, though, work hard. One of the younger men *jokingly* pushes the button that lets loose a sharp whistle against the flat blast of the emergency buzzer. A foreman hustles down from the mixer. He asks, "Who done it?". . . The above observations reveal . . . that energetic and cooperative work efforts on the surface were not even brought about by an emergency situation' (Gouldner, 1964, p. 140 italics in original).

Additional quotes are used in the *Results* section below to illustrate the meanings and relationships of key concepts.

The means, ranges and standard deviations for the ethnographic and survey variables are provided in Tables 1 and 2, respectively. The key employee dignity and management competence variables are all measured with scales tapping their underlying components. The weights for these scales are based on factor loadings derived from principal components analysis (results reported in Tables 1 and 2). The means and standard deviations for both the ethnographic data and the survey variables suggest that these data are broadly representative of the broader organisational and labour force populations. A notable exception is the 50 per cent unionisation rate for the ethnographic cases, which is well in excess of the U.S. average.

Results

The regression of our three facets of employee dignity on management competence and other organisational, job and labour force character-istics is presented in Table 3. Two models are presented for each of the three facets of dignity – one for the ethnographic data and one for the survey data. All six models are highly statistically significant, even given the relatively small sample sizes involved.[3]

Management competence and establishment size, in particular, are observed to be strong influences on employee dignity. Management competence has significant positive effects in all six models estimated and establishment size has significant negative effects in four of the six models. The strength and consistency of these findings provide strong support for Hypothesis 1, which argues that management competence will have strong effects on employee dignity relative to other organ-isational and labour force determinants, as well as for Hypothesis 2, which argues for the replication of these effects across methods of observation.

Table 1 Variable ranges, means, standard deviations and factor scores, organisational ethnographies ($n = 204$)

Variables	Factor loadings	Range	Mean	SD
Working with dignity				
Organisational citizenship (alpha = 0.84, first and second eigenvalues = 3.06 and 0.60)		Standardised	0.00	1.00
Cooperation	0.801	1–3	2.47	0.59
Extra effort	0.842	1–3	2.41	0.68
Pride	0.770	1–3	2.24	0.78
Enthusiasm	0.712	0,1	0.32	0.47
Commitment	0.779	0,1	0.58	0.49
Conflict with management[a]		1–5	2.97	0.80
Conflict with supervisors		1–5	3.01	1.06
Conflict with management		1–5	2.92	1.05
Co-worker infighting (alpha = 0.79, first and second eigenvalues = 2.16 and 0.99)		Standardised	0.00	1.00
Within group conflict	0.728	1–3	2.06	0.56
Within group gossip	0.621	0,1	0.84	0.37
Between group conflict	0.720	1–3	2.10	0.61
Between group gossip	0.854	0,1	0.81	0.40
Organisational characteristics				
Local ownership		0,1	0.51	0.50
Establishment size (ln)[b]		0–11	5.80	2.20
Unionisation		0,1	0.51	0.50
Management competence (alpha = 0.81, first and second eigenvalues = 2.82 and 0.82)		Standardised	0.00	1.00
Abuse (reverse coded)	0.713	1–5	2.45	1.15
Leadership	0.823	1–5	3.05	0.99
Communication	0.711	1–3	1.87	0.79
Repair	0.669	1–3	2.22	0.76
Organisation of production	0.822	1–5	3.06	1.01
Job and labour force controls				
Skill		1–3	2.07	0.77
% female in work group		0–100	33.88	37.51
% minority in work group		0–100	17.74	28.75

[a]Conflict with management in the ethnographic data is computed as the numeric average of its two components.

[b]The unlogged mean and (standard deviation) of establishment employment are 2144 (4753).

An example of the positive effect of management competence on worker cooperation and enthusiasm (core elements of OCB) is provided by an ethnography of a North Atlantic freighter:

> [A sailor reports,] ''I like it that the captain doesn't put anyone down. He's keeping the whole trip together, but he doesn't bark or growl at anyone. He seems to be drawing everyone's ideas out...''

Table 2 Dependent variable ranges, means, standard deviations and factor scores, survey data (n = 371)

Variables	Factor loadings	Range	Mean	SD
Working with dignity				
Organisational citizenship (alpha = 0.61, first and second eigenvalues = 1.86 and 0.82)		Standardised	0.00	1.00
Help out	0.618	1–4	3.57	0.64
No damage	0.575	1–4	3.34	0.85
Avoid work (reverse coded)	0.765	1–4	2.83	1.08
Others avoid work (reverse coded)	0.754	1–4	2.50	1.07
Conflict with management				
Concern with management direction		1–4	2.93	1.02
Co-worker infighting (alpha = 0.64, first and second eigenvalues = 1.92 and 0.86)		Standardised	0.00	1.00
Bickering	0.720	1–4	2.11	1.02
Favouritism	0.723	1–4	2.42	1.14
Extra credit	0.608	1–4	2.35	0.96
Satisfaction with co-workers (reversed coded)	0.714	1–4	1.51	0.62
Organisational characteristics				
Local ownership		0,1	0.60	0.49
Establishment size (ln)[a]		7–9	5.01	2.29
Unionisation		0,1	0.21	0.41
Management competence (alpha = 0.73, first and second eigenvalues = 2.25 and 0.84)		Standardised	0.00	1.00
Treats workers with respect	0.816	1–4	3.53	0.71
Asks opinions	0.728	1–4	3.11	0.94
Opportunity to learn	0.610	1–4	3.35	0.74
Satisfaction with supervisor	0.824	1–4	3.42	0.78
Job and labour force controls				
Skill		1–4	3.13	0.93
Female		0,1	49.06	50.06
Minority		0,1	7.61	26.55

[a]The unlogged mean and (standard deviation) of establishment employment are 1318 (2766).

Indeed we were impressed by the high degree of cooperation and cohesion among the crew...Everyone understood his job. Everyone was doing his job. This is the true test of any working community – how well they do their jobs, and how effectively their skills come into play, how easily they work with each other in their cooperative endeavour' (Schrank, 1983, pp. 39, 60).

Conversely, an ethnography of a pickle factory with low levels of management competence (standardised management competence

Table 3 Regression of three facets of employee dignity on workplace characteristics, organisational ethnographies ($n = 204$) and survey data ($n = 371$)

Variables	Organisational citizenship		Conflict with management		Co-worker infighting	
	Ethnography	Survey	Ethnography	Survey	Ethnography	Survey
Year study ended	0.061		0.154[c]		0.020	
Organisational characteristics						
Local ownership	0.073	0.092[d]	−0.065	−0.010	0.073	−0.030
Establishment size	−0.065	−0.100[c]	0.102	0.169[b]	0.225[b]	0.155[b]
Unionisation	−0.115	−0.039	0.151[c]	0.074	0.032	−0.024
Management competence	0.324[a]	0.384[a]	−0.545[a]	−0.120[c]	−0.236[b]	−0.470[a]
Job and labour force controls						
Skill	0.362[a]	0.009	0.064	−0.078	0.141	0.082[d]
Female	−0.061	0.050	0.082	−0.107[c]	0.061	−0.022
Minority	−0.089	−.007	−0.056	−0.021	−0.096	0.056
Multiple regression	0.651[a]	0.449[a]	0.616[a]	0.299[a]	0.335[b]	0.504[a]

The table reports standardised regression coefficients.
Statistical significance (2-tailed t-tests) denoted by:
[a] $p \leq 0.001$.
[b] $p \leq 0.01$.
[c] $p \leq 0.05$.
[d] $p \leq 0.10$.

score $= -0.97$) illustrates how working in a poorly managed workplace, and the resulting lack of opportunity for taking pride in one's work, can be devastating to morale:

'There isn't anyone among us who doesn't resent how the factory is operated so fast and sloppy, because there's no way to respect what we're doing and what we're making. In fact, most people here like it best when things don't work right and production goes to hell, and I'm right along with them. And that's a crummy way to waste your working time' (Turner, 1980, p. 61).

The role of management incompetence in engendering conflict among co-workers is evidenced in a study of a steel mill (management competence $= -1.20$). The ethnographer reports on numerous episodes of abusive actions on the part of management. For example, aggravated by a minor complaint from a worker, a supervisor 'flew into a rage, and shouted, "Get back on your job. You don't know what-in-hell you're talking about. I've been watching you, and you've been sitting on your [expletive deleted] all morning" (Spencer, 1977, p. 171). In this abusive setting, animosity and jealousy also characterise relations between workers. For example, millwrights are secretive in their knowledge and unwilling to share it with apprentices:

> 'Steve [the apprentice] was beginning to boil over, and one morning when the millwright was thumbing over a blue print, holding it purposely out of Steve's view, as though it were personal and confidential, he popped off, ' . . . I'm gonna' learn everything there is to know about this [expletive deleted] job, no matter what you think' (Spencer, 1977, p. 64).

Establishment size reduces OCB and increases both vertical and horizontal conflict. This finding is consistent with a large body of prior research that has identified organisational size as a key contributor to disaffection from work (Kalleberg et al., 1996). Chronic infighting among co-workers is clearly evident in an ethnography of a large electronics factory (employment = 800):

> 'On our line all this was complicated by the conflict between the electrical checker and the reject operator. Sharon, the reject operator . . . was very bossy . . . She also stirred up trouble by telling tales on us to Eamonn [the foreman] and interfered in our work. Sharon tried to cut down on her own work and kept saying the UMOs I put out for her weren't faulty. She wanted me to send them down the line "to see if Joyce puts them out" . . . It got to the stage where she wouldn't take any reject of mine for a mechanical fault unless I had already . . . rechecked it – this meant twice as much work for me and none for her' (Cavendish, 1982, pp. 36–37).

In general, the organisational variables have larger effects on working with dignity than the job and labour force characteristics. This finding is particularly important given the common practice of evaluating models of organisational outcomes *within* organisations. It appears that such practices may actually result in the underestimation, or inability to estimate, many of the effects that are most important to the theoretical traditions being evaluated (see Heath and Sitkin, 2001).

The year the ethnographic study was completed is also included as a control in the model for the ethnographic data. The effect of time trend is significant only for conflict with management, where a positive trend is evidenced. The observed increase in conflict with management over time may reflect increasingly tense relations with management in the workplace in recent decades because of increased competition, downsizing and outsourcing. The coefficient should probably not be overinterpreted, however, because of its modest size and limited replication across dependent variables. The positive time trend for conflict with management does nevertheless provide a rare glimpse into trends that would otherwise be difficult to observe.

The effects of the skill and labour force characteristics on employee dignity are more limited than the effects of the organisational characteristics. Skill is a significant positive contributor to OCB as evaluated in the ethnographic data. But skilled workers are more given to infighting as evidenced in the survey data. The role of skill and autonomy in encouraging pride in work (an aspect of employee citizenship) is illustrated in an ethnography of construction workers:

> 'At the sewage treatment plant, there were several occasions when the men placed a thousand yards of concrete in a single day. No one from management told them to do it. The superintendent, foremen, and key journeymen decided and planned it on their own initiative. One evening, at the local bar... after one of the thousand-yard pours, Pete expressed the pride and satisfaction that comes from extraordinary accomplishment, and said: "If they'd leave us alone, we can take care of the work and make money for the company. We did a thousand yards today. But I've done better. As long as Carmen (the employer) leaves Earl (the superintendent) alone we can turn out the work"' (Applebaum, 1981, p. 63).

Race and gender are also evaluated as influences on working with dignity and are significant in only one of the models estimated – female workers evidence less conflict with management in the survey data. The limited effects of race and gender are consistent with prior research on employee dignity, which has argued that working with dignity is largely a result of organisational dynamics that operate above and beyond work force characteristics (but see Tsui and Gutek, 1999).

Overall, the effects of the job characteristics, including skill and labour force characteristics, on working with dignity are both less significant and smaller than the effects of the organisational characteristics and are less consistently replicated across methods.

Discussion

Supported by a cross-methods validation of findings, the crucial determinants of working with dignity appear to be management competence, which exerts a positive influence, and organisational size, which exerts a negative influence. Management competence has the strongest effects in the model, effects which are validated across methods and which are evidenced for all three dignity facets – citizenship behaviour and horizontal and vertical conflict. Skill also has a positive effect on the citizenship aspect of working with dignity, although this relationship is only significant in the ethnographic data.

Workers appear to be keenly interested in and motivated by management competence. We thus need appropriate conceptualisations of appropriate management behaviour if we are to adequately understand the nature of work and its dynamics in the contemporary economy. The results presented in the current analysis suggest that the most significant determinant of working with dignity is working in an organisation in which management supports a productive work environment and abides by norms that respect workers' rights and interests. Without consistent management competence, worker citizenship and the productivity promises of the flexible workplace may be undermined.

There are substantial benefits to be attained by including an explicit conceptualisation of management competence in discussions of employee dignity and well-being. By explicitly identifying norms of management behaviour and establishing the centrality of these to the success of job redesign programs, we can begin to specify the foundation for realisable improvements that can be attained in the contemporary workplace. Identifying and abiding by such organisational norms is essential for the success of new production systems based on high trust and high commitment. If organisations are to achieve competitive advantage by cultivating dense networks of social capital (Nahapiet and Ghoshal, 1998), then it appears that management must take the lead by convincingly demonstrating its own citizenship (Leana and Van Buren, 1999; Smith, 2001).

There are also substantial benefits to be attained by validating findings about the workplace across research methods whenever possible. Only in this way can we distinguish between findings that are conditional on the method of observation and those that are repeated across methodologies. Our confidence in the positive effects of management competence and the negative effects of organisational size on working with dignity is thus strengthened by their replication across methods of observation and analysis.

Limitations

An important limitation of the current analysis concerns the relationship of the population of organisational ethnographies to the population of organisations. Organisational ethnographies do not represent a random draw from the population of organisations but were undertaken for a variety of theoretical and practical reasons, including access. For this reason, analysis of the populations of ethnographies cannot be statistically generalised to all organisations based on conventional sampling theory. Rather, analysis of the population of organisational ethnographies tells us quite precisely (without sampling error) *what ethnographers have observed about organisations.* Nevertheless, the amalgamation of ethnographic case studies of organisations and their simultaneous analysis does address the core limitation of single case studies through the introduction of explicit comparison groups and controls. Cross-methods validation of the core ethnographic results with survey data further supports their credibility.

Conclusions

Our analysis of workplace ethnographies summarises what 200 trained observers have reported about organisations and organisational life. The conclusion from these findings is that competent and respectful managerial behaviour is crucial for working with dignity. This research responds to the call for organisational researchers to breathe life into their scholarship by grounding it in lived experiences on the job (Dutton, 2003). Our research also highlights the simple, but sometimes questioned, observation that management *is* important in the workplace and that their actions set the tone that defines the experience of work for those under their supervision (see Lockett and McWilliams, 2005). It is therefore important that organisational researchers continue to include a central focus on managers and supervisors and their interactions with employees as a core topic in organisational research and to theoretically integrate these insights with broader concerns of technology, globalisation, labour force dynamics and profitability.

The research presented here also suggests several directions for future research. The finding that management competence is crucial for working with dignity could and should be replicated with other data sets based on other methodologies. Perhaps more importantly, the concepts of *management competence* and *employee dignity* can and should be further refined and their relations with other concepts in organisational literature explored. Management behaviour that is competent and respectful of employees is a central aspect of effective leadership and a requirement in modern organisations that rely on stakeholder commitment (Gruber and Coleman, 2005). The linking of managerial competence and important outcomes for employees and organisations is thus an important endeavour for organisation studies (Gomez and Rosen, 2001). While the current findings may not justify some of the boldest claims for the centrality of leadership (Fulmer and Goldsmith, 2001; Kanter, 1983), they, nevertheless, do reinforce the importance of managerial competence for employee dignity. Working with dignity is also a broad concept with multiple facets and implications. Exploring the meaning and experience of working with dignity can further contribute to the breathing of life into organisational studies.

References

Ackroyd, S. and Thompson, P. (1999) *Organizational Misbehaviour*, London: Sage.

Adler, P. S. (2001) 'Markets, Hierarchy and Trust: The Knowledge Economy and the Future of Capitalism', *Organization Science*, **12**, 215–234.

Anderson, L. M. and Pearson, C. M. (1999) 'Tit for Tat? The Spiraling Effect of Incivility in the Workplace', *Academy of Management Review*, **24**, 452–471.

Applebaum, H. (1981) *Royal Blue: The Culture of Construction Workers*, New York: Holt.

Applebaum, H. (1992) *The Concept of Work: Ancient, Medieval, and Modern*, Albany, NY: State University of New York Press.

Barley, S. R. and Kunda, G. (1992) 'Design and Devotion: Surges of Rational and Normative Ideologies of Control in Managerial Discourse', *Administrative Science Quarterly*, **37**, 363–399.

Barnard, C. I. (1950) *The Functions of the Executive*, Cambridge, MA: Harvard University Press.

Bass, B. M. (1985) *Leadership and Performance beyond Expectations*, New York: Free Press.

Becker, T. E. (1998) 'Integrity in Organizations: Beyond Honesty and Conscientiousness', *Academy of Management Review*, **23**, 154–161.

Besser, T. L. (1996) *Team Toyota: Transplanting the Toyota Culture to the Camry Plant in Kentucky*, Albany, NY: State University of New York Press.

Bies, R. J. (1987) 'The Predicament of Injustice: The Management of Moral Outrage', in *Research in Organizational Behavior*, Volume 9 (Cummings, L. L. and Staw, B. M. eds), Greenwich, CN: JAI, pp. 289–319.

Bolton, S. C. and Boyd, C. (2003) 'Trolley Dolly or Skilled Emotion Manager? Moving on From Hochschild's Managed Heart', *Work, Employment and Society*, **17**, 289–308.

Bommer, W. H., Miles, E. W. and Grover, S. L. (2003) 'Does One Good Turn Deserve Another? Coworker Influences on Employee Citizenship', *Journal of Organizational Behavior*, **24**, 181–196.

Cavendish, R. (1982) *Women on the Line*, Boston: Routledge and Kegan Paul.

Cherry, M. (1974) *On High Steel: The Education of an Ironworker*, New York: Quadrangle.

Cornfield, D. B. and McCammon, H. J. (eds) (2003) 'Labor Revitalization', *Research in the Sociology of Work*, Volume 11, Amsterdam: JAI/Elsevier.

Cropanzano, R., Prehar, C. A. and Chen, P. Y. (2002) 'Using Social Exchange Theory to Distinguish Procedural from Interactional Justice', *Group & Organization Management*, **27**, 324–351.

Cummings, T. G. (1993) *Organizational Development and Change*, Minneapolis, MN: West.

Drucker, P. F. (1993) *Post-Capitalist Society*, New York: Harper.

Dunlop, P. D. and Lee, K. (2004) 'Workplace Deviance, Organizational Citizenship Behavior, and Business Unit Performance: The Bad Apples Do Spoil the Whole Barrel', *Journal of Organizational Behavior*, **25**, 67–80.

Dutton, J. E. (2003) 'Breathing Life into Organizational Studies', *Journal of Management Inquiry*, **12**, 1, 5–19.

Edwards, P. K. and Wajcman, J. (2005) *The Politics of Working Life*, Oxford: Oxford University Press.

Fink, D. (1998) *Cutting into the Meatpacking Line: Workers and Change in the Rural Midwest*, Chapel Hill: University of North Carolina Press.

Fox, A. (1974) *Beyond Contract: Work, Power and Trust Relations*, London: Faber and Faber.

Fulmer, R. M. and Goldsmith, M. (2001) *The Leadership Investment*, New York: American Management Association.

Gomez, C. and Rosen, B. (2001) 'The Leader-Member Exchange as a Link Between Managerial Trust and Employee Empowerment', *Group & Organization Management*, **26**, 53–69.

Gouldner, A. (1964) *Patterns of Industrial Bureaucracy*, New York: Free Press.

Gruber, D. A. and Coleman, M. S. (2005) 'Inspired Leadership in Challenging times', *Journal of Management Inquiry*, **14**, 4, 338–342.

Hackman, J. R. (2003) 'Learning More by Crossing Levels: Evidence from Airplanes, Hospitals, and Orchestras', *Journal of Organizational Behavior*, **24**, 905–922.

Hammersley, M. (1997) 'Qualitative Data Archiving: Some Reflections on its Prospects and Problems', *Sociology*, **31**, 1, 131–142.

Heath, C. and Sitkin, S. B. (2001) 'Big-B versus Big-0: What is Organizational About Organizational Behavior?' *Journal of Organizational Behavior*, **22**, 43–58.

Hodson, R. (1999) *Analyzing Documentary Accounts. Quantitative Applications in the Social Sciences*, Volume 128, Thousand Oaks, CA: Sage.

Hodson, R. (2001) *Dignity at Work*, New York: Cambridge University Press.

Jackall, R. (1978) *Workers in a Labyrinth: Jobs and Survival in a Bank Bureaucracy*, Montclair, NJ: Allanheld and Osmun.

Jehn, K. A. (1995) 'A Multimethod Examination of the Benefits and Deter-minants of Intragroup Conflict', *Administrative Science Quarterly*, **40**, 256–282.

Juravich, T. (1985) *Chaos on the Shop Floor: A Worker's View of Quality, Productivity, and Management*, Philadelphia: Temple University Press.

Kalleberg, A. L., Knoke, D., Marsden, P. and Spaeth, J. L. (1996) *Organizations in America*, Newbury Park, CA: Sage.

Kanter, R. M. (1983) *The Change Masters*, New York: Simon and Schuster.

Knights, D. and McCabe, D. (1999) '"Are There no Limits to Authority?": TQM and Organizational Power', *Organization Studies*, **20**, 197–224.

Kolb, D. M. and Bartunek, J. M. (1992) *Hidden Conflict in Organizations*, Newbury Park, CA: Sage.

Kunda, G. (1992) *Engineering Culture: Control and Commitment in a High-Tech Corporation*, Philadelphia: Temple University Press.

Lamont, M. (2000) *The Dignity of Working Men*, Cambridge, MA: Harvard University Press.

Leana, C. R. and Van Buren, H. J., III. (1999) 'Organizational Social Capital and Employment Practices', *Academy of Management Review*, **24**, 538–555.

Lee, C. K. (1998) *Gender and the South China Miracle: Two Worlds of Factory Women*, Berkeley: University of California Press.

Lee, T. W. (1999) *Using Qualitative Methods in Organizational Research*, Thousand Oaks, CA: Sage.

Lincoln, J. R. and Kalleberg, A. L. (1990) *Culture, Control, and Commitment*, New York: Cambridge University Press.

Lockett, A. and McWilliams, A. (2005) 'The Balance of Trade Between Disciplines: Do We Effectively Manage Knowledge?' *Journal of Management Inquiry*, **14**, 2, 139–150.

McNally, F. (1979) *Women for Hire*, New York: St. Martin's.

Mouly, V. S. and Sankaran, J. K. (1997) 'On the Study of Settings Marked by Severe Superior-subordinate Conflict', *Organization Studies*, **18**, 175–192.

Nahapiet, J. and Ghoshal, S. (1998) 'Social Capital, Intellectual Capital, and the Organizational Advantage', *Academy of Management Review*, **23**, 242–266.

Nord, W. R., Brief, A. P., Atieh, J. and Doherty, E. (1990) 'Study of Meanings of Work: The Case of Work Values, in *Meanings of Occupational Work* (Brief, A. P. and Nord, W. R., eds), Lexington, MA: Lexington, pp. 21–64.

Organ, D. W. (1988) *Organizational Citizenship Behavior*, Lexington, MA: D.C. Heath.

Pfeffer, J. (1998) *The Human Equation: Building Profits by Putting People First*, Boston: Harvard Business School Press.

Podsakoff, P. M., MacKenzie, S. B., Paine, J. B. and Bachrach, D.G. (2000) 'Organizational Citizenship Behaviors: A Critical Review of the Theoretical and Empirical Literature and Suggestions for Future Research', *Journal of Management*, **26**, 513–563.

Pollert, A. (1981) *Girls, Wives, Factory Lives*, London: MacMillan.

Prasad, A. (2002) 'The Contest Over Meaning: Hermeneutics as an Interpretative Methodology for Understanding Texts', *Organizational Research Methods*, **5**, 12–33.

Prasad, P. and Prasad, A. (2000) 'Stretching the Iron Cage: The Constitution and Implications of Routine Workplace Resistance', *Organization Science*, **11**, 387–403.

Pratt, M. G. (2000) 'The Good, the Bad and the Ambivalent: Managing Identification Among Amway Distributors', *Administrative Science Quarterly*, **45**, 456–493.

Roethlisberger, F. J. and Dickson, W. J. (1939) *Management and the Worker*, Cambridge, MA: Harvard University Press.

Schnake, M. (1991) 'Organizational Citizenship: A Review, Proposed Model, and Research Agenda', *Human Relations*, **44**, 735–759.

Schrank, R. (1983) *Industrial Democracy at Sea: Authority and Democracy on a Norwegian Freighter*, Cambridge, MA: MIT Press.

Seider, M. (1984) *A Year in the Life of a Factory*, San Pedro, CA: Singlejack.

Selznick, P. (1969) *Law, Society, and Industrial Justice*, New York: Russell Sage Foundation.

Shore, L. M. and Coyle-Shapiro, J. A.-M. (2003) 'New Developments in the Employee-Organization Relationship', *Journal of Organizational Behavior*, **24**, 443–450.

Smith, V. (2001) *Crossing the Great Divide: Worker Risk and Opportunity in the New Economy*, Ithaca, NY: Cornell University Press.

Smith, C. A., Organ, D. W. and Near, J. P. (1983) 'Organizational Citizenship Behavior: Its Nature and Antecedents', *Journal of Applied Psychology*, **68**, 653–663.

Spencer, C. (1977) *Blue Collar: An Internal Examination of the Workplace*, Chicago: Lakeside Press.

Tekleab, A. G. and Taylor, S. M. (2003) 'Aren't There Two Parties in an Employment Relationship? Antecedents and Consequences of Organization-Employee Agreement on Contract Obligations and Violations', *Journal of Organizational Behavior*, **24**, 585–608.

Tsui, A. S. and Gutek, B. A. (1999) *Demographic Differences in Organizations: Current Research and Future Directions*, New York: Lexington.

Tsui, A. S., Pearce, J. L., Porter, L. W. and Tripoli, A. M. (1997) 'Alternative Approaches to the Employee-Organization Relationship: Does Investment in Employees Pay Off?' *Academy of Management Journal*, **40**, 1089–1121.

Turner, S. (1980) *Night Shift in a Pickle Factory*, San Pedro, CA: Singlejack Books.

Tyler, T. R. (2001) 'Why do People Rely on Others? Social Identity and the Social Aspects of Trust' in *Trust in Society* (Cook, K. S., ed.), New York: Russell Sage Foundation, pp. 285–306.

Van Maanen, J. (ed.) (1998) *Qualitative Studies in Organizations*, Thousand Oaks, CA: Sage.

Weber, R. P. (1990) 'Basic Content Analysis', 2nd ed. *Quantitative Applications in the Social Sciences*, Volume 49, Newbury Park, CA: Sage.

Whitener, E. M., Brodt, S. E., Korsgaard, M. A. and Werner, J. M. (1998) 'Managers as Initiators of Trust: An Exchange Relationship Framework for Understanding Managerial Trustworthy Behavior', *Academy of Management Review*, **23**, 513–530.

Wood, S. (2000) '*The British Journal of Industrial Relations* and Industrial Relations in the New Millennium', *British Journal of Industrial Relations*, **38**, 1, 1–5.

8

Best companies, best practice and dignity at work

Sharon C. Bolton and Gemma Wibberley

Management practice and dignity

Despite the apparent importance and universal acceptance of the 'inherent dignity of the human person' (*The International Bill of Rights* in Perry, 2005), dignity is not something that is generally referred to within management texts. When the word dignity is used, it tends to be linked with the subjective elements of dignity at work – self-esteem, autonomy and meaningful work. For instance, an early focus on the 'humanization of work' formed the basis for the introduction of new softer management practices; developing through several phases of job enlargement, teamwork, industrial democracy and responsible autonomy (Agassi, 1986; Fox, 1994; Freidman, 1977; Gemmill, 1977; Gini, 2001; Hodson, 1996, 2001; Hodson and Roscigno, 2004; Khan, 1981; Kornhauser, 1964; Rosow, 1979; Ryan, 1977; Schumacer, 1979). The most recent prescriptions from management gurus tend to mirror early human relations writings in their call for management practice to create employee engagement and cohesive corporate cultures (Peters, 1995; Reeves, 2001). From a different perspective, though directly linked with varied calls for building cultures of respect (Ishmael, 1999; Rennie Peyton, 2003; Tehrani, 2004; Wright and Smye, 1997), is the high-profile campaign for 'dignity at work' (cf. AMICUS and The Andrea Adams Trust) that draws attention to everyday bullying behaviours that occur in the workplace serving to intimidate and oppress employees. Some of the core concerns of this campaign are clearly related to substantive matters not dissimilar to earlier concerns relating to autonomy and worth. From whatever angle, it would seem that, though only ever referred to loosely, dignity at work is closely associated with management practice – its design, implementation, effect on the workforce and, ultimately, its impact upon performance.

This chapter seeks to explore the association between the implementation of various management practices and the achievement of dignity at work by examining the approach of companies that are known for the implementation of 'best practice' management. The 10 companies examined in this chapter are recognised for their exemplary approach to managing employees through inclusion in *The Sunday Times 100 Best Companies to Work For* (2006) list. Despite protracted debate concerning the universal applicability of best practice and doubts concerning empirical verification of its link with performance, there is ample evidence to suggest that a consequence of achieving at least some elements of best practice management is that organisations are seen as good corporate citizens, employers of choice, superior performers and, hence, best places to work (Department of Trade and Industry, 2002a,b, 2004b; Leary-Joyce, 2004; The Work Foundation and The Future Foundation, 2002; The Work Foundation, 2005). *The Sunday Times 100 Best Companies to Work For* is a large scale survey that gathers core information from nominated companies known for their 'best practice' approach to people management. It therefore offers valuable information on working conditions, health and well-being and organisational diversity and why and how companies are perceived as 'the best' and the type of people employed. Whilst not searching for generalisable knowledge, the *Best Companies* survey data allow an exploration of how people might experience dignity at work and how this might be related to different organisations' approaches to people management.

A best practice framework for dignity at work

Best practice people management (BPPM) is often proposed as a means of valuing and respecting people in an organisation, hence offering opportunities for the creation and maintenance of dignity at work. And this is precisely what 'best companies' proclaim lies at the heart of their success. Of course, BPPM also has a sound business case to make. The adoption of a best practice approach to people management has been widely advocated as a means of increasing innovation and performance in UK business, and a broad consensus has emerged that investment in various human resource management (HRM) practices will create a high-performance workplace (HPWP) (Applebaum et al.,

2000; DTI 2004a,b; Guest, 1997; Guest et al., 2003; Huselid, 1995; Pfeffer, 1994; Sung and Ashton, 2005).

The focus on best practice draws heavily from the resource-based view of the firm (Barney, 1991; Mueller, 1996) that offers an inside-out version of strategic management, quite different from the contingency view (i.e., Porter, 1985) in the way it emphasises 'softer' people management practices involving learning and development, involvement and empowerment and a strong focus on people as the organisation's most important asset. Closely associated with a move towards bundles of softer HRM practices is the focus on leadership as a defining feature of successful organisations. Strong leadership is represented as a creative force and prime motivator for change and quite different to the functional direction of management (Barker, 2001; Kotter, 1990; Senge, 1996). In line with the resource-based view of the firm, leadership is portrayed as strategic but with a gentle touch as charismatic leaders create and espouse organisational vision and values within a unitary framework of what good leadership might be. In essence, leadership is seen as an essential prerequisite for the implementation of innovative people management practices leading to best practice and increased performance. The concentration on transformational, rather than transactional, leadership and softer management practices that focus more on the intrinsic rather than extrinsic needs of employees clearly reflects the broader move towards changing organisational forms, flatter hierarchies, networked organisations and knowledge-intensive industries where more traditional 'macho management' techniques are deemed no longer applicable.

The best practice approach emphasises the need to 'bundle' people management practices in order to achieve maximum effectiveness (Pfeffer, 1994). For instance, recruitment practices need to be linked to retention issues of learning and development and performance and reward. In isolation, each practice may have some effect, but its impact on overall performance will be minimal. Various approaches to strategic HRM have suggested model approaches to the adoption of bundles of best practice, and this has become a popular means of linking people and performance in corporate strategy. The UK government have drawn from this theme, endorsing links between management practices that enable employees to develop and fulfil their potential and successful organisations. The Department of Trade and Industry (DTI) offers BPPM as a key benchmark for companies to follow, thus leading to best practice organisations (see Table 1).

The list the DTI offers is far more comprehensive than many advocates of BPPM, and its close cousin HPWP, would suggest as it goes beyond the mere change of organisational culture and the tweaking

Table 1   DTI best practice people management indicators

- Recognise and reward employees' contributions
- Encourage equal opportunities for all
- Promote learning
- Instigate internal communication systems
- Ensure effective employee consultation arrangements
- Empower employees
- Maintain constructive relationships with trade unions
- Provide as much employment security as possible

Defined by the Department of Trade and Industry (DTI, 2004a).

of reward packages and involvement systems to deal with issues of collective voice, security and equality. The BPPM framework offered by the DTI reflects a comprehensive 'bundle' of people management practices that help to support both objective and subjective dimensions of work, recognising as it does the need to offer job security, equal opportunities and collective voice but also the importance of building a learning organisation where employees feel empowered and able to communicate with colleagues and management at all levels. There are clear similarities between this list and the defining features of what is understood as 'decent' and 'good work' (see also Bolton, Coats, Philpott and Wallace, this volume).

As the International Labour Organisation's decent work indicators (see Table 2) signify, there are large areas of overlap between what is internationally recognised as fundamental factors that contribute to good work and the DTI's best practice framework. Overall, it would appear that the DTI list offers a management framework that aims at creating the conditions for empowered workers, recognised, rewarded

Table 2   International labour organisation decent work indicators

- Employment opportunities
- Unacceptable work
- Adequate earnings and productive work
- Decent hours
- Stability and security
- Balancing work and family life
- Fair treatment in employment
- Safe work environment
- Social protection
- Social dialogue and workplace relations
- Economic and social context of decent work

From Anker et al. (2003, p. 153).

and respected within a culture of diversity; the central ingredients most frequently recognised as contributing to the achievement of dignity at work (Bolton, 2007, this volume; Hodson, 2001, 2007, this volume; Rayman, 2001).

Best companies and the Times' list

The Sunday Times 100 Best Companies to Work For is a large scale survey that gathers core information from nominated companies known for their exemplary approach to people management. The research is carried out by *Best Companies Ltd* (http://www.bestcompanies.co.uk), and the list is sponsored by the DTI. Best 100 companies are defined by their approach to key areas: *well-being*, work–life balance issues; *leadership*, the integrity and involvement of the senior management of the company; *belonging*, teamwork and immediate colleagues; *giving something back*, whether the company contributes to society and/or the local community; *personal growth*, opportunities to learn, grow and be challenged; *immediate manager*, day-to-day management issues; *fair deal*, pay and associated benefits, and *my company*, the company and the overall impression of how it treats its staff (*The Sunday Times*, 2005, 2006). Clearly, this list represents the expected attributes of BPPM which is widely recognised as firmly making the link between 'best companies: best practice' (DTI, 2004a,b) and is described by the British government as a 'key benchmark' (Kearns, 2004).

Lists such as *The Sunday Times 100 Best Companies to Work For* are evidence of the desire of organisations to be seen as 'best' in their employment practices (*The Sunday Times*, 2005, 2006). The strength of the brand of being a 'best' company to work for also indicates that employees view this list as a guide when making decisions concerning changes in employment. It is interesting to note that questions asked by the *Best Companies* survey clearly reflect the best practice approach to people management. Though there is some available factual data concerning organisational demographics, length of service and paid holidays, the vast amount of data collected from employees represent their subjective interpretations of various facets of their work and working relationships with colleagues and with managers (line managers) and leaders (senior managers). As the following analysis will show, overwhelmingly, *Best Companies* appear to be judged as 'best' based on intrinsic value as perceived by employees which clearly reflects the move towards a 'softer' focus on management and the growing appreciation of the importance of respect and recognition and successful working relationships – ideas that are firmly embedded in the philosophy of the best practice approach to people management and leadership.

Methodology

The Sunday Times 100 Best Companies to Work For (2006) list is the sixth in the annual series. *The Times* list represents 100 Best small companies (50–250 employees), 100 best mid-sized companies (employees 250–5000) and 20 best big companies (over 5000 employees), thus offering insights into a range of companies. Companies who appear on the list must be at least five years old and have a minimum of 50 employees. Companies are ranked based on responses from an employee survey and company survey. The employee survey contributes 90 per cent of the final assessment for ranking. Staff who participate are randomly selected and asked to answer 70 questions relating to their workplace. There must be at least a 40 per cent return rate on the employee questionnaire for a company to be eligible for consideration as a 'best' company. Company survey data counts as the additional 10 per cent of the assessment for ranking.

For the analysis presented here, we chose to analyse mid-size companies (250–5000 employees), as the majority of the working population are employed by companies of this size. The top 10 mid-sized companies will be the focus of the analysis for this chapter (see Table 3). Overall, the *Best Company* list is dominated by professional service firms, law, media, IT (33 per cent) and also financial and business services – recruitment agencies, call-centre sales and queries (27 per cent) with caring, community and public services coming in third at 13 per cent. The top 10 companies, therefore, do not directly represent various sectors in the same way as the *100 Best Companies* list, containing as it does only two professional firms and three caring and public service organisations along with manufacturing and retail companies. However, the list is representative in the way it represents mainly 'feminised' industries, that is, care, retail, business services, a relatively youthful workforce and an overall focus on intrinsic employee satisfaction as a measure of the success of best practice management.

As an analytical scaffold for *The Sunday Times* data, a table has been created using the *Best Practice Management* guidelines produced by the DTI as a basis for conceptualising dignity at work. Interpretation of the data in the analysis relies heavily upon that which is published by *The Sunday Times*. The complete data sets are not made

Table 3 The top 10 mid-sized companies 2006

			Recognise and reward employees' contributions (must apply to all staff)						Encourage equal opportunities for all					Provide as much employment security as possible		Involvement and voice		Promote learning	
Rank in Sunday Times 2006	Sunday Times Best Companies in the NW	Industry	% earning more than £35,000 pa	25 days or more leave	Pension (a)	Private health care (b)	Gym facilities (c)	% who say appreciation is expressed for a good job done (top 10 scores)	% of female employees (* at least 33% of senior management are women)	% employees under 35 yrs old	% of employees over 55 yrs old	At least 10 weeks maternity leave on full pay	On site nursery or vouchers	40% of workforce have been there more than 5 years	Staff turnover (%)	Share option scheme	% who say managers are open and honest (top 10 score)	Top 25 personal growth	% think their job is good for personal growth (top 10 score)
1	W L Gore	Manufacturer	n/a	Yes	Yes			82	35	23	11	Yes		Yes	7	Yes	88	Yes	92
2	Sandwell Community Caring Trust	Personal care and support	2	Yes	Yes			82	85*	32	14	Yes			12		85	Yes	82
3	Pannone	Legal firm	32		Yes		Yes		69*	58	5				5			Yes	84
4	Beaverbrooks	Retailer	6		Yes			80	84	66	6		Yes		19		82	Yes	
5	Data Connection	Computer software	49	Yes	Yes	Yes			20	59	4		Yes	Yes	5		87	Yes	
6	Lindum Group	Construction and housing	5				Yes		19	34	24		Yes	Yes	8	Yes	83	Yes	
7	Badenoch and Clark	Recruitment Consultancy	66		Yes			84	60*	94	0		Yes	Yes	28			Yes	
8	Office Angels	Recruitment Consultancy	10				Yes	82	92*	80	0		Yes		39		83	Yes	84
9	St Anns Hospice	Hospice	3	Yes					93*	12	24		Yes	Yes	14			Yes	
10	Southdown Housing	Housing Association	2						66*	32	10		Yes		15			Yes	

(a) Non contributory pension or firms pay double staff contribution
(b) Private health care for employees and their family
(c) On site gym/subsidised membership for off site

available and not all questions are published and some answers are only published by top 10 scores. In addition, the data do not reveal any information concerning some very important workplace issues such as race, bullying and harassment, sickness policies, absenteeism rates, average salaries or trade union involvement. The published data from the *Best Companies* survey are organised under the headings of each of the points of best practice in the DTI framework, for instance 'promote leaning' draws on published responses to questions as to whether employees feel their job is good for personal growth or managers support them when they need to learn new skills. Some sections report objective data such as demographic figures or measurements of pay and reward, but many rely on assessing employees' feelings regarding certain aspects of their work. Therefore, some sections have more reliable data available than others, and the analysis of some aspects of BPPM is necessarily limited. Where complete data are available, it is presented in Table 1. Where data are not available for all companies but some interesting 'spotlights' on various companies are offered, these are presented in boxes where relevant to the ongoing analysis. Despite some limitations in the data available, *The Times* lists do offer a valuable opportunity to appraise what is seen as the 'best' and how companies use the brand of 'Best 100' to firmly place themselves as good organisation citizens via their ethical approach to people management, their inspirational leadership and as 'employers of choice' in a competitive labour market.

Best practice in action

The DTI's BPPM framework is used to analyse data derived from *The Sunday Times 100 Best Companies to Work For* (2006) list. It will examine the occurrence of various policies and practices and employees' feelings regarding various aspects of people management in order to identify which companies are achieving bundles of BPPM and where gaps in the bundles might occur. Each of the DTI's elements of BPPM will be analysed discretely.

Reward

There are various questions in the *Best Companies* survey that cover issues relating to recognition and reward. There are objective measurements of pay and conditions regarding paid holidays and pensions for instance, but also employees' subjective interpretations of feeling valued via questions that cover feeling appreciated and suitably rewarded.

The most extensive data presented detail an array of material benefits available to employees. Unsurprisingly, over 80 per cent of employees at Gore, Sandwell and Pannone, and 74 per cent at Data Connection express satisfaction with pay and benefits and these are the companies who offer pension and reasonable paid holiday arrangements. Sandwell Community Trust is relatively unusual in the low-paid care work sector in offering a range of material benefits, as highlighted by the contrast of Southdown housing reporting less than 25 days paid holiday and no pension scheme.

Clearly, the levels and availability of these benefits are not as high or as universally available across all the companies as one might expect of a *Best Company* list. Office Angels, for example, provide gym facilities but do not offer more than 25 days paid leave nor do they provide a company-sponsored pension plan, and yet over 80 per cent Office Angel employees believe good work is rewarded appropriately and 82 per cent say appreciation is expressed for a good job done. At the same time, Office Angels are highlighted as a company that fosters a particularly inclusive company culture that celebrates successes and employee loyalty with social activities. Employees are rewarded with active engagement programmes and performance linked awards such as weekends in Barcelona and New York.

Reward

- Over 80 per cent of employees are happy with pay and benefits at Pannone (87 per cent), W. L. Gore (83 per cent) and Sandwell Community Caring Trust (82 per cent)
- Over 80 per cent of employees believe good work is rewarded appropriately at Pannone and Office Angels

---

Equality

Published data offer some demographic detail on gender and age and women and management. It also offers information on the availability of child-care vouchers or onsite nursery and whether at least 10 weeks fully paid maternity leave is available to employees. Unfortunately, there are no data available concerning disability or ethnicity. The lack of comprehensive data in these areas necessarily limits any analysis of equal opportunities in 'best' companies. However, some interesting insights on age and gender can be derived. For instance, it is interesting to note recruitment consultancy companies report that all of their employees are under the age of 35 and the professional companies (law and IT) have only 4 or 5 per cent of their workforce who are over 55 years old. This is compared to a 20 per cent employment rate for the over-55s in the labour market in general (Labour Force Survey, 2005).

Upon closer examination, the demographics of these companies are a little less surprising. Employee engagement practices employed by these companies very much emphasise 'fun' activities which serve to propagate 'youth' cultures (Bolton, 2006; Partridge, 2006). For instance, professional companies such as Pannone are very proud of their youthful 'work hard, play hard' culture. A total of £48,000 was spent during 2005 on social events such as shopping trips, days at the races and barbeques. Not surprisingly, 86 per cent of Pannone employees report having fun at work. Similarly, Data Connection offer a social fund of £1500 per person to be spent on weekends away and skiing trips. Of course, not all employees in professional service firms are under the age of 30; nevertheless there is a definite emphasis on youth as exemplified by this Data Connection employee talking about the culture at Data Connection:

'So I bet you're thinking, so this guy's now a middle aged BMW-driving company director with a family and a mortgage. Ok, I confess. It's true. But I still retain the skills from my youth-such as being able to prop up bars in Monte Carlo and Marbella after six hours drinking' (A Data Connection employee with 18 years service).

As mentioned in the section on reward, social activities are an inherent part of the incentive and reward mechanisms of professional and business service firms. For instance, Badenoch and Clark's top performers receive evenings in high-class restaurants in recognition of their hard work and Office Angels hold performance competitions, with the winner receiving extra paid leave and long weekends in Barcelona. It all sounds like one long round of fun, fun, fun, but it also begs the question of who these inclusive cultures actually exclude. Not everyone is able to party all weekend – especially the over-35s with family commitments – and may well be discriminated against in terms of opportunities, incentives and rewards if there is an over-reliance on a 'fun' culture. And yet very specific approaches to best practice prevail in some best companies, and this is despite companies apparently working very hard to promote images as equal opportunity employers. As the Badenoch and Clark web site proclaims:

'We do not discriminate on any basis, including race, colour, sex, age, religion, natural origin, sexual orientation, disability or marital status'.

And, somewhat paradoxically, Office Angels have been publicly endorsed as an 'Age Positive Employer Champion' who 'are employers and organisations who have demonstrated their commitment to tackling age discrimination and promoting age diversity in the workplace' (http://www.agepositive.gov.uk/).

In terms of opportunities for gender equality, the top 10 best companies appear to offer good prospects for women, with 7 of the top 10 company workforces being dominated by women and 6 of those companies also reporting more than 33 per cent of senior management are women. However, Beaverbrooks, despite a feminised workforce, is the exception to this. Classed as the best retail employer for three years running, its web site proclaims opportunities for 'sparkling careers' for all:

'Everyone has the opportunity to apply for our Management Development Programme and given our extension plans and the fact that 100 per cent of our Management positions are filled internally, the opportunities for a sparkling career are excellent'.

The figures, however, tell us something very different: 84 per cent of employees at Beaverbrooks are female, but at less than 33 per cent of senior management women are no where near reaching proportional representation in the senior ranks. Particularly striking is the fact that internal promotions are the norm, and yet they appear to be promoting solely from the ranks of young male employees, who are a minority group at Beaverbrooks. One also wonders what happens once promotion takes place as there are only 6 per cent of employees over the age of 55 and 66 per cent under 35.

It would seem that diversity is not necessarily a feature of best companies. Given the dominance of young women employees in the top 10 mid-sized companies, fully paid maternity leave of at least 10 weeks is only available at one of the companies with a dominantly feminised workforce, Sandwell Trust, and only Pannone and St Ann's Hospice report the availability of flexible work arrangements. Interestingly, there appears to be a strong relationship between gender and age when assessing whether child-centred policies will be put into place, with companies reporting a larger proportion of the workforce being between 35 and 55 years of age, the most vital years for combining career and child-rearing in the UK, also providing childcare support.

Promote learning

Learning

- Over 80 per cent of employees believe that training provided is helpful at Lindum Group, Southdown Housing and St Ann's Hospice.

Findings from the *Best Companies* survey tend to support existing research that laments the lack of investment by companies in employee learning and development. Though some companies are endorsed by *Best Companies*, with all top 10 mid-sized companies appearing in the top 25 list for 'personal growth', only three companies are listed as providing 'useful training' (see above). Those that do receive a mention have transparent and active learning and development policies in place: Beaverbrooks have a policy to promote all managers from within the company; St Ann's Hospice has a 'dedicated institute of learning' to ensure staff are kept up-to-date with innovations in hospice care; and at Southdown Housing staff development is considered a priority. There are few companies that stand out in the area of learning and development, and none of the companies receive a mention regarding Leadership support for learning. The top 10 mid-sized companies are not unusual in this as the notion of learning companies or learning cultures does not seem to be a prevalent feature of *Best Companies*.

Instigate internal communication systems, ensure effective employee consultation arrangements, maintain constructive relationships with trade unions

The *Best Company* survey does not include information on collective communication, via Trade Unions for instance, but it does ask employees if they feel listened to by management and if they feel their organisation is open and honest with them. The large companies that are cited, that is, Beaverbrooks, appear to make the effort to communicate directly with employees via regular (monthly) face-to-face meetings with senior management and Pannone's confidence in management as 'good listeners' derives from the extensive social networks built within the firm.

Voice

- Over 80 per cent of employees say their manager is a good listener at Pannone and Beaverbrooks
- Over 85 per cent say managers are open and honest at W. L. Gore, Data Connection and Sandwell Community Caring Trust
- At Office Angels and Data Connection, over 80 per cent of staff feel fully involved at work

---

Six of the overall top 10 of employees who believe managers are open and honest are situated in the top 10 mid-sized companies (see Table 1), Pannone and Beaverbrooks report 80 per cent of employees feel their manager is a good listener and 80 per cent of Office Angels and Data Connection staff feel fully involved in work – findings which signify the existence of cultures of trust and openness in some best companies that create opportunities for employee voice and involvement. However, from information available, non report recognised Trade Union activity and only two offer a share option scheme (W. L. Gore and Lindum Group), indicating a lack of collective voice in the *Best Companies* to work for.

Empower employees

Empowerment

- At W. L. Gore and St Ann's Hospice, over 80 per cent of staff feel that they are able to make a difference
- Over 80 per cent feel trusted to do their job by their leaders, at W. L. Gore, Office Angels and Beaverbrooks

---

Empowered employees are those who say that they can make a valuable contribution to the success of their organisation and who feel trusted to do their job well. Not surprisingly, companies cited positively by employees for empowerment are those who offer community services, caring for the terminally ill, deal with social housing tenants or offer business support services to clients. All of these are people-centred occupations where employees clearly feel they are able to have an impact on client experience of services offered. Those who are listed also appear as 'best' in relation to other dimensions such as equality, communication and development, indicating that trust and empower-ment emerge as a result of policies, practices and procedures being put into place and regularly endorsed by management which builds a culture of trust (see Hodson, this volume).

Provide as much employment security as possible

Security

- 89 per cent of staff at Data Connection feel that they have job security
- See also Table 3 for further details

Job security is cited by Rayman (2001) as a major factor in achieving a sense of dignity at work. Turnover is exceptionally high in some companies: 39 per cent at Office Angels and 28 per cent at Badenoch and Clark. There are also only four companies in the top 10 who have over 40 per cent of the workforce with five or more years of service. In some cases, it simply reflects the various industry standards. Those with long service tend to be in the professional groups, and this is reflected in comments made by employees at Data Connection who feel relatively secure in their employment. However, employees at Data Connection also report high levels of satisfaction with pay and benefits (77 per cent) and enjoy an array of material benefits as well as feeling full involved with work, indicating that in many cases the high staff turnover appears to represent people's dissatisfaction with work–life balance issues and reward packages (Swan, 2005). Staff at Badenoch and Clark, for example, believe they spend too much time at work, and this is reflected in the high turnover figures. Whilst Office Angels report involvement with work (85 per cent), feeling appreciated (82 per cent), believe good work is rewarded appropriately (81 per cent), that their job is good for personal growth (84 per cent), they also report almost double the industry standard staff turnover rate (Paton, 2006). This appears something of a mystery as reportage for Office Angels is generally positive; however, it is a high-pressure work environment with salaries almost entirely reliant on bonus systems, and a long hours culture is an inherent part of the 'work hard, play hard' mindset of the company. Combined, this data would appear to support Swan's (2005) thesis that people who are dissatisfied with work–life balance issues do not stay in a company to change the culture but simply move on.

On the other hand, Beaverbrooks reports a relatively low turnover for the retail sector whilst also reporting high levels of employee satisfaction with pay and benefits (74 per cent) and feeling appreciated at work (80 per cent). St Ann's Hospice ranks ninth in the *Best Companies* list but has relatively poor pay and conditions offering no contributory pension scheme or paid maternity leave (despite this being a dominantly female workforce) and only 3 per cent earn more than £35,000. Their high position in the Top 100 relies a lot on high returning scores for community, colleagues, positive difference and stimulating work. As an in-patient manager at St Ann's proudly proclaims: 'If you asked me which I'd rather – a fat salary or job satisfaction, I know which I'd choose'. The people who work for St Ann's find their work stimulating and feel they contribute something special to their clients and society as a whole.

Best practice, best companies and dignity at work

From the analysis of the *Best Companies* data presented in this chapter, it would appear that the majority of *The Sunday Times Ten Best Companies to Work for* would have difficulty in delivering effective bundles of best practice that would underpin a rounded definition of dignity at work. Whilst fulfilling many individual elements contained in the DTI's best practice framework, only one company, W. L. Gore, appear to offer a range of management practices and employee benefits that might be described as a bundle of best practice. It can be no coincidence that they are also at the top of *The Times* list and have been consistently for the past three years (*The Sunday Times*, 2004, 2005, 2006). Their long history and reputation as a 'good' employer places them firmly in employees' minds as a dignified workplace as they proclaim they are proud to work for Gore, believe the company has strong values and that their organisation makes a positive difference to the world.

Looking at companies through the lens of dignity at work via best practice management highlights the different reasons why organisations may be cited as *100 Best Companies* when they are obviously lacking in some regards. For instance, Data Connection rates very highly on the objective factors of work, offering paid holidays, a pension scheme, private health care, opportunities for personal growth, help with childcare and low staff turnover, and yet there are reports of poor work–life balance and an exclusive company culture that potentially undermines the achievement of dignity at work for all employees. As the status of St Ann's Hospice in *The Times* list shows, in the eyes of employees it is not always material reward that contributes the most to achievement of dignity at work. As Randy Hodson (2001) points out, people seek out their own paths to finding dignity in work and clearly we see this from the voices of the people who work in these sectors. But it is not necessarily the company that offers this – more the nature of the work itself. Though it does seem from comments made by workers that St Ann's fosters 'caring' as a valued attribute and creates a supportive environment for staff.

Similarly, Beaverbrooks ranks highly as the fourth 'best' company to work for, and yet they do not appear to offer what is often regarded as a vital ingredient of dignified work: interesting work. However, qualitative accounts from workers report that they feel they have some discretion in how they deal with customers and report good communication with managers and opportunities for personal growth, indicating that despite the reputation of retail work as monotonous and gruelling, Beaverbrooks do attempt to implement management practices that empower staff and make them feel valued. Beaverbrooks also offers slightly above-average salaries for the retail sector and also a non-contributory pension, thus meeting many aspects of the DTI's BPPM framework and apparently offering opportunities to attain dignity at work. However, they are not alone in the *100 Best Companies* in not dealing with issues of age and gender equality, thus potentially excluding some groups from the opportunity to gain from a 'best' company's often exemplary approach to BPPM. For example, women make up approximately half of the workforce in *100 Best Companies*, but they are more often to be found in peripheral positions or in the feminised professions, both of which rarely offer comprehensive bundles of BPPM and are often more likely to be linked with denials of dignity. Similarly, people over 55 are clearly not welcome in the 'best' companies. Where they do appear, they are settled into managerial and professional groups but remain a very small minority of the *100 Best Companies*. Given the constant references to the aging workforce, a demographic time bomb and growing structural inequalities (Taylor, 2002), this seems to be a neglected aspect of best practice for many *100 Best Companies*.

The multidimensional analysis of dignity at work via the DTI's BPPM framework also highlights the interrelatedness of many management practices and how the long hours cultures prevalent in many of the professional and business service companies deny opportunities for dignity at work to many groups – women who cannot balance domestic responsibilities with 'work hard, play hard' cultures and both men and women over 35 who seek to value their family lives and therefore cannot and will not work for 'best practice' companies. However, we need to be careful of painting too positive a picture for those under-35s who enjoy their work and receive high material rewards; they appear to have no other life – 'willing slaves' as Madeleine Bunting (2004) describes them. In return for autonomy, value and material reward in work, they have lost the chance for autonomy and freedom in their personal lives. Where, we must ask, is the dignity in that?

Concluding remarks

Many companies may not have a complete bundle of BPPM, but they are moving in a promising direction. The notion of a multidimensional view of dignity at work builds on the DTI list of BPPM and emphasises the need for a holistic approach – small bundles of discrete practices which focus too much on organisational culture and do not deal with structural issues such as collective voice, equality of opportunity and security of employment will not hold the promise for dignity at work. However, there is every reason to believe that management practices that create and maintain dignity at work have very real potential to create a dignified workplace that is held in esteem in society and the global marketplace. If a business case must be made for dignity at work, and it appears that it must, then clearly bundles of effective BPPM offer an employer brand as companies are seen as *employers of choice* attracting and retaining high-calibre employees, *good organisational citizens* gaining a reputation that supports good relationships with suppliers and as *ethical producers* of goods and services that attract a loyal customer base (The Work Foundation and The Future Foundation, 2002; Leary-Joyce, 2004).

The danger is that in using *Best Companies* as a benchmark of best practice, it becomes a demi-God of management practice, with many companies feeling it has no relevance to the reality of their operations. However, there is ample empirical evidence to suggest that valuable lessons can be learnt from holistic analyses of what companies may, or may not, be doing regarding BPPM and that bundles of effective practices do make a very real difference to the success of the company and the well-being of the people who work there.

Acknowledgements

This research was supported by an Economic and Social Research Council (ESRC) Grant (no: RES-000-22-1048): 'Dignity in and at Work'.

References

Agassi, J. B. (1986) 'Dignity in the Workplace. Can Work be Dealienated?' *Journal of Business Ethics*, **5**, 4, 271–285.

AMICUS. http://www.amicustheunion.org

Andrea Adams Trust. http://www.andreaadamstrust.org

Anker, R., Chernyshev, I., Egger, P., Mehran, F. and Ritter, J. (2003) 'Measuring Decent Work with Statistical Indicators', *International Labour Review*, **142**, 2, 147–177.

Applebaum, E., Bailey, T., Berg, P. and Kalleberg, A. L. (2000) *Manufacturing Advantage: Why High Performance Work Systems Pay Off*, Ithaca, NY: Cornell University Press.

Barker, R. (2001) 'The Nature of Leadership', *Human Relations*, **54**, 4, 469–494.

Barney, J. B. (1991) 'Firm Resources and Sustainable Competitive Disadvantage', *Journal of Management*, **17**, 1, 99–120.

Bolton, S. (2006) 'The UK's Best Could Do So Much Better', *Opinion, Personnel Today*, 10 March.

Bunting, M. (2004) *Willing Slaves: How the Overwork Culture is Ruling our Lives*, London: Harper Collins.

Department of Trade and Industry (2002a) 'Alan Johnson's (MP) Speech on Fit for the Future Northern Conference on People and Performance – A Winning Combination', Oulton Hall, Leeds, Tuesday, April 16. http://www.dti.gov.uk

Department of Trade and Industry (2002b) 'The Rt. Hon. Patricia Hewitt's speech on the Council for Excellence in Management and Leadership Report', London, Monday, May 13. http://www.dti.gov.uk

Department of Trade and Industry (2004a) 'Achieving Best Practice in Your Business. High Performance Work Practices: Linking Strategy to Performance Outcomes'. http://www.dti.gov.uk, URN 05/665.

Department of Trade and Industry (2004b) 'Best Companies: Best Practice'. http://www.dti.gov.uk/bestpractice, URN 04/813.

Fox, M. (1994) *The Reinvention of Work*, San Francisco: Harper.

Freidman, A. (1977) *Industry and Labour: Class Struggle at Work and Monopoly Capitalism*, London: Macmillan.

Gemmill, G. (1977) 'Postscript: Toward the Person-Centred Organization', in *A Matter of Dignity: Inquiries into the Humanization of Work* (Heisler, W. and Houck, J., eds), London: University of Notre Dame Press, pp. 197–205.

Gini, A. (2001) *My Job, My Self. Work and the Creation of the Modern Individual*, London: Routledge.

Guest, D. (1997) 'Human Resource Management and Performance', *International Journal Human Resource Management*, **8**, 263–276.

Guest, D., Michie, J., Conway, N. and Sheehan, M. (2003) 'Human Resource Management and Corporate Performance in the UK', *British Journal of Industrial Relations,* **41**, 2, 291–314.

Hodson, R. (1996) 'Dignity in the Workplace under Participative Management: Alienation and Freedom Revisited', *American Sociological Review*, **61**, 5, 719.

Hodson, R. (2001) *Dignity at Work*, Cambridge: Cambridge University Press.

Hodson, R. and Roscigno, V. J. (2004) 'Organizational Success and Worker Dignity: Complementary or Contradictory?' *American Journal of Sociology*, **110**, 3, 672.

Huselid, M. (1995) 'The Impact of Human Resource Management Practices on Turnover, Productivity and Corporate Financial Performance', *Academy of Management Journal*, **38**, 635–672.

Ishmael, A. (1999) *Harassment, Bullying and Violence at Work*, London: The Industrial Society.

Kearns, P. (2004) 'Beyond the Spin'. http://www.personneltoday.co.uk

Khan, R. (1981) *Work and Health*, New York: Wiley.

Kornhauser, A. (1964) *Mental Health of the Industrial Worker: A Detroit Study*, New York: Wiley.

Kotter, J. (1990) *Force for Change. How Leadership Differs from Management*, New York: Free Press.

Labour Force Survey (2005) (Quarterly), Autumn (September 2005–November 2005), accessed from the UK Data Archive http://www.data-archive.ac.uk and Labour Force Survey Quarterly Supplement accessed from National Statistics http://www.statistics.gov.uk

Leary-Joyce, J. (2004) *Becoming an Employer of Choice. Making your Organisation a Place where Great People Want to do Great Work*, London: CIPD.

Maslow, A. (1965) *Management*, Homewood, IL: Irwin-Dorsey Press.

Moynagh, M. and Worsley, R. (2005) *Working in the Twenty-First Century*. Leeds: Economic & Social Research Council, Future of Work Programme, and the Tomorrow Project. http://www.esrctoday.co.uk

Mueller, F. (1996) 'Human Resources as Strategic Assets: An Evolutionary Resource Based Theory', *Journal of Management Studies*, **33**, 757–785.

Partridge, C. (2006) 'When Best Practice is not Best for All Staff', *The Times*, 24 October.

Paton, N. (2006) *Plugging the Performance Gap*, 14 February. http://www.personneltoday.com

Perry, M. (2005) 'The Morality of Human Rights: A Nonreligious Ground?' *Emory Law Journal*, **54**, 97–150.

Peters, T. (1995) *The Pursuit of Wow*, New York: Macmillan.

Pfeffer, J. (1994) *Competitive Advantage Through People*, Boston: Harvard University Press.

Porter, M. (1985) *Competitive Advantage*, New York: Free Press.

Rayman, P. (2001) *Beyond the Bottom Line*, New York: Palgrave.

Reeves, R. (2001) *Happy Mondays. Putting the Pleasure Back into Work*, London: Pearson Education Limited.

Rennie Peyton, P. (2003) *Dignity at Work: Eliminate Bullying and Create a Positive Working Environment*, London: Routledge.

Rosow, J. M. (1979) 'Human *Dignity* in the Public-Sector Workplace', *Vital Speeches of the Day*, **45**, 6, 66.

Ryan, J. (1977) 'Humanistic Work: Its Philosophical and Cultural Roots', in *A Matter of Dignity: Inquiries into the Humanization of Work* (Heisler, W. and Houck, J., eds), London: University of Notre Dame Press, pp. 11–22.

Schumacer, E. F. (1979) *Good Work*, New York: Harper Colophon Books.

Senge, P. (1996) 'The Leaders' New Work: Building Learning Organizations', in *How Organizations Learn* (Starkley, K. ed.), London: Thompson Business Press.

The Sunday Times 100 Best Companies to Work For (2004) Published with the Sunday Times on March 7, 2004.

The Sunday Times 100 Best Companies to Work For (2005) Published with the Sunday Times on March 6, 2005.

The Sunday Times 100 Best Companies to Work For (2006) Published with the Sunday Times on March 5, 2006.

Sung, J. and Ashton, D. N. (2005) *Achieving Best Practice in Your Business. High Performance Work Practices: Linking Strategy and Skills to Performance Outcomes*, London: Department of Trade and Industry in association with CIPD.

Swan, J. (2005) 'Inflexibility Drives Out Silent Majority', *People Management*, **11**, 10, 101.

Taylor, R. (2002) *'Britain's World of Work – Myths and Realities'*, Economic and Social Research Council. http://www.esrctoday.co.uk

Tehrani, N. (2004) *Bullying at Work: Beyond Policies to a Culture of Respect*. http://www.cipd.co.uk/NR/rdonlyres/D9105C52-7FED-42EA-A557-D1785DF6D34F/0/bullyatwork0405.pdf

The Work Foundation (2005) Cracking the Performance Code: How Firms Succeed. http://www.theworkfoundation.com/publications/

The Work Foundation and The Future Foundation (2002) *The Ethical Employee*. http://www.theworkfoundation.com/publications/

Wright, L. and Smye, M. (1997) *Corporate Abuse*, New York: Simon and Schuster.

9

Information technology at work: the implications for dignity at work

Bill Doolin and Laurie McLeod

Why is it important to address the implications of information technology in a consideration of dignity and work? The more one considers this question, the more one is struck by the great extent to which information technology underpins and is interwoven with the arrangement and practice of work in organisations. Technology permeates society and our lives. Our actions and interactions are increasingly mediated by information technology. As Asaro (2000, p. 258) observes, there is a 'deep connection between the form of technology and the form of human life'. Work and organisations are important arenas in which this occurs.

Bloomfield et al. (1994, p. 495) put this nicely when they talk about how 'there is no technology without organisation and no organisation without technology'. What they are saying is that information technology and organisations both presuppose each other. It would be hard to imagine a modern organisation or workplace that is designed without consideration being given to the use of some form of information technology. Similarly, when information technologies and systems are developed, their designers have in mind some idea of the organisational and work environment in which they will be used.

If information technology is so pervasive and so intimately intertwined with organisations, then it must surely have some implications for dignity in the workplace. But in what way, and how? The answer lies in the way that we, as designers and users of technology, delegate a social or moral order to technology. In particular, the way in which information technology 'in use' helps to produce and maintain social structures and power relations in organisations.

In their fabrication, information technologies and systems are 'inscribed' with their designers' assumptions and knowledge about the intended users and their world (Akrich, 1992). As such, they imply a delegated social or moral order that presupposes, mediates and reinforces social relations. The French sociologist, Bruno Latour (1992), gives the example of speed bumps, or 'sleeping policemen', constructed to slow traffic on certain roads. Here, the technological artefact stands in for a human policeman. Speed bumps achieve their effect because we, as drivers, understand and acknowledge the implicit moral directive to slow down.

Similarly, various values, beliefs, norms and rules that reflect existing structures of knowledge, authority and relations within an organisation become inscribed in an information system. When we use an information system, we interact with and draw upon these interpretive resources in a way that shapes our situated use of the technology (Orlikowski, 2000). In many ways, information systems mobilise a particular view of organisational reality. This representation constitutes the 'truth' of organisational reality, informing our actions and behaviour as we act in relation to it (Bloomfield, 1995). In turn, the recurrent and routine use of an information system tends to reproduce and maintain the social structures that these values, beliefs, norms and rules constitute. We can sometimes see this in the implementation of 'enterprise resource planning' (ERP) information systems. These software packages integrate information flows across functional areas in an organisation and are based on generic representations of 'best practice' business processes. The standardisation of business processes associated with these large information systems often produces considerable changes in work organisation and practices, with disciplining and centralising tendencies (Hall, 2005).

Of course, our use of a technology is neither deterministic nor inflexible. Through our actions, whether deliberately, inadvertently or by improvisation in response to unexpected events, we may appropriate a practice or use of an information system in ways that were not necessarily intended by its designers (Orlikowski, 2000). If this change in use or practice is sustained over time and adopted more widely in an organisation, it becomes institutionalised, modifying or transforming the social structures associated with it. Thus, in implementing the ERP information systems described above, an organisation may attempt to customise the software package to better align it with existing practices and processes (Soh and Sia, 2004). Alternatively, users of the information system may develop 'workarounds' that circumvent the intentions of the package designers and may eventually become accepted practice (Orlikowski, 1992).

All of this suggests that, despite popular perceptions, information technology is not neutral (Winner, 1980). Its development, deployment and routine use in workplaces and organisational settings reflects, reinforces and even transforms particular social and moral orders, and thus has real consequences for people in those organisations. As the philosopher, Martin Heidegger, observed in his essay, *The Question Concerning Technology*:

> 'Everywhere we remain unfree and chained to technology, whether we passionately affirm or deny it. But we are delivered over to it in the worst possible way when we regard it as something neutral; for this conception of it, to which today we particularly like to do homage, makes us utterly blind to the essence of technology' (1977, p. 311).

Sharon Bolton (preface, this volume) makes a useful distinction between *dignity in work*, in the sense of worthwhile and meaningful work, and *dignity at work*, in the sense of being treated with dignity as a human being in the work environment. In this chapter, we utilise this conceptualisation of dignity to examine the implications of information technology for dignity both in and at work. The next two sections present some underlying theoretical ideas that help us understand how information technology might have implications for dignity in both the senses that Bolton discusses. Following this, we look at four examples of workplaces where information technology has been introduced in order to explore how these implications may occur in practice, before attempting to draw together some common themes and conclusions on this topic.

Information technology and *dignity in work*

In terms of information technology, *dignity in work* is related to issues such as professional autonomy, the ability to control one's own work and the opportunity to participate in work and information systems design. At its heart are questions of empowerment. Are users of an information technology or system best qualified to determine how to improve their work and their working life? Should workers have access to upskilling and empowering tools instead of having their work automated and deskilled?

The former concerns what Clement (1994) terms democratic empowerment. Its underlying principle is that workers should have control over important aspects of their work environment and be able to participate in decisions on technological choice. With respect to information technology, it sees expression in a call for greater participation of users in the design and development of information systems. In particular, the 'participatory design' philosophy encourages active user participation both to improve the system developed and to allow users to co-determine the effect of the system on their workplace (Clement and Van den Besselar, 1993). It is intended to give 'practical form to the philosophy of humanism by providing employees with an opportunity to influence the work systems that surround them' (Mumford, 1997, p. 309).

Ideally, participation by the eventual users of an information system in its design and development should be meaningful, involving significant consultation, communication, personal autonomy, decision-making, responsibility and control. In practice, however, the nature and extent of user participation in information systems development and its influence on the development outcome varies considerably between projects, organisations and national contexts.

Often, it is management that defines the boundaries of user participation. As a consequence, participation may fail to engage with users' personal and professional values, individual and collective identity, roles and work practices (Riley and Smith, 1997). Participation may also be more symbolic or rhetorical than actual. Howcroft and Wilson (2003) caution that, while from the espoused humanistic and democratic agenda, user participation enhances the personal dignity of employees, much of the benefit accrues to a managerial agenda based on encouraging commitment to and compliance with a process of change in an increasingly competitive, global economy.

In contrast to democratic empowerment, functional empowerment in relation to information technology involves extending the capabilities of users through tools that supply relevant information, implement users' decisions and provide feedback (Clement, 1994). Functional empowerment can be related to what Zuboff (1988) calls the 'informating' potential of information technology when it is used to mediate work processes. Rather than simply automating work, information technology can generate information about underlying production and administrative processes that can be used by workers as a basis for skilled and informed decision-making and intervention in the work process. Of course, this information can also be used by management to monitor and control production and administrative processes.

From this perspective, information technology can be either empowering and upskilling, or disempowering and deskilling, depending on how it is applied and whether its informating potential is utilised. Zuboff (1988) argues that traditional management control perverts this potential of information technology. Instead, information technology can and should be designed with the intention to 'informate' work, thereby enhancing worker flexibility and autonomy.

It is likely to be the intentions and decisions of senior management that influence job content and work organisation surrounding the implementation of information technology in organisations. However, technological change is a negotiated outcome, shaped by individual users' appropriation of the technology, collective action by the workforce or unions and by the actions of middle and lower managers responsible for implementing the decisions.

If *dignity in work* involves the opportunity and ability to do 'good work', then information technology has both enabling and constraining potential. The deployment of information technology in organisations is more likely to enhance dignity in work where users have the opportunity to participate and influence decisions on its design and where it is designed to increase the skilled and informed intervention of its users in work processes.

Information technology and *dignity at work*

Information technology is implicated in *dignity at work* in the increasing trend towards electronic surveillance in the workplace, in which a variety of information technologies and systems may be used to monitor and survey the activities of employees. Of particular interest are information systems that facilitate the comparative application of performance information. Such information systems operate by measuring, calculating and making visible the extent to which work behaviour departs from norms of performance. Examples include the comparative application of performance information in fields as diverse as lawyers' billable hours, call centre operators' response times, surgeons' morbidity rates, and academics' research outputs! The information generated by such information systems renders individuals calculable, and thus knowable and governable, enabling management to make stronger truth claims (Boland and Schultze, 1996) in intervening in and controlling work.

The routine use of these information systems mobilises a particular representation of organisational reality, underpinning the framework of meaning within which organisational participants orient their daily work and behaviour (Bloomfield et al., 1994). In other words, individuals are made not only calculable but also more calculating with respect to their own actions (Miller, 1994). They learn to survey and discipline themselves through forms of self-monitoring and self-control rather than direct control and supervision. This subtle exercise of 'disciplinary power' (Foucault, 1977) constitutes a new, internalised, discipline of norms that influence individuals' judgements about what is legitimate and non-legitimate behaviour at work (Bloomfield et al., 1994; Clegg, 1989).

The use of comparative information systems is often linked to wider changes in management control, such as the simultaneous operational decentralisation of decision-making and responsibility, and centralisation of strategic control through extensive monitoring and enhanced control over expenditure. Rather than suppressing individuals' autonomy, such comparative information systems utilise it, 'extending spheres of discretion and choice, while at the same time helping to ensure that actions are taken in accordance with broader economic, financial and social objectives of government' (Humphrey et al., 1993, pp. 16–17).

At the same time, computerised surveillance through comparative information systems requires an involvement with the technology that mediates the work of those managing, as well as those managed. Managers' actions become caught up in the reproduction of the mechanisms used to discipline and control others (Bloomfield and Coombs, 1992). As Foucault (1980, p. 156) notes, 'everyone is caught, those who exercise power just as much as those over whom it is exercised'. Further, the use of information systems to monitor and control organisational activity does not constitute employees as passive victims of computerised surveillance. There is a tendency among those subject to power and control to resist by challenging, circumventing or appropriating the systems and rules imposed on them (Clegg, 1989). Comparative information systems are not exclusively repressive or constraining. Indeed, such systems are 'double-edged', available to both the controlling and the controlled (Bloomfield and Coombs, 1992). They potentially empower employees in the way that they open up legitimate spaces for action, for example, in arguing for sufficient resources to perform recorded activities.

If *dignity at work* is related to how we are valued and treated as workers, then the implications of comparative information systems for dignity lie in the way that they create conditions of possibility within which work and workers are made more visible, transparent and controllable. As we will see, in certain workplace contexts, the use of information systems to tightly monitor and control workflow can have some arguably undignified consequences for workers.

The discussion in the preceding sections has laid out some conceptual and theoretical ideas about how information technology might have implications for dignity both in and at work. To explore how this can occur in practice, we will examine how information technology has been introduced to mediate the work processes of call centre operators, ambulance service dispatchers, mobile sales representatives and hospital nurses. The examples used in the following discussion are drawn from empirical research on these workplace contexts.

Call centres

Call centres, whether outsourced service operations or the rationalisation and centralisation of an organisation's customer relationship functions, integrate communication and information technologies. Within a call centre, operators deal constantly with customers, making or receiving telephone calls and processing the information generated from these calls using computerised information systems. The relatively recent development of call centres as a new workplace environment has attracted a great deal of interest among a range of commentators and researchers. Some are optimistic, seeing call centres as exemplifying the 'knowledge economy', offering a source of skilled and flexible employment in economically depressed areas. Others are deeply critical, seeing call centres as representing a new form of Taylorism, involving standardised and routinised work with little worker autonomy and subject to close monitoring and surveillance (Belt et al., 2000).

Call centres use a range of information technologies and systems both to increase the efficiency of the operators' work and to facilitate a variety of monitoring and control practices. Automated call distribution systems process incoming calls and distribute them to available operators. These systems may be connected to computer databases, providing relevant customer or technical information to operators' computer screens. The systems are also used to monitor and measure workflow in the call centre, generating statistical information about individual and team performance. This might include what each operator is working on at a particular time, the number of calls made by an operator, the length of each call, the time taken to process information after a call, the number of unanswered customers and so on. Information such as this is available to managers and supervisors in real time and in many call centres is displayed on electronic wall boards visible to all employees (Belt et al., 2000).

In their study of European call centres, Belt et al. (2000, pp. 372–373) describe the typical work organisation as follows:

'The vast majority of agents spent all of their working day solely speaking to customers over the telephone, and most worked on a very narrow of range of tasks. Work processes were also heavily monitored and controlled. Information was regularly collected on the number of calls made by each agent and on the timing of these calls. Supervisors and team leaders also routinely listened in to telephone conversations between agents and customers in order to ensure that the correct procedures were being followed and that the required standards of service were being met. In addition, most agents were required to follow computerized 'scripts' designed to control the content, pace and structure of the telephone conversation'.

The tightly controlled and repetitive nature of call centre work described above is a far cry from the picture painted by some commentators of highly skilled 'knowledge workers'. Indeed, Belt et al. (2000) note that many of the call centre workers they talked with found the work tiring, stressful and lacking in stimulation, with generally little variation or opportunity for employee discretion. The high level of monitoring and surveillance increased the pressure to keep working. These conditions tended to lead to employee demotivation and a high level of staff turnover. Employees, particularly women and part-time or temporary workers, often felt that their work was considered low status by the rest of their organisation and by society. The managers that the researchers talked with had little intention of changing the work process, emphasising the need to 'maximise the hours that people stay on the phone' and achieve 'certain quantifiable metrics' (Belt et al., 2000, p. 374).

The emphasis on meeting performance targets was reflected in another study of UK call centres by Taylor et al. (2002). They described a common experience of work in the call centres 'which is driven by quantitative imperatives, most manifest in the pervasive implementation of targets' (p. 133). The researchers found that many call centre operators had little or no control over performance targets and were subject to considerable managerial and supervisory pressure to meet or exceed externally imposed individual and team productivity targets. The display of quantitative performance data of electronic wall boards in one call centre further added to the pressure employees were under. Importantly, Taylor et al. describe how implicit norms and expectations about operator performance were part of the organisational culture, even at a call centre where explicit targets were supposedly discouraged:

'Powerful implicit expectations of acceptable output levels are embedded in the culture of each workflow, with managers and, particularly, team leaders applying performance norms in the course of their supervisory activities. These norms are reinforced through the practice of writing up the daily outputs of teams/sections and individuals on whiteboards, specifying the percentage achievements in relation to SLA [service level agreement] standards' (Taylor et al., 2002, p. 145).

It is important to note, however, that while the experience of work in call centres described above may be a common one, differences do exist between call centres and also between 'workflows' within a call centre. In particular, Taylor et al. (2002) distinguish between *quantity* and *quality* in call centre work. The former relates to volume-driven, routine calls requiring standard or scripted responses and subject to close time and statistical control. The latter relates to more complex customer interactions requiring more operator discretion and experience or skill, where the emphasis is more on the quality of interaction with the customer. Belt et al. (2000) observed a similar difference in call centre work between industry sectors. For example, while work in financial services call centres was highly repetitive and standardised, utilised a narrow range of skills and was subject to tight monitoring and control, operators in more specialised technical roles in computer services call centres needed more detailed product knowledge and exercised a greater range of skills. In this case, their work was monitored and controlled to a lesser extent.

Another important qualification to make is that, as noted earlier in the chapter, the subjects of information systems that measure and compare performance are not passive or incapable of resisting or subverting the application of such systems. There is evidence that individual and informal collective workplace resistance is occurring in some call centre contexts (Taylor et al., 2002; Mulholland, 2004). In other cases, where the dominant organisational culture emphasises quality and employee autonomy, attempts to impose rigid monitoring and control may be unsuccessful (Burns and Light, 2006).

Ambulance service control rooms

Ambulance services provide emergency paramedical assistance via a fleet of ambulance vehicles dispersed across a large urban area.

The movements of these ambulances are generally coordinated from a control centre somewhere in the region. Control room dispatchers receive emergency calls and need to decide the optimal allocation of an available ambulance to respond to the emergency. Given the emphasis on human safety and the critical element of time in responding to emergencies, work in these control rooms can be very stressful. Wastell and Newman (1996) present a comparison of two projects involving the introduction of information technology into the control rooms of the London and Manchester ambulance services in the UK. In both cases, new computer-aided dispatch systems were intended to optimise resource allocation and replace existing manual dispatch processes.

The London case experienced severe operational problems, and the project was ultimately terminated in a high-profile public failure. In a climate of tense industrial relations, management ran the project in an autocratic and adversarial way. When control room staff raised concerns, these were dismissed by management as 'politically motivated subversion' (Wastell and Newman, 1996, p. 285). There was little participation from the control room workforce in the design and development of the new system, and users became alienated rather than interested in the project. They resisted the change, either by sabotaging the effectiveness of the new information system or by working around it so as to accommodate their established and preferred work practices. Wastell and Newman suggest that the system in the London project was machine centred and Tayloristic in its design, intended to reduce, constrain and automate many of the human operator functions:

'It is clear from the [Government] Inquiry's report that management saw the new system as a "control device" for enforcing correct procedures (e.g. over the choice of which ambulance to mobilise) upon an undisciplined workforce, to take away what was seen as an excessive degree of discretion' (Wastell and Newman, 1996, p. 285).

In contrast, the new Manchester computer-aided dispatch system resulted in improved service performance, user support and reduced staff stress levels. Wastell and Newman attribute a major cause of the different outcomes in the two cases to the management styles and intentions underlying the implementation and use of the respective systems. They argue that, in contrast to the London ambulance service, Manchester management viewed staff joint ownership of the new system as critical. They maintained a consultative approach to the project, keeping the system users well-informed and including their active participation in some design work. Overall, 'relations between staff and management were characterised by trust, constructive cooperation and open communication' (Wastell and Newman, 1996, p. 295). Further, the Manchester system was more human centred in its design; intended to support and augment the role of the control room operators:

> 'Through supportive information displays and the removal of unskilled secondary work (e.g., transcribing messages), [the system's] role was to support operators in their primary task of despatching ambulances. By deliberate design, [the system] did not encroach on the problem-solving kernel of the operator's job . . . decision-making remained solely the prerogative of the operator' (Wastell and Newman, 1996, p. 296).

Wastell and Newman conclude that in the Manchester case, the introduction of information technology improved working conditions in the control room. They argue that the design quality of information systems should be evaluated not just on improvements in work performance but importantly on their impact on users' well-being.

Mobile sales representatives

Blosch and Preece (2000) describe the information technology-mediated working practices of sales representatives in a UK retail company. For the company's senior management, information technology played an important role in the centralised decision-making approach they adopted in a highly competitive and rapidly changing market. A 'state-of-the-art' management information system was used by a small central group of senior managers to analyse the market, make decisions and control the organisation. This centralised control structure was consistent with a company management style that Blosch and Preece describe as autocratic and Tayloristic. Employees were described as 'worker bees', presumably paid to work and not to think. Blosch and Preece (2000, p. 96) report the comments of a sales representative on the implications of this approach:

> 'We are just the hired hands, we are paid well to do our job well, and that's it. They [senior management] don't want us to take part in the running of the company in any way . . . As long as you can detach your self esteem from your job, then its bearable, otherwise you can end up feeling demoralised'.

The data used to drive the management information system was generated by the work of sales representatives working from their homes dispersed over a wide geographic area. Sales representatives received details of the day's sales calls via a small laptop computer, which they subsequently used to enter their sales results into the company's marketing database. The sales representatives' interaction with their computers was controlled by a software program, which guided them through a series of defined screens, each to be completed before the next could be accessed. Sales calls could not be closed until all screens were completed. In this way, the information technology imparted a discipline on the sales representatives, constantly mediating their work.

The data the sales representatives entered into the system were used to measure their performance against targets and key factors captured in statistics. Each week, sales representatives received a printout of their performance, comparing them against other representatives in a sales territory. The sales representatives were not privy to the means used to calculate these targets and performance measurements. Embedding these in the computer system made them less visible and less open to question or criticism – what Orlikowski (1991, p. 26) calls 'control over the premises of decisions and actions'.

Once a month, the area manager chaired a meeting of all the sales representatives within a sales territory, at which the comparative performance of each representative was reviewed and commented upon openly by the area manager. A sales representative described the experience as follows:

'It's rather like standing naked in front of a group of strangers – they can see all your embarrassing details. Though you know these people, it's done in a way so you feel exposed and ashamed... The whole process is rather like getting an enema in public, you know its going to happen, all you wish is for your turn to be over as quickly as possible' (Blosch and Preece, 2000, p. 98).

This use of comparative performance information is a clear example of computer-based monitoring and control. Blosch and Preece note that company management regarded such surveillance practices as necessary and made no effort to conceal their use. What is interesting is that not only were the sales representatives made more calculable with respect to their performance, but they also became more calculating, disciplining themselves in a bid to meet sales targets in order to retain their lucrative remuneration. As a sales representative reflected:

'It makes me laugh, 1984 isn't a work of fiction – it's our management handbook. Big Brother watches us all the time... But the sweetest paradox of this is our desperate compliance, we engage in this insanity because our very lifestyle depends on it... We are trapped by our own greed!' (Blosch and Preece, 2000, p. 97)

Through their use of the various company information systems, the sales representatives and their managers reproduced and reinforced the existing organisational structures and power relations of hierarchical authority, centralised decision-making and the organisational culture in which sales representatives were relatively isolated from each other and from control over their work.

Nursing information systems

In recent years, the governments of many countries have been struggling with the problem of reconciling increasing public expectations over health care expenditure with limited economic growth. The increasing expectations are typically the result of an ageing population with an increased life expectancy and the increased opportunities for diagnosis and treatment offered by (expensive) advances in medical technology and practice. Hospitals are a major source of health care expenditure in most countries. Driven by the view that most of the resource allocation in these settings is determined by patient care and treatment decisions made by health professionals, the problem of health care is translated into one of a lack of the appropriate information required to control costs and to enable more efficient use of existing resources.

This translation is accompanied by an implicit delegation to information technology which involves keeping track of resource usage (Bloomfield, 1995). As a consequence, hospital management have often introduced a range of 'resource management' information systems to monitor, manage and control the limited resources available for health care provision. These information systems make health care activity visible, providing management with both the technology and a rational justification for increased intervention in medical practice in order to persuade health care professionals to conform to standard or 'normal' work practices. Placing health care activity under such scrutiny increases the transparency of professional knowledge, expertise and work processes (Bloomfield and Coombs, 1992; Davies and Kirkpatrick, 1995).

The work of hospital nurses has not been exempt from the introduction of such information systems. Their implementation occurs in a context of increasing professionalisation as nurses attempt to improve their employment situation, but also one in which the notion of 'care' is still the defining characteristic of nursing (Wilson, 2002). Wilson (2002) presents a case study of the implementation and use of a nursing management information system in the UK National Health Service.

The new system included a care planning function that provided a database of 'care libraries' that could be edited by nurses to produce a printed and standardised document. The idea was to replace the handwritten notes used by nurses to record their intended patient care delivery. As noted above, the new system was part of a broader programme to standardise health care practice and thus improve financial and resource management in hospitals.

The automated care plans were intended by management to be the only record of nursing work, providing both a record for legal considerations and an accurate picture of nursing activity. Nurses were led to believe that the new information system would make their administrative tasks more efficient, freeing up time to spend on patient care. However, the new system encountered resistance and hostility from the nurses who were supposed to use it. Some nurses felt that the standard care plans were, to an extent, deskilling. Others felt that despite the espoused user representation and participation in the system development project, 'they were not "really" consulted about what they wanted – they had not been asked nor listened to' (Wilson, 2002, p. 151).

Wilson reports that the main reason for the hostility was that, in practice, complying with the requirements of the system took nurses away from direct patient care, in terms of both the time taken to use the system and the physical location of the computer terminals away from patients' beds. While the nurses agreed that care planning was important, the reality of their ward workloads limited the time they could spend on this function. Nurses resisted using the new information system and continued using their existing manual systems. Slow network speeds, insufficient access to computer terminals and the fact that most nurses were not trained to type, all contributed to this situation.

Doolin (1997) describes a similar situation in the introduction of a computerised nursing resource planning system in a New Zealand hospital. The new system was intended to track nursing resources used on a daily basis in each hospital ward. Individual nurses were supposed to enter details of planned and actual nursing hours spent in direct patient care into the system via computers located on each ward. This information would be available to charge nurses to assist them in planning their ward nursing workloads. It would also enable management to monitor consumption of nursing resources over time and to intervene to optimise ward staffing levels.

Despite the fact that the cooperation of nurses was needed to enter reliable data into the system, nurse users were not significantly involved in the development and implementation of the nursing information system. Many of the data terms and categories used by the system were unfamiliar to the nurses or meaningless in the local hospital context. Nurses remained unconvinced that the new system would facilitate better patient care. Even though nurses routinely use various clinical technologies, in a dominant culture of 'hands-on care' (Wilson, 2002), many nurses did not see information technology as useful or relevant. An information systems analyst at the New Zealand hospital observed that:

'Nurses actually don't like using it. Nurses actually resist using it very much. They have an attitude of "I don't need the computer to do my job, so why should I use the computer to help you keep your data up to date?" That's the general, pervasive attitude' (Doolin, 1997, p. 109).

The time spent by nurses to collect and enter the information to feed the nursing information system was seen as a distraction from their primary focus of patient care. Further, it was perceived as a duplication of established patient management procedures and an imposition on their professional expertise and practice. As one charge nurse commented:

'The majority of my nursing staff see it as just another thing that they have to do. . . They still feel that the patient is their primary responsibility and if patient care is going to be neglected in favour of the computer, then they are not going to do the computer. The patient comes first. And it's really funny, because you have this kind of difference between a nursing perspective and a management perspective. I mean, the management perspective is really aimed at the financial side, and you start to think that the financial side is all that matters. And then you have the nurses, who feel that the patient is the only one that matters' (Doolin, 1997, p. 109).

A shortage of computer terminals on the wards, inadequate physical locations for the terminals that were available, difficulties in nurses attending user training during the busiest time of the year (during a influenza epidemic in winter) and increasing demands on nurse time exacerbated the negative reaction to the new information system by nurses. Data accuracy also suffered during busy periods on the wards as recording of activity was postponed or delegated to a single nurse who entered data at the end of a shift.

From the perspective of charge nurses responsible for managing the wards, the nursing information system did not match how nursing work on the wards actually occurred. Nor did it necessarily accurately reflect how hard their nurses worked. They became adept at manipulating the system to portray what they considered to be a realistic consumption of nursing resources, at times building 'slack' into the system in order to rest staff after busy and tiring episodes. Consistent with the 'double-edged' nature of such comparative information systems (Bloomfield and Coombs, 1992), one charge nurse was able to successfully use the information generated by the nursing information system to negotiate for increased nursing resources:

> 'I've been able to use the Nursing Resource Planner to increase the established staff here by proving that we consistently don't have enough hours to meet the needs that we're programming. So we've been able to use it to prove that. But the nurses almost resent it because it's a commitment that they have to come and feed the information in. . . And they probably don't always see the relevance. However, the days that we can't get staff to match the needs, they're very quick to see the relevance' (Doolin, 1997, p. 130).

In both of the nursing information systems described here, the introduction of the new system was problematic because it challenged a strong professional nursing culture with a distinctive collective identity. The espoused benefits of the new systems conflicted with the perceived values and roles of their nurse users.

Discussion

How can we make sense of the empirical examples described above in terms of the implications that information technology can have for *dignity in and at work*? With some important exceptions, the examples are rather negative in their portrayal of information technology in the workplace. This is not to suggest that information technology cannot be enabling and empowering, constitutive of dignified work and the dignified treatment of workers. We can see this clearly in the example of the Manchester ambulance service, where both democratic and functional empowerment, to use Clement's (1994) terms, occurred. The active participation of employees in the development of the information system that would affect their work practices occurred in an environment of trust. Further, the technology was intended to support and augment, rather than replace, their role as human decision makers. Wastell and Newman (1996) were able to present a 'win-win' situation where both organisational performance and the well-being of the control room workers improved. What comes through strongly in this case, and in the counter example they use, is the way that the intentions behind how an information technology or system is designed, developed and deployed can shape the outcome of its introduction into a workplace.

Too often, however, the design and arrangement of an information system produces consequences, either intended or unintended, which favour certain social interests or at least create conditions of possibility, within which particular kinds of social relations are able to occur to the detriment of *dignity in and at work*. This is shown in the examples involving information systems that monitor, measure and compare work performance in various ways. In the case of the mobile sales representatives, the information system that mediated their work was intended to be an extension of the centralised control exercised by the company's senior management. Its routine operation by both managers and those managed served to maintain and reinforce the dominant organisational culture. The information system that the sales representatives used structured both their interaction with it and the way they carried out their daily work. Further, it made visible their activity in ways that enabled some rather undignified management practices to be enacted, as the sales representatives interviewed by Blosch and Preece (2000) attested.

The difficulty is that, to an extent, the sales representatives complied with the information system and its associated practices in order to maintain relatively high levels of remuneration. The company's human resources manager pointed out that employees were made aware of how the company operated before they joined, and that 'their emotional and spiritual welfare is not our problem' (Blosch and Preece, 2000, p. 96). Unfortunately, this seems to not be an isolated response to claims of undignified working conditions. For example, while differences in call centre work do exist, the dominant experience seems to be one of tightly controlled and routinised work. Belt et al. (2000, p. 374) note that, in their study of call centres, managers frequently commented that the working conditions in call centres were made clear to prospective employees and that call centre workers 'knew what to expect'. One could argue that this is an abrogation of responsibility by management. The point that we are trying to make is that in these cases the information systems created specific conditions of possibility within which management could operate certain practices of monitoring and control.

Even when information systems designed to measure and monitor work activity are ostensibly intended to assist the employees they survey, such as in the nursing information systems discussed above, they render social phenomena visible in a particular way. Some activities are given an existence and attention, while others are unrecognised. Complex or ambiguous phenomena are quantified and made subject to calculation. The very existence of the information these systems generate increases the transparency of work, knowledge and expertise, affording management the opportunity to intervene more directly in the control of professional work processes. In some cases, we can observe that the routine use of these information systems may act to reinforce dominant values or norms, mobilising a particular representation of organisational reality with which workers and managers inform their actions. For example, the explicit display of performance data on electronic wall boards in many call centres reinforces norms and expectations about appropriate levels of performance, increasing the pressure on employees to conform. However, comparative information systems are not always exclusively constraining or repressive. By generating information that may be acted on, they open up a legitimate space for action, within which employees may utilise the information for their own purposes, such as the charge nurse who was able to negotiate increased staffing levels for her ward.

What is ironic in the cases of the two nursing information systems described above is that, although their effective operation relied to a large extent on the willing cooperation of the nurses themselves, meaningful participation by nurses in the design and development of these systems did not occur. The result was information systems that challenged the values, identity and work practices of these health care professionals. The lack of participatory design can also be seen in how the implementation of these systems failed to consider the demands and actual organisation of nursing work, for instance the physical space constraints on computer installation and use in existing wards, the time involved in nurses' compliance with using the information system and the inappropriate scheduling of training. In many ways, it becomes a question of whose values are 'inscribed' in information systems. In both nursing information systems, it was management's concern with cost control or the standardisation of work practices that dominated the design of the systems. The dominant values and professional identity of nurses based around patient care were not supported by the new systems, which seemed to take nurses away from direct patient care and undermine their professional autonomy.

It is important to remember that workers are capable of action themselves, whether in appropriating the information technology for their own purposes or circumventing its application in their workplace. In fact, resistance figures in almost all the empirical examples described above. People seem able to find ways to assert their dignity in and at work, either individually or collectively. One example is the charge nurse who managed to 'work' the nursing information system so as to organise the work of her staff in a dignified way, taking into account variations in levels of work and stress and enacting a form of professional autonomy. In other cases, existing work processes and systems continued to be used, with management unable to persuade or compel users to move from established cultures and routines, often reinforced by the perceived negative qualities of the new system (Wilson, 2002).

Conclusion

In this chapter, we argue that the information technologies and systems encountered in work environments can have implications for *dignity in and at work*. Specifically, we suggest that in terms of dignity in work, in the sense of being able to undertake worthwhile and meaningful work, users of an information system ought to have some control over how they interact with the system. This includes the opportunity to participate in the design of a new information system and in decisions on technological choice that will affect their work practices and conditions. Further, we believe that human *dignity in work* is enhanced when the information technology used to mediate work practices is designed and implemented in ways that support and extend human work roles, rather than deskill, replace or restrict the work performed by their human users.

We also suggest that an increasing trend towards the use of information systems that monitor and survey the work of employees has implications for *dignity at work* in the way that such systems facilitate the comparative application of performance information. These systems increase the visibility of work, providing management with both the opportunity and the justification to intervene more closely in the control of work practices. Their use on a routine basis may also reinforce dominant organisational norms and values 'inscribed' within them.

In this, we agree with Winner (1980) that technology is political and that consequently we need to take technology seriously. Winner concludes that societies choose structures for technologies that influence how people work and live. Commonly, these structuring decisions are made by people with unequal degrees of power and levels of awareness. Thus, it becomes important to recognise a moral dimension to the introduction and use of information technology in organisations.

We do not want to usurp the right of information technology users to speak for themselves, or to privilege our academic perspective over the lived experience of workers in the information technology mediated contexts we describe in the chapter. Our own motivation is to adopt a critical and reflective stance in relation to the role that information systems may play in (re)producing social orders and power relations in organisations (Doolin and McLeod, 2005). Similarly, we suggest that workers, system designers and managers should be aware of and reflect on the potential applications and implications of the information technologies they introduce, design and use in the workplace. In this way, they can make more informed choices and decisions as to how they engage with information technology in and at work.

Acknowledgements

We thank Sharon Bolton for the opportunity to contribute to this volume and for her understanding, support and helpful comments. The quote used from Martin Heidegger's The Question Concerning Technology was first encountered in Asaro (2000).

References

Akrich, M. (1992) 'The Description of Technical Objects', in *Shaping Technology/Building Society: Studies in Sociotechnical Change* (Bijker, W. E. and Law, J., eds), Cambridge, MA: MIT Press, pp. 205–224.

Asaro, P. M. (2000) 'Transforming Society by Transforming Technology: The Science and Politics of Participatory Design', *Accounting, Management and Information Technologies,* **10**, 4, 257–290.

Belt, V., Richardson, R. and Webster, J. (2000) 'Women's Work in the Information Economy: The Case of Telephone Call Centres', *Information, Communication & Society*, **3**, 3, 366–385.

Bloomfield, B. P. (1995) 'Power, Machines and Social Relations: Delegating to Information Technology in the National Health Service', *Organization*, **2**, 3/4, 489–518.

Bloomfield, B. P. and Coombs, R. (1992) 'Information Technology, Control and Power: The Centralization and Decentralization Debate Revisited', *Journal of Management Studies*, **29**, 4, 459–484.

Bloomfield, B. P., Coombs, R. and Owen, J. (1994) 'The Social Construction of Information Systems: The Implications for Management Control', in *The Management of Information and Communication Technologies: Emerging Patterns of Control* (Mansell, R., ed.), London: Aslib, pp. 143–157.

Blosch, M. and Preece, D. (2000) 'Framing Work Through a Socio-Technical Ensemble: The Case of Butler Co', *Technology Analysis & Strategic Management*, **12**, 1, 91–102.

Boland, R. J. and Schultze, U. (1996) 'From Work to Activity: Technology and the Narrative of Progress', in *Information Technology and Changes in Organizational Work* (Orlikowski, W. J., Walsham, G., Jones, M. R. and DeGross, J. I., eds), London: Chapman and Hall, pp. 308–324.

Burns, B. and Light, B. (2006) *Rewriting the Rules: Professionals, Technologies and Call Centre Working*. Paper presented at the European Association for the Study of Science and Technology Conference, 23–26 August, Switzerland: University of Lausanne.

Clegg, S. R. (1989) *Frameworks of Power*, London: Sage.

Clement, A. (1994) 'Computing at Work: Empowering Action by "Low-Level users"', *Communications of the ACM*, **37**, 1, 53–63.

Clement, A. and Van den Besselar, P. (1993) 'A Retrospective Look at PD Projects', *Communications of the ACM*, **36**, 4, 29–37.

Davies, A. and Kirkpatrick, I. (1995) 'Performance Indicators, Bureaucratic Control and the Decline of Professional Autonomy: The Case of Academic Librarians', in *The Politics of Quality in the Public Sector: The Management of Change* (Kirkpatrick, I. and Lucio, M. M., eds), London: Routledge, pp. 84–107.

Doolin, B. (1997) Discourse, Technology and Organisation in a New Zealand Crown Health Enterprise, Unpublished PhD thesis. New Zealand: University of Waikato.

Doolin, B. and McLeod, L. (2005) 'Towards Critical Interpretivism in IS Research', in *Handbook of Critical Information Systems Research: Theory and Application* (Howcroft, D. and Trauth, E. M., eds), Cheltenham: Edward Elgar, pp. 244–271.

Foucault, M. (1977) *Discipline and Punish: The Birth of the Prison*, London: Penguin.

Foucault, M. (1980) *Power/Knowledge: Selected Interviews and Other Writings 1972–1977*, New York: Pantheon.

Hall, R. (2005) 'The Integrating and Disciplining Tendencies of ERPs: Evidence from Australian Firms', *Strategic Change*, **14**, 5, 245–254.

Heidegger, M. (1977) *The Question Concerning Technology and Other Essays*. Translated by W. Lovitt. New York: Harper and Row.

Howcroft, D. and Wilson, M. (2003). 'Paradoxes of Participatory Practices: The Janus Role of the Systems Developer', *Information and Organization*, **13**, 1, 1–24.

Humphrey, C., Miller, P. And Scapens, R. W. (1993) 'Accountability and Accountable Management in the UK Public Sector', *Accounting, Auditing and Accountability Journal*, **6**, 3, 7–29.

Latour, B. (1992) 'Where are the Missing Masses? The Sociology of a Few Mundane Artifacts', in *Shaping Technology/Building Society: Studies in Sociotechnical Change* (Bijker, W. E. and Law, J., eds), Cambridge, MA: MIT Press, pp. 225–258.

Miller, P. (1994) 'Accounting and Objectivity: The Invention of Calculating Selves and Calculable Spaces', in *Rethinking Objectivity* (Megill, A., ed.), Durham: Duke University Press, pp. 239–264.

Mulholland, K. (2004). 'Workplace Resistance in an Irish Call Centre: Slammin', Scammin' Smokin' an' Leavin', *Work, Employment and Society*, **18**, 4, 709–724.

Mumford, E. (1997) 'The Reality of Participative Systems Design: Contributing to Stability in a Rocking Boat', *Information Systems Journal*, **7**, 4, 309–322.

Orlikowski, W. J. (1991) 'Integrated Information Environment or Matrix of Control? The Contradictory Implications of Information Technology', *Accounting, Management and Information Technologies*, **1**, 1, 9–42.

Orlikowski, W. J. (1992) 'The Duality of Technology: Rethinking the Concept of Technology in Organizations', *Organization Science*, **3**, 3, 398–427.

Orlikowski, W. J. (2000) 'Using Technology and Constituting Structures: A Practice Lens for Studying Technology in Organizations', *Organization Science*, **11**, 4, 404–428.

Riley, L. and Smith, G. (1997) 'Developing and Implementing IS: A Case Study Analysis in Social Services', *Journal of Information Technology*, **12**, 4, 305–321.

Soh, C. and Sia, S. K. (2004) 'An Institutional Perspective on Sources of ERP Package-Organisation Misalignments', *Journal of Strategic Information Systems*, **13**, 375–397.

Taylor, P., Hyman, J., Mulvey, G. and Bain, P. (2002) 'Work Organisation, Control and the Experience of Work in Call Centres', *Work, Employment and Society*, **16**, 1, 133–150.

Wastell, D. and Newman, M. (1996) 'Information System Design, Stress and Organisational Change in the Ambulance Services: A Tale of Two Cities', *Accounting, Management and Information Technologies*, **6**, 4, 283–300.

Wilson, M. (2002) 'Making Nursing Visible? Gender, Technology and the Care Plan Script', *Information Technology and People*, **15**, 2, 139–158.

Winner, L. (1980) 'Do Artifacts Have Politics?' *Daedalus*, **109**, 1, 121–136.

Zuboff, S. (1988) *In the Age of the Smart Machine: The Future of Work and Power*, New York: Basic Books.

10

Preparing for dignity: tackling indignity at work

Charlotte Rayner

Achieving dignity at work is desirable, but it is necessary to examine the full spectrum of the employee 'dignity' experience in order to grasp the challenge of providing dignity to employees. It is tempting to think that employees experience dignity or not, however the reality is more complex (see Bolton, Chapter 1). Most of us have parts of our job where we could tick the dignity box, and other aspects of our work where we could not. This chapter reviews the contemporary debates around indignity and specifically tackle the issue of defining workplace bullying. It will present original empirical evidence drawn from a large, well-supported research project. The findings from the research will be discussed in the context of the challenge for employers in providing workplaces free of indignity.

In approaching this chapter, some assumptions have been made. First, that we can experience dignity, indignity and also a neutral state where we would claim neither. Second, that our experience at work is variegated, and some of us may experience all three states to varying degrees. Third, that the sources of dignity and indignity come from either interpersonal experience or structural aspects of work (i.e., how the work is organised).

Taking these together, one begins with a potentially complex situation where to ask if one is achieving *dignity at work* for employees appears a rather simplistic notion. Further, different experiences within a variegated reality may tradeoff against each other so that a positive or negative experience offsets the effect of other experiences. For example, an inspiring but 'difficult' boss might be acceptable to some of us if the opportunities s/he provides are sufficiently high. Finally 'contagion' within an individual's experience might occur where one area of dignity or indignity produces dynamics that may affect others.

For example, Bowen and Blackmon (2003) describe how a gay man perceived himself to be in an unsafe working environment to 'come out' and did not attend informal social gatherings of work colleagues, subsequently failing to develop relationships effectively which led to further negative experiences. Here his reticence to reveal his sexuality contaminated workplace relationships beyond the initial issue of sexuality.

This chapter focuses on situations where the source of indignity is at the interpersonal level of experience – what is often referred to as bullying or interpersonal harassment. The chapter has three sections. The first section, by attempting to understand how people conceive and define bullying behaviours, examines negative experiences as they appear in our workplaces. The analysis reveals considerable confusion over what constitutes workplace bullying. The confusion over definition, in terms of its effect on the challenge of tackling workplace bullying, will then be examined in the second section. The final section of the chapter makes suggestions as to how these difficulties may be overcome.

What is bullying?

This section of the book is concerned with applications into work, and thus one need be concerned with how human resource (HR) management professionals, trade union representatives, other associated professionals and employees themselves understand what is bullying, as their understanding will trigger them to take action. If action is taken at an early point, it is assumed that the action will limit the damage to employees' health and clear the ground for the notion of *dignity* to further permeate their working life. Which behaviours should we be considering and over what frequency should we 'count' people as having been bullied?

The academic study of workplace bullying began in the early 1990s and has been dominated by European studies. As with any 'new' area of academic study, researchers initially concentrated on establishing the incidence of this negative experience. In order to legitimise the issue, measurement – usually through surveys – was a focus. In academic research, respondents to surveys are typically asked how frequently they experience a set of negative behaviours, and (separately) whether they think they have been bullied in a certain period of time usually against a definition (which is referred to as a 'labelling' question). Early studies in the UK (e.g., UNISON, 1997) only 'counted' respondents who both labelled themselves as having been bullied and also reported the experience of weekly negative behaviours. The weakness of this methodological approach is put into perspective when we see that it has been noted elsewhere that only around half of those who experience frequent (weekly) negative behaviours also label themselves as 'bullied' (Rayner, 1997). In addition, a study by Hoel and Cooper (2000) found that the health of individuals who reported the experience of negative behaviours at work was significantly worse than those who did not report such recent experiences, regardless of whether they labelled themselves as bullied or not (Hoel et al., 2004). Their study shifted the focus of academic definitions to those individuals who report the experience of behaviours, rather than those who currently label themselves as bullied.

The positivist quantitative surveys utilised lists of interpersonal behaviours reported by badly damaged targets of bullying (e.g., The Leymann Inventory of Personal Terrorization, Leymann, 1996; The Negative Acts Questionnaire, Einarsen et al., 2003). In contrast, qualitative studies which have chosen working people as their sample (e.g., Harlos and Pinder, 1999; Liefooghe and MacKenzie Davey, 2001) have used an inductive approach. These inductive studies have enriched our understanding of workplace bullying by asking employees what they find negative in their experience at work. Broadly speaking, they revealed two types of bullying – negative interpersonal behaviour by another person or a group of people and negative organisational practices such as unfair reward systems (e.g., Liefooghe and MacKenzie Davey, 2001) or appraisal practices (e.g., Harlos and Pinder, 1999). These have been considered as negative interpersonal behaviour and negative organisational behaviour (Rayner, 2005). This chapter is concerned with situations where the perceived source of bullying is negative interpersonal behaviour; however, it will be seen that the two aspects (interpersonal and organisational) appear to be irrevocably intertwined, especially when attempting to seek solutions.

Definitions: The options

Taking a stimulus–response model, one could define bullying either by focusing on the behaviours which an employee experiences (i.e., the stimulus) or by their reaction to that behaviour (i.e., the response). The former would provide a list of negative behaviours which were 'not-OK' in a workplace. Such a list would give a cornerstone of clear guidance for employees seeking to ensure they were not bullying and to label a bullying experience before they became damaged. The challenge is to establish an exhaustive list of behaviours (e.g., Brodsky, 1976; Adams, 1992). Generating such a list is problematic largely because bullying is rarely concerned with single dramatic events. Instead it is usually a collection of small events which on their own appear innocuous, but taken together form a pattern of potentially oppressive behaviour. Also many of these 'behaviours' are the absence of action – not being included in email lists, not invited to useful networking events or having information withheld which is essential to do one's job. All of these are hard to identify and complain about as well as define. As such, a definitive list of bullying behaviours as a practical approach has been abandoned by those in the field.

The response model requires individuals to have a negative response to their treatment and also presents challenges. People differ in their response to stressors (McKay et al., 2004) which could impact upon the response approach. For example, a target might be perceived as 'sensitive' (Adams, 1992) and thus responsible for their reaction (and thus the bullying). As such, the target is blamed. The academic and popular literature holds an assumption of blamelessness on the part of the target (e.g., Rayner et al., 2002). Such a stance might be naïve in reality, and this aspect will be returned to in the later sections.

Operationally, the response approach may be less effective at preventing damage as someone would already have experienced a negative effect (likely damage). From a health and safety perspective, one is looking to risk assess and prevent occurrence prior to damage (McKay et al., 2004). Thus, the response approach may not be acceptable as the damage process is already underway. One might use the response approach in a risk-based approach, and thus look for 'early' signs before significant damage is done. However, studies have yet to extend to such aspects; thus the identification of these parameters still requires investigation.

One positive aspect of the stimulus approach is that a set of behaviours can be used by everyone to check their own actions to ensure they are not bullying. In the response approach, those who are concerned their behaviour could be bullying would need to anticipate how others were feeling. Predicting negative reactions is clearly more problematic for individuals than with the stimulus approach.

There is also a potential for 'borrowing' related, and perhaps less emotive, concepts in definition. For example, Rayner used 'management style' (Rayner and Cooper, 2003), finding that coercive management style could account for some bullying, although by no means all. Harlos and Pinder's (ibid.) study looked at 'Injustice' – potentially one might be able to refer to better-established concepts such as fairness and justice in order to define bullying at work for employees (e.g., Colquitt et al., 2001).

The problem with policies

Anti-bullying polices are highly functional in that they give a clear unequivocal statement that the organisation is against this behaviour and provide the steps for tackling it (Tehrani, 2001). Whilst it is generally agreed that such policies need to exist (Richards and Daley, 2003; Vartia et al., 2003), the issue of definition is not an easy one. When examining definitions used in workplace policies, it is common to find both the stimulus and response approaches used in order to create a broad definition. In this way, exemplars of bullying behaviour are used (and it is made clear that there are many forms of bullying) and also exemplars of negative effect (response) such as humiliation and loss of confidence (Richards and Daley, 2003).

In a positive sense, generalised definitions can be highly functional for HR and trade union representatives so that they are not exclusionary for employees who feel they have a negative interpersonal experience at work, and a broad definition can be highly functional. Perceptions of bullying may change over time, and thus broad definitions allow such evolutions to take place without triggering the need to rewrite the policy. However, very broad definitions may not be effective in enabling employees to interpret their experience as bullying. Does this matter, or are employees able to work within these broad behavioural definitions to locate their experience?

Recent evidence regarding definitions

In 2004, the UK Department of Trade and Industry, together with AMICUS, Britain's largest private sector trade union, sponsored an initiative aimed at implementing better intervention practices for workplace bullying and harassment in UK workplaces. At the time of writing, this is an ongoing project. A research study by Portsmouth University was undertaken to establish current practices in tackling bullying and harassment (Rayner and McIvor, 2006). The research included focus groups with individuals in employment who had positive contributions to make regarding interventions into workplace bullying. The research provided complete anonymity to participating individuals who were recruited through a marketing agency and were paid a small inducement in shopping vouchers. Eleven groups were held in December 2005 and were run in Glasgow, Leeds, London and Cardiff including over 100 individuals from over 80 organisations.

The focus groups began with a facilitated discussion on what comprised bullying and harassment. Originally planned as a warm-up question, and contrary to the researchers' assumptions, considerable and genuine debate occurred regarding the definition of workplace bullying. The concept of harassment appeared to be better understood. Focus group members acknowledged the difference and accounted for their better understanding of harassment through many years of dealing with it in a legislative framework.

The discussion amongst focus group members revealed a real need for clarity, as exemplared in the following quotes (the specific focus group is identified by the number in brackets):

'Bullying is hard to define and therefore difficult'. (FG11)

'People don't know what bullying is'. (FG01)

'Bullying is subtle – people don't realise it is happening to them or they are doing it'. (FG02)

'Often people don't know they are being bullied, if there's nothing written down to define it, they might not know they are being bullied'. (FG04)

Others assigned less importance to definition:

'Even if you can't define bullying that's okay if people can discuss all their concerns'. (FG01)

Many members suggested that awareness raising or another method was necessary to help people recognise the experience:

'But some people don't have skills to recognise they are being bullied or are in denial'. (FG09)

'We need to raise self-awareness because people need to understand themselves before they can understand others. This is the only way that people will learn to see that their behaviour may come across as offensive'. (FG10)

Group members also suggested that the stimulus approach would be effective in defining behaviours:

'It would be good to give an example of good behaviour and bad behaviour as well; making a distinction between the two'. (FG08)

Some focus group members thought that labelling and reaction (response) was the most important issue:

'If people are being bullied but don't recognise it, managers should ignore it'. (FG01)

'(Bullying is) any thing that makes an employee feel uncomfortable'. (FG07)

Many focus group members made reference to organisational culture as a direct facet of definition:

'If it's an overall cultural thing which is accepted, then it's difficult to stop'. (FG07)

'If the culture promoted bullying then it's much bigger than personality, it's about culture'. (FG09)

'Nobody sets it (Culture) up to be abusive. It's how people use it. Over time, actions and activities that lead to bullying become accepted – because it's not discouraged it becomes the culture'. (FG09)

If bullying is within a culture, the locus of the problem shifts to the organisation rather than the individual level. As such, we are taken closer to negative organisational behaviours as exposed by Liefooghe and MacKenzie Davey (2001) and Harlos and Pinder (1999). The following excerpts are relevant:

'If you don't have the right culture, no amount of training will make a difference. A blame culture versus problem-solving culture'. (FG04)

'The last intake sees it as their right of passage to bully the new intake'. (FG05)

'It gets acceptable when it's always been like this. . . . That is institutional bullying – the way they treat all the staff'. (FG03)

Acceptability pervaded comments from those reflecting on areas of their organisations which experienced entrenched bullying. Acceptability applied to the broad occupational culture, and also showed that certain groups of individuals were 'accepted' when they exhibited bullying behaviours. A trade union representative worked in an organisation where a senior staff member had been caught on video camera kicking a member of security staff in the car park, but was not sacked for the attack, which she said 'sends a bad message' (FG05). A focus group member working in HR for a charity engaged in high-level research also reported exceptions being made for academics as

'The 'that's just them' approach. . . everyone seems to accept it from certain individuals. Then it gets brushed under the carpet . . . They think because they are the brains of the world they can do anything they like'. (FG07)

Similar stories concerned 'excellent' sales managers, 'very good' computer chiefs and 'creatives' whose work would be hard to replace and who were all somehow immune from criticism. As such, we can observe respondents struggling with definition by seeing behaviours they themselves label as 'bullying' but not receiving organisational reaction (all had policies), and hence their own definition becomes questionable. When acceptance comes into play, multiple definitions may be being used. Exemplars so far identify that there may be an espoused policy, but it is ignored because of the occupational climate, or because there are different levels of acceptability depending on job role and replaceability of staff, creating 'immune' groups.

A variation commonly reported by focus group members in larger organisations was local interpretations of policy definitions, summarised by the following quote from Focus Group 10:

'We have three basic working environments: an office environment, factories and distribution centre. The notions of acceptability changes between these and we recognise that as a fact'. (FG10)

In some instances, this was applied into specific environments, such as either side of the restaurant kitchen door.

'In a restaurant, the kitchen area has very bad language even though there are young people working there (fourteen year olds cleaning the dishes), but this is seen as acceptable. However, the same language would never be used in the restaurant part'. (FG05)

In the statements above, such delineation appears acceptable, but it was not always the case. We must question whose definition of bullying should be used – local staff, centralised head office staff, industry and professional standards or local workplace traditions?

The description so far has been somewhat negative, identifying confusion and unease in the identification of bullying. The researchers were unable to find an employer with a recognisable set of stimulus behaviours. The focus groups produced significant discussion on what behaviours constituted bullying. In reviewing the material from the focus groups, the only behaviour agreed by all was bullying as physical abuse, which is very uncommon in UK workplaces (e.g., UNISON, 1997). Swearing produced the discussion below in Focus Group 05 and is typical of other exchanges.

'There is a difference between bad language used around the organisation and bad language directed at the individual (singling out)'.

'Legally this doesn't stand up. If bad language is accepted in practice and tolerated over a period of time you can't then discipline an individual for doing it'.

'Even bad language directed at you might be acceptable as long as it wasn't meant personally. People tend not to complain'.

'There is a difference between swearing and aggressive language'. (FG05)

This exchange shows how hard it is to place definitions around specific behaviours, and go to the heart of the challenge for those involved in organisations that are responsible for tackling workplace bullying as a form of indignity.

During the research, it became apparent that vague definitions, while potentially set up with the best of intentions, held a potentially negative effect. They could act to create a vacuum of clarity which employees sought to fill through their own judgements on the one hand, and their observations of actions taken by the organisation on the other hand. In the best organisations, these coincided to establish a strong understanding of levels of acceptable behaviour that prevented situations of indignity for staff. In the worst organisations, employees observed no action to tackle workplace bullying. In such situations, although the bullying might be interpersonal in nature, the organisational systems meant that situations of indignity were being accepted through lack of action; thus there was a blurring between interpersonal and organisational bullying.

We will now turn to the challenge that generalised definitions place on those who are responsible for tackling bullying as a source of indignity at work.

The organisational challenge

The virtues of loose definitions of workplace bullying have been outlined in that they provide practitioners with flexibility to be able to act whatever the nature of the formal or informal complaint provided by an employee. What was surprising in the AMICUS/DTI-sponsored research was the genuine lack of clarity that exists surrounding this issue. The confusion provides a classic case where those at distance from dealing directly with problems in the workplace (e.g., academics, centralised policy makers in large organisations) need to take into account the challenges faced in real-life face-to-face situations. A loose definition without sufficient guidelines for interpretation effectively pushes real definitions to the level of those engaged in workplace interactions, who in turn may have expected such difficult decisions to have been taken by those more specialised than themselves (usually the HR department). How can one be sensitive to local interpretation, but also provide standardisation across an organisation? The challenge is found in the following quote:

> 'Multiple sites can be a problem. They don't all adhere to the same rules. Policy might be there but isn't used. There is resentment from sites because the policy gets imposed by the centre without consultation'. (FG04)

This shows that a standard set of 'rules' are required, but at the same time remonstrates against standardisation being imposed. It was generally agreed that the HR department were seen as the policy makers. Many employees held sympathy with the need for different standards in different working contexts. How HR manages such variegation without being 'blamed' for ineffectiveness through enabling different cross-organisational standards is very problematic.

The notion of policy being 'imposed' provides a useful pointer to the need for consultation, a process which many focus group members suggested was the first step to achieving an appropriate definition. The quote below exemplars consultation in a large organisation:

> 'Ours (policy) is new. It's about behaviour and about how people treat each other. It's also about whether people take ownership of their own behaviour. It was written in consultation with the TU. (It was) published as a draft for everyone to see (several thousand staff) and all comments back to HR. They still know they didn't get to everyone, but they did take account of the feedback'. (FG04)

It is therefore possible to undertake consultation even in large organisations, but one can imagine the time and effort put in by the HR group was substantial.

If policy is to be retained as having generalised definitions, then operational definitions will be left to those closer to the incident. In such circumstances, one becomes dependent on local staff to interpret effectively. Local interpretations may be skewed such that the 'exemptions' of senior or valuable staff are continued, or that some behaviour fails to be labelled at all as it has been present for such long periods of time. Consider the following example provided by a public health inspector:

> 'I know of an environmental health officer who was thrown into a vat of blood at an abattoir as a sort of initiation. It's brutalising for

the people themselves and for the people that they do it to. I'm not saying we should all go in for aromatherapy and I don't want to lose the humour but we do need to think'. (FG11)

One can see how easy it is for an organisation to become 'stuck' in its current behaviour and interpretation of definition, as it is constantly following current practice rather than taking the bolder step of considering indignity, its causes and therefore its constitution to be applied to workplace definitions. There is a strong case for HR to be placed with the responsibility of ensuring that indignity is an issue tackled on a level playing field. The author finds it difficult to see how else one can achieve this other than take a standardised approach, thus ignoring local practices (Richards and Daley, 2003).

The final point in this section is to return to the issues highlighted in the introduction – those of a variegated experience and also the notion of weakness on the part of targets, thus blame being attributed to them. It has been troubling to academics to find a way of explaining why only around half of those who report negative behaviour at work also experience themselves as being bullied. Both the variegation of experience and the notion of blame issues may come into play in mediating or confounding judgements on whether people label themselves as bullied when being treated negatively.

Assuming that most workplaces hold positive *dignity* experiences for individuals, they may tradeoff against the 'indignity' of negative behaviours that employees' experience which typify bullying. Unfortunately, academic researchers in the area tend to only ask about negative experience and it is an area for future research to understand whether such a cognitive process is in action and the dynamics held within it. Further, blame and shame are both known to be present in bullying situations (Adams, 1992; Brodsky, 1976; Lewis, 2004; Rayner et al., 2002). Such emotional attributions may mitigate against labelling and have a part to play in operational definitions being applied by individuals to their own working situations. These comments lend support to the suggestion that it would be very positive to study the whole spectrum of experience (McKay et al., 2004).

Meeting the organisational challenge

Given the problem of applying generalised definitions and the likely confounding cognitive dynamics occurring at the individual level, the challenge concerning definition becomes easier to understand. The need for HR and other policy-related job holders (such as trade union-ists and health and safety professionals) to assist all employees and especially those in a management capacity to understand bullying becomes essential (Lewis and Rayner, 2003).

In the AMICUS/DTI-funded research, several suggestions were made. First was the need to generate working definitions through con-sultation. Such workshops, engaging with all staff or employee group representatives to discover what is 'OK behaviour' within the cul-ture, were important both for the outcome (sets of behaviours which apply the policy) and for getting staff to consider the question of what causes indignity. Sometimes, workshops led to the creation of Codes of Behavioural Conduct, and the consultation process assisted buy-in from employees at all levels.

Having identified a working definition, it was suggested that it needed then to be constantly reinforced which could be done in a number of ways. First, that core values are expressed during selection interviews, and later reinforced at induction. Second, that employees are encouraged to raise potential problems informally and gently before the situation escalates and that they can do so without their action being career limiting or attracting blame and shame to themselves. Third, that any situation is dealt with by managers in an overt way so that it is clear that the operationalised policy is being reinforced. In this way, the traditionally exempt staff will need to be dealt with which may require supportive action from HR for the local manager taking action. And finally, that indignity issues are embedded into training programmes, cascade communication sessions and other managerial messages with the no-blame, no-shame approach reinforced.

Summary

Larger UK organisations are concerned to retain their staff, and as we compete in a knowledge economy, the issue of staff retention becomes a matter of competitive advantage (Boxall and Purcell, 2003). Considerable research has shown that workplace bullying leads to employees finding alternative employment. Minimising bullying and other indignities are coming into the foreground where employers are working in an economy which holds significant competition for talent and also demands low costs.

While it has been shown that indignity can be found at an inter-personal level and also at an organisational level, most employers are focusing on interpersonal bullying. However, to start tackling this type of indignity, we must have some shared understanding at a local level of what workplace bullying is. Recent research sponsored by AMICUS and the DTI have shown how generalised definitions used in policies have contributed to confusion amongst employees regarding the nature of workplace bullying in particular. Resolving such confusion, together with the need to take a more realistic approach to the variegated nature of the workplace experience, requires organisations to grasp the nettle of definition and take active steps. It is only on the basis of a clear understanding of what constitutes this type of indignity that intervention and preventative activities can take place. If an organisation has a variety of workplaces (such as the goods yard, the office and the shop), it is likely that different levels of tolerance will be in existence. A strategic decision will be needed as to whether to allow for variegation in acceptance within the workforce. The AMICUS/DTI research has shown that those employers who have done this have eventually found such differences difficult to justify.

Our increased understanding of intervention mechanisms shows that employers need to provide effective policy, support and complaints systems for individual employees to repair their situation. Where these are not in place, the individual finds themselves not only bullied by other employee(s), but that their experience is echoed by organisational (in)action. Such a situation begins to blur the line between interpersonal and institutional bullying. When organisations get to grips with the challenge of providing adequate systems, management and individual support to enable the resolution of interpersonal bullying, so the far more complex issues of organisational bullying will also begin to be tackled.

References

Adams, A. (1992) *Bullying at Work – How to Confront and Overcome It*, London: Virago.

Bowen, F. and Blackmon, K. (2003) 'Spirals of Silence: The Dynamic Effects of Diversity on Organizational Voice', *Journal of Management Studies*, **40**, 6, 1393–1417.

Boxall, P. and Purcell, J. (2003) *Strategy and Human Resource Management*, Basingstoke: Palgrave MacMillan.

Brodsky, C. M. (1976) *The Harassed Worker*, Toronto: Lexington Books, DC Heath & Co.

Colquitt, J. A., Conlon, D. E., Wesson, M. J., Porter, C. O. L. H. and Ng, K. Y. (2001) 'Justice at the Millennium: A Meta-Analytic Review of 25 years of Organizational Justice Research', *Journal of Applied Psychology*, **86**, 3, 425–445.

Einarsen, S., Hoel, H., Zapf, D. and Cooper, C. (2003) 'The Concept of Bullying at Work, in *Bullying and Emotional Abuse in the Workplace: International Research and Practice Perspectives* (Einarsen, S., Hoel, H., Zapf, D. and Cooper, C., eds), London: Taylor Francis, pp. 3–30.

Harlos, K. and Pinder, C. C. (1999) 'Patterns of Organizational Injustice: Taxonomy of What Employees Regard as Unjust', *Qualitative Organizational Research*, **2**, 97–125.

Hoel, H. and Cooper, C. L. (2000) *Destructive Conflict and Bullying at Work*, Unpublished manuscript.

Hoel, H., Faragher, B. and Cooper, C. L. (2004) 'Bullying is Detrimental to Health, But all Bullying Behaviours and Not Necessarily Equally Damaging', *British Journal of Guidance and Counselling*, **32**, 3, 367–387.

Lewis, D. (2004) 'Bullying at Work: The Impact of Shame Among University and College Lecturers', *British Journal of Guidance and Counselling*, **32**, 3, 281–299.

Lewis, D. and Rayner, C. (2003) 'Bullying and Human Resource Management: A Wolf in Sheep's Clothing?' in *Bullying and Emotional Abuse in the Workplace* (Einarsen, S., Hoel, H., Zapt, D. and Cooper, C., eds), London: Taylor Francis, pp. 370–383.

Leymann, H. (1996) 'The Content and Development of Mobbing at Work', *European Journal of Work and Occupational Psychology*, **5**, 2, 165–184.

Liefooghe, A. P. D. and Mackenzie Davey, K. (2001) 'Accounts of Workplace Bullying: The Role of the Organization', *European Journal of Work and Organizational Psychology*, **10**, 4, 375–393.

McKay, C. J., Cousins, R., Kelly, P. J., Lee, S. and McCaig, R. H. (2004) 'Management Standards and Work-Related Stress in the UK: Policy Background and Science', *Work and Stress*, **18**, 2, 91–112.

Rayner, C. (1997) 'Incidence of Workplace Bullying', *Journal of Community and Applied Social Psychology*, **7**, 3, 199–208.

Rayner, C. (2005) 'Reforming Abusive Organizations', in *Workplace Violence: Issues, Trends and Strategies* (Bowie, V., Fisher, B. and Cooper, C. L., eds), Cullompton, UK: Willan Publishers, pp. 60–73.

Rayner, C. and Cooper, C. L. (2003) 'The Black Hole in "Bullying at Work" Research', *International Journal of Decision Making*, **4**, 1, 47–64.

Rayner, C., Hoel, H. and Cooper, C. L. (2002) *Workplace Bullying: What we Know, Who is to Blame and What Can We Do?*, London: Taylor Francis.

Rayner, C. and McIvor, K. (2006) *Report to the Dignity at Work Project Steering Committee* available on http://www.port.ac.uk/workplacebullying.

Richards, J. and Daley, H. (2003) 'Bullying policy: Development, Implementation and Monitoring', in *Bullying and Emotional Abuse in the Workplace: International Research and Practice Perspectives* (Einarsen, S., Hoel, H., Zapf, D. and Cooper, C., eds), London: Taylor Francis, pp. 127–144.

Tehrani, N. (2001) *Building a Culture of Respect*, London: Taylor Francis.

UNISON (1997) *UNISON Members' Experience of Bullying at Work*, London: UNISON.

Vartia, M., Korppoo, L., Fallenius, S. and Mattila, M. (2003) 'Workplace Bullying: The Role of Occupational Health Services', in, *Bullying and Emotional Abuse in the Workplace: International Perspectives in Research and Practice* (Einarsen, S., Hoel, H., Zapf, D. and Cooper, C. L., eds), London: Taylor Francis, pp. 285–298.

11

Is that something we used to do in the 1970s?: The demise of 'good work' in the Volvo Corporation

Terry Wallace

Ramsay's (1977) *Cycles of Control* thesis argues that patterns of employee participation have not followed linear trajectories towards some idea of industrial democracy. The evidence draws from a study of the UK over a 150-year period and suggests a cyclical trajectory in which participation has been used by organisations in those specific circumstances when labour has challenged managerial prerogative. When those circumstances no longer exist, enterprise management are less enthusiastic about employee participation and withdraw support for it (Harley et al., 2005). In developing the now classical *Cycles of Control* thesis, I truncate its temporality and transpose its spatiality towards analysing Volvo Truck Corporation's development of work organisation from the 1970s onwards. The analysis traces Volvo's trajectory over a 35-year period, from being a Swedish multinational towards its becoming a global, transnational organisation. I take the *Cycles of Control* thesis a step further through isolating three additional explanatory factors over and above that of the strength of organised labour. I suggest that at the microlevel, the development of work organisation is also dependant upon: (i) the socioeconomic and political environments in which the firm operates, (ii) the level of its globalisation strategy, and (iii) the nature of the market places in which it operates.

By incorporating a wider conceptual framework, we are better able to counter those who suggest that work organisation has undergone a permanent shift away from the dominance of 'instrumental' views of work associated with Taylorist and Fordist modes of production (Applebaum, 1998; Katzenbach and Smith, 1993; Pulignano and Stewart, 2006; Thompson, 2003; Womack et al., 1990). I therefore suggest that Volvo's development of work organisation, specifically its 'good work' strategy, is little more then a set of contingent responses to its location within specific socioeconomic, labour and product market conditions. As these conditions change and develop, the necessity for 'good work' diminishes and organisations such as Volvo, operating in increasingly globalising market places, are able to mould their employee relations and production strategies to suit these changing conditions.

The evidence draws from a longitudinal study of work organisation, industrial relations and management systems within the manufacturing units of the Volvo Truck and Bus Corporation. The study, following the seminal work of Blackler and Brown (1978), has reflected on the leading role that the organisation has taken in developing what Svenska Metall (SM), the leading Swedish blue-collar trade union, has called 'det goda arbetet' or 'good work'. In this context, 'good work' is defined in terms of increased cycle times, task and knowledge sharing, parallel or cell-based forms of production technology and payment systems linked to knowledge (Berggren, 1992, 1995; Engström and Medbo, 1995; Nilsson, 1995; Svenska Metall, 1985; Wallace, 2000; for an extended definition of 'good work' see Coats in this collection). New production regimes in Volvo were designed around both managerial and trade union imperatives and implemented through autonomous self-directed teams taking high levels of responsibility for the everyday operation of the workplace (Wallace, 2000).

The chapter is ordered around four key themes. First, I identify those socioeconomic, political and sector conditions that led Volvo to develop its model of 'good work'. Second, through tracing the trajectory of its usage within Volvo, the specific role of trade unions and management in its implementation and growth will be identified. Third, those conditions which have led to its dismantling will be identified and analysed to assess how far changes in the firm's environment have affected the further implementation of 'good work'. Fourth, I will ask: is there a future for 'good work' and if so on whose terms will it develop in the twenty-first century?

Good work: socioeconomic and sectoral environments

The genesis of 'good work' within Volvo's Swedish plants came from three quite distinct sources. First, in the 1970s, it arose as the latest stage in the neo-corporatist Swedish model of political economy (Misgeld et al., 1988). Since the 1930s, the 'Swedish Model' consisted of a vibrant welfare state (Himmelstrand et al., 1981; Korpi, 1978), the centralisation of its collective bargaining system (Kjellberg, 1992; Lash, 1985; Wise, 1993) and, more latterly, its support for innovations in the human-centred organisation of shop-floor work (Berggren, 1992; Sandberg, 1995). By the 1970s, this had resulted in a highly educated population, relatively low levels of unemployment, welfare payments amongst the highest in Europe, with, for example, unemployment benefit paid at 90 per cent of previous year's salary, extensive sick-pay schemes and active labour market policies facilitating occupational and geographical mobility (Anxo and Niklasson, 2004). The investment in retraining, high unemployment benefit and generous sick-pay schemes facilitated the relative ease in which blue-collar employees were able to absent themselves from work and/or change jobs on a regular basis. Volvo, suffering from these high levels of labour turnover and absenteeism, felt they could no longer rely on Taylorist management techniques and assembly line technology.

Second, from within the realm of production, there was pressure on the organisation for it to develop different solutions to the rapidly changing markets sectors in which it operated. For example, the markets for trucks had historically been dominated by fleet customer demands for low specification, standard vehicles manufactured and assembled in high volume and mass production environments utilising assembly line technologies. In the late 1960s, these markets began to change with an increasing critical mass of smaller, non-fleet-based customers, demanding high-specification, low-volume vehicles. For technical reasons, existing flow-line assembly technologies were unable to satisfy these demands and increased the necessity for additional forms of production technologies.

Third, in the arena of employee relations, AB Volvo was a key player in the growth and eventual demise of centralised bargaining during the latter half of the twentieth century. During the 1950s and 1960s, Volvo had experienced significant domestic growth in sales, productivity and employment and was increasing its penetration into export markets (Axelopolous and Cohen, 2003; Delsen and van Veen, 1992). At the same time, SM was arguing that wage compression was affecting the ability of high-skilled workers to maintain differentials with both sides agreeing that increased absenteeism and labour turnover were the result. They both felt that centralised bargaining was limiting Volvo's ability to attract high-calibre employees, and as a consequence they jointly withdrew from centralised bargaining in 1983 in order to develop their own internal bargaining model. This, alongside the increasing internalisation of the Swedish economy, its growing dependence on foreign markets and increasing levels of foreign investment in production facilities led the SAF to officially pronounce the end of the Swedish Model in 1990 (SAF, *Tidning* 16/2/1990 cited in Persoff, 1999 op. cit. p. 2; Thörnqvist, 1999). Although the end of centralised agreements *de jure* signalled the end of the Swedish Model, *de facto*, the model, in its industrial form, continued to operate at plant level throughout most of Volvo's Swedish operations and actually led to the development of innovations over and above anything achieved within the centralised bargaining model. These innovations were introduced, and to some extent, designed through tri-partite co-operation between Volvo management, Svenska Metal, local and regional state bureaucracies and external consultants largely drawn from the university sector.

Volvo and 'good work'

In order to safeguard the recruitment and retention of blue-collar employees, middle-level managers within Volvo began to look towards developing production systems that had the potential for lessening the monotony of assembly line production. Initially, they looked at innovating around issues of job rotation, individual learning programmes and group working with ensuing experiments conducted without changes in production technologies, the technical division of labour or organisational structure. They only began to have a wider purchase when, in the early 1970s, executive level management switched the focus of the company towards more human-centred values through the recruitment of specialist personnel. A senior manager, recruited in the 1970s specifically to drive forward the work organisation agenda, said that at the time he was told by a colleague:

> 'You know there are people coming here from the outside and... they have homes, families, children (and) they are taking care of their own lives. They are chairmen of different types of organisation. When they come here and they pass this gate they cannot take any responsibility at all. There is something happening at the gate and we have to redesign the gate. Inside here they cannot even pick up a screw they have dropped on the floor. That was a tough way of describing the culture we had inside. The unions had a view that we were not developed to use the brain, only their hands and legs. What they did was to show that we can do something else – that was a very important start' (Lars Krister Jonsson, September 1995).

Over the next 15 years, they began to address these problems through innovations in three distinct areas. First, at the level of work organisation, there was a noticeable shift towards production environments in which cycle times on the shop floor increased from between three and 12 minutes to, in some cases, up to four hours resulting in blue-collar workers assuming a range of non-traditional roles in their everyday work environments. This was facilitated through the increasing use of 'assembly docks' – more or less static or cell-based assembly technologies – providing an increased range of solutions to the changing demands of the market place. In the truck sector, one of the driving forces for cell-based production in the 1980s was the reduction in balance losses through increased demand for high-specification, low-volume products from an increasing number of small operators. Although flow-line assembly techniques were suitable for mass production, they are less efficient in the production of more customised ranges of vehicles. Consequently, 'dock assembly' techniques, following work experiments carried out in 1973 and 1974 at the Arendal plant in Gothenburg, were introduced into final assembly plants at Umeå, Boras, Tuve as well as car plants at Uddevalla and Kalmar (Berggren, 1992, p. 109). It was assumed blue-collar workers would take more responsibility for the production agenda rather than be dictated to by line speed. The dock philosophy was described by one of the engineers responsible for its development as 'a wide open door to the production of a post-industrial society where we will engineer, produce and market better trucks with lower prices and with happier people' (Johannson, 1975). Although Volvo introduced cell-based production, this was parallel to, and did not replace, assembly lines, with standard vehicles still built using flow-line technologies.

By 1989, these changes in the technical division of labour led Roger Holtback, President of Volvo's Car Division, to suggest that Volvo was 'saying farewell to the traditional assembly line' with the 'hope that one day in the future somebody will be able to stand here and say "Henry Ford invented the assembly line but Volvo did away with it – in a profitable way" ' (Taylor, 1989). It was argued at the time that Volvo was challenging many of the 'fundamental assumptions that have dominated managerial thought about mass production since the beginning of the century and return car manufacture to the made by hands in teams approach that existed before Henry Ford's assembly line methods began in 1914' (ibid.). Although Holtback's comments were specifically directed at the Car Division, it is generally agreed within Volvo that much of the design and implementation of these technical innovations had their genesis within the Truck Division.

Second, the introduction of knowledge or competence-based reward systems began to link pay to the acquisition of job-related skills and was supported by continuous training and education (Wallace, 2000). This enabled an expansion of the skills base of the organisation, the flexible utilisation of labour and an enhanced capacity to manage change processes from below. Competence-based pay was introduced across most of the firm's Swedish plants during collective negotiations in the late 1980s and early 1990s. It was based on a 'ladders' metaphor in which enhanced skill levels led to increases in pay. Depending on the specificity of the needs of individual plants, the number of steps in each ladder ranged from 5 at the Tuve Final assembly plant (Ahlstrand, 2000) to 15 at the Skövde engine plant (Wallace, 2000). Movement through the steps was meritocratic with an operator's ability to increase their skill profile and reach the highest pay levels wholly dependent on their technical, cognitive and intellectual competence. Operator pay was based around what 'they knew' as well as what 'they did'. Local union officials at the Tuve and Umeå plants argued that this 'open' system of wages and skills enhancement reduced competition between blue-collar workers and allowed them to reach the optimum skill levels in which both the employee and the organisation benefited.

Third, the organisational vehicle utilised for the development of production technology and competence pay was that of team- or group-based forms of work organisation. The development of group work erased most of the boundaries between skilled and non-skilled labour and, more recently, those between blue-collar and white-collar staff's terms and conditions of employment. Initially, groups at Volvo were seen as significantly different from the idea of teams, a concept Volvo argued had more to do with Japanese systems of lean production. Volvo's specific focus on 'group work' and its distinctiveness compared to lean production was also articulated by the trade unions who argued that its vision of group work was distinct from the Japanese notion of team work. Their vision was to give all employees the chance to develop 'as a whole person', to take more responsibility for their workplace, to have more room to decide on what work they do and to have more control of their own working environment (Trade Union activist, Volvo Umeå). SM linked Japanese ideas of team work to high-performance production teams having the effect of increasing the competition between groups of workers on the shop floor. They argued against a move in that direction because for them developments in work organisation should be in the interests of their members and not just increasing the profitability of the company. Although working in partnership with Volvo, they had to argue strongly for a core definition of group work that accounted for employee development and

increasing blue-collar competence. This was a result of their perception that production management's interest in developing the human
side of production was over-shadowed by their over-riding interest in
technical and productivity issues. The union's interest in 'good work',
orientated around the need for a non-competitive wage system, was
equally concerned with developing the technical organisation of production (Wallace, 2000). With significant levels of task, cognitive and
governance responsibilities devolved down to shop-floor level, there
was a danger of an intensification of work. However, the presence of
the open access and transparent competence pay system meant that
there was no compulsion for employees to take on an increased workload, with those that did being incrementally compensated (Thompson
et al., 1995, Wallace, 2000).

Changing contexts – The erosion of 'good work'

The chapter thus far has traced the context of the introduction of 'good
work' and traced its changing usage across three clear areas. This
section begins to chart the changes within Volvo's environment and
the impact these changes have had on the continuance or otherwise of
'good work' innovations.

Socioeconomic changes resulting from Sweden's incorporation into
the European Union were indicative of a shift away from Keynesian
macroeconomic regulation towards a more market orientated economy.
This has led to increasing unemployment and to a reduction in benefit
payment from 90 to 80 per cent of previous year's salary, the introduction of a 5-day waiting period, reductions in other social and welfare
benefits and the parallel reduction in income tax (Anxo and Niklasson,
2004). Despite Volvo's attempt to reduce sickness absenteeism through
developing 'good work', absenteeism generally within the Swedish
economy continued to remain problematic throughout the 1990s and
the early years of the twenty-first century. The state's response was to
lower rates of sickness benefit, introduce waiting periods prior to payment of benefits and instigate the usage of 'return to work' programmes
(Anxo and Niklasson, 2004). This market-led approach to employment has impacted upon labour mobility with turnover, sickness and
other forms of absenteeism in Volvo becoming less problematic for
the firm, thus lowering the necessity for further development of 'good
work' strategies. These macroeconomic influences were described by
a leading plant-based union activist within Volvo as the 'ethics of
a new thinking . . . from the employers organisations (and) . . . some

sort of death of the Swedish model' with 'the government (and) the trade unions listening more to the employer's organisation than to the workers' (Trade Union activist, Volvo Umeå).

There have also been significant changes in the global market place for trucks. Historically, truck buyers in Europe, South America and North America have tended to be loyal to indigenous manufacturers. In the 1960s, there were around 40, largely regionally based, truck manufacturers spread across the globe all offering individual solutions to their customer's transportations problems. Volvo's factories in Europe, and North and South America designed and manufactured discrete trucks for each of these markets. By 2005, outside of Japan, the global market place was dominated by one North American multinational and five European multinationals, leading to wider processes of convergence within the industry. With the introduction every seven or eight years of new truck families, Volvo, following the sector norm, has moved towards the 'global truck' concept through modularising and standardising the structural base of its full product range. At the same time, the trend in the truck market has shifted back towards large, fleet-based orders, lessening the demand for production systems able to manufacture high-specification, low-volume items (Volvo, 2003). Demands for increased standardisation on truck manufacturers remain, with large-scale investment in product development and rational production systems increasingly seen as crucial to meeting customer demands for efficient and cost-effective, capital goods. Developments in the global reach of the company, the importance of its 'Global Truck Concept' and its presence as producer in five continents make the requirement for 'good work' in its Swedish plants less of an issue. It is now better able to switch production between its assembly units in Australia, Brazil, the USA, Belgium, Poland, and more recently in Russia.

The percentage of Volvo's employees in Sweden has fallen from 73.6 per cent in 1985 to 33 per cent in 2005. Although figures for employees working in the truck corporation have not been disaggregated, the production figures for trucks indicate a decreasing reliance on its Swedish assembly plants. By the early twenty-first century, the sale of Volvo's Car Division to Ford and its acquisition of the truck division of Renault/Mack in 2000 lessened its reliance on Swedish production units. In the 1970s although producing only 50 per cent of its global truck capacity in Sweden, it was more or less wholly reliant on its other main production markets (Volvo Company Report, 1989). But by 2005, with trucks constituting its major business area, production in Sweden had reduced to 17 per cent of Volvo's global capacity, a figure that reduces to less than 10 per cent when we include figures for Renault/Mack production (Volvo Annual Reports, 1989–2005; www.Volvo.com.). The shift of production away from Sweden means that Volvo is less reliant on developing 'good work' as there is little to suggest that in its other main production areas it has been central to the development of the employment relationship.

In France, there is little evidence of the development of 'good work' (Boyer and Freyssenet, 2002; Linhart, 1980). This is indicative of French employee relations traditions dominated by employer attitudes of paternalism, low union density, arms-length bargaining and the legacy of communist and anarchist influences on the CFDT and CDT, the leading French union confederations (Goetschy and Rozenblatt, 1992). From conversations with key personnel in the organisations, there is a perception that one of the more significant consequences of the take-over of Renault/Mack is the increasing influence of French managerial philosophy within Volvo. It does seem to the be case that it is French managers from Lyon who are leading the crusade for Volvo to take up more and more of the techniques of the Toyota Production System (TPS) and to shed its reliance on 'good work'.

Historically, innovations in the Brazilian automotive industry have not come from employee relation strategies but from the growth of new business models such as the modular consortium, material supply systems and the use of the techniques of lean production (Wallace, 2004). Employee relation problems have tended to be addressed through shifting production away from trade union strongholds within Sao Paulo to less well-organised areas such as Resende in Rio de Janeiro province and Curitiba in the province of Parana. The Volvo truck plant, located at Curitiba in the southern state of Parana, although headed by senior Swedish executives, exhibits little evidence of developments in the area of work organisation. Indeed, one senior manager at the plant told me in 2003 'Of course the labour relations here – the union is pretty tolerant. You can get away with a lot of things here that you cannot get away with in Europe. I mean hiring and firing is pretty easy'.

Team working at the Ghent plant has developed more around ideas of lean production than work organisation. So, for example, whilst they built a single dock in the final assembly area, it had a limited use with a shelf life of only a couple of years. Equally, like the Curitiba plant, they have a remuneration system structured around basic pay, supplemented by a series of bonuses linked to key performance indicators. During my visits to the plant in 1994 and 1997, senior management stressed the Flemish nature of the plant, with the production manager pointing out that Flemish people are:

'rather hard working . . . We don't need systems to make industrial work attractive which was one of the main reasons why they introduced dock work in Sweden. If you were that stupid that you did not find anything else to work for, then you went to the assembly line at Volvo. Sorry to say it so black and white. To attract people they really had a lot of nice thinking, they have to make work attractive. That is why they have introduced docks' (Production Manager, Volvo Ghent, 1994).

So what have been the effects on 'good work' of these changes in the internal and external environments in which Volvo Truck operates? In terms of competence pay, the company is attempting to introduce a performance dimension by attempting to abandon the philosophy of payment for knowledge and returning to a 'payment for work done' system. In the late 1990s, it became clear that HR managers in the Truck Corporation were not prepared to pay just for competence itself and began to insist that competencies had also to be used. They argued that pay for knowledge was an inefficient use of labour because although those higher up the ladder got competence pay, there was nothing in the system forcing them to use these competencies. In its place, they wanted a wage system that was 'about what you do and how you do it' organised and confirmed by line management and not by the team and the trade union (HR Manager, Volvo Köping). The implication being that the system as it stood put too much power into the hands of the trade unions and blue-collar operators.

Of the plants who introduced Dock technology in the 1980s and 1990s, Workington, Irvine, Kalmar and Uddevalla have closed; Borås has moved from a two-step dock towards a mini-line philosophy; the six finally assembly docks at Tuve moved from a two- to a four-stage format before finally closing in 2002; the 'short flows' at Umeå were replaced by a segmented line between 2003 and 2005; and, the chassis docks at Tuve and the small assembly docks at the Skövde engine plant have also been closed. The evidence clearly suggests that experimentation with parallel production flows is at an end. This is despite a barrage of evidence that suggests cell-based or parallel forms of production, even for low variant models, are more productive than traditional assembly lines (Engstrom et al., 1996, 2004; Medbo, 1999; Nilsson, 1995). From many conversations with senior management across a range of Swedish final assembly plants, it has been suggested that cell-based production systems are not cost-effective and are more difficult to manage than traditional line systems. However, it could also be argued that management philosophy was driven more by a need to challenge the power of the trade unions within Volvo. At Umeå, there is no doubt that management on the shop floor lost control of the production agenda to the union and they felt that they had little input into local production and compensation strategies. As a leading member of SM at Umeå put it

> 'I think that one of the real crucial issues . . . is that the management felt that they were not in command – it was not them who decided everything. There was too much power, not in the union but on the floor. The team members and the teams were too strong. I think that was the main – really the main issue was about this. They have said it – many times the company – we will take back the power from the union but mainly from the floor' (Member A, Svenska Metall Committee, Umeå).

This has been a brief sketch of the global context within which attempts to dismantle cell-based production and competence pay over the last five years have taken place. The consequences are that the specificity of the Swedish model of group work has been diminished, with the remnants resembling more the TPS than the traditional Volvo system of work organisation. During its earlier stages, 'good work' was developed with active participation of the blue-collar trade union in their design, implementation and management. Attempts by Volvo to modify its employee relation strategy through incremental changes in production technology and competence pay has met with significant trade union resistance. The trade unions still speak about 'good work' in terms of lessening competition between workers, payment linked to skills development and an increased knowledge base of its members.

Is there a future for 'good work'?

So where does all this leave the prospects for the continuance of 'good work'? Through applying an adapted model of the *Cycles of Control* thesis, the chapter has highlighted the fluidity of the employment relationship. It has allowed us to go beyond a purely internal analysis by taking into consideration a range of contingent factors that have impacted upon the development, and demise, of 'good work' within the Volvo Truck Corporation. The unfolding narrative in this chapter would not be significant except for the fact that Volvo has been seen by trade unions, progressive management, critical sociologists and organisation theorists alike as the exemplar of 'good work'. Over the past 30 years or so, sociological, psychological and organisational analysts of the 'new workplace' have been directing their critical attention towards what have been variously labelled 'high-performance work systems' (HPWS) (Jenkins and Delbridge, 2007), the 'TPS'

(Pulignano and Stewart, 2006), 'hybrid factories' (Boyer et al., 1999) and the 'knowledge economy' (Thompson, 2003). In these contexts, Volvo has been absolved from criticism by omission and, within a largely Swedish-based literature, has been presented as the beacon of best practice (Sandberg, 1995). This is indicative of the way HPWS and the TPS have been seen as distinct from what we might want to call Volvoism; a distinctiveness the evidence presented here suggests is in the process of being eroded. It is therefore legitimate to ask if current practice in Volvo, the exemplar of 'good work', signals its demise, with little or no opportunity for its widespread incorporation into the strategic development of large multinational organisations. Although a pessimistic picture has been painted here, as we have seen, product and labour markets are in constant flux not just in Sweden, but in all of the markets in which Volvo operates. To write off 'good work' on the basis of a 20-year longitudinal study may be premature.

Volvo, like most large multinational organisations, consists of shifting power relations between different organisational interest groups. Ironically, it is the success of 'good work' over the last 20 years that may have planted the seeds of its own destruction (Schumpeter, 1934). Trade Union activists in Gothenburg and Umeå have suggested that the consequences of 20 years of 'good work', high levels of trade union influence in the development of payment systems and work organisation and the lack of overt conflict have led to a de-politicisation of the workforce. 'Good work' was taken for granted and without the hindsight of experience, younger workers are more willing to accept individualised pay systems in which they are more highly rewarded for increased individual performances, thus laying the foundations of a shift towards the TPS.

Recent struggles over work organisation and payment systems at Tuve and Umeå have, activists suggest, led to a re-politicisation in which they have been 'staggered' by the response of their membership. At Umeå for instance, managerial attempts to dismantle competence pay met with more or less 100 per cent blue-collar resistance and a unified trade union committee. The three-year struggle between SM and the company although resulting in modifications to the competence pay system left its structure relatively unchanged. However, the union was unable to stop the dismantling of cell-based production. The reason why it was successful in one and not in the other simply reflects the fact that wage systems are part of the collective bargaining process whilst production systems are wholly in the ownership of the company.

The firm's current strategic positioning is structured around the recruitment of a new cadre of young production workers, and personnel management convinced that labour relations problems are a thing of the past. One such middle-level manager remarked to a colleague 'work organisation – is that something we used to do in the 1970s?' (Technical Manager, Volvo Borås, 2005). But how strong is this feeling amongst more senior mangers in the company? In 2004, I edited a special edition (SE) of the *International Journal of Operations and Production Management* entitled 'The End of "good work"' in which a group of influential European scholars argued that Volvo's commitment to 'good work' was coming to an end. In response, the CEO of Volvo sanctioned the spending of around £100,000 on a conference in which around 100 senior managers and trade unionists from Brazil, France, Sweden, the USA, Belgium and the UK met with around 30 researchers from Europe.

During the conference, it became clear that executive level management within the company did indeed feel that Volvo's response to globalisation and changes in labour and product markets was necessary and overdue. However, they suggest that this, in itself, does not indicate the end of 'good work'. Paraphrasing Winston Churchill, the head of human resources for the global organisation argued in response to the SE that the current period was not the 'end of the end of the "good work", it was not even the beginning of the end of "good work", but was the end of its beginning' (Kjell Svensson, Volvo, Gothenburg). So there is still some commitment at senior level within Volvo to 'good work'. However, the problem is with its implementation and continuance at plant and shop-floor level. Volvo is a de-centred organisation, with large amounts of autonomy devolved down to plant level and functional management. Talking to American, French, Belgian, and mid-level Swedish managers at the conference, it was clear that they wanted Volvo to switch more towards the TPS and leave behind their historical commitment to work organisation. The danger for 'good work' is that those at the top are near retirement and the environment it which Volvo is operating shows no sign of deviation from its current trajectory. Even those managers I spoke to at the conferences who are sympathetic to the ideas of 'good work' are now talking in terms of Organisational Development Teams, Business Models, TPS and Lean Production. In the presentation of a senior production executive, it was suggested that in the past Volvo was 'so much influenced by (Swedish) problems (and) solutions that we didn't take on influences from the rest of the world'. They wanted to create 'good work', but mixed up direct and indirect work in a way that gave them problems with efficiency. In moving away from line production, he argued that they did not take advantage of high-volume standardised products when solving the production of low-volume complex products. So the return to line production has 'to be seen in a broader context than just the technical system', it is more about becoming a learning organisation in which 'learning from the past' enables them to 'focus on the future' (Hultman, 2006; Senge, 1990).

It seems that learning from the past means that they want to wrestle the 'good work' agenda away from the trade unions and redefine it from a managerial perspective. The debate within senior management is how to incorporate the TPS through identifying 'common targets and priorities for development, purchasing and production; more focus and eagerness to work with small step improvements, lowering of lead times and standardised ways of working' (Hultman, 2006).

In the early 1990s, a leading figure at Volvo argued that he had seen:

> 'Work organisation... at the end of the 60s we had problems in Paris, the student revolution and there were in Sweden a lot of strikes. After that the pendulum came over and the emphasis was on new work organisation, new situations for the employee. Productivity was not necessary, only for us to have good people, to have human relations, to be the best. We took from Norway and tested the ideas of work organisation and built up groups. But that was the beginning of the 1970s. We were a little bit naïve in Sweden; we thought work organisation would resolve all the problems we had. I think the 1980s was better when we found the right balance between work organisation and productivity'.

Of course, the ultimate danger is that although docks and wage systems had a large input from the union activists, they can easily be incorporated into a managerial agenda. For the past 15 years or so, the management strategy in the employment relations has tended to be reactive to trade union pressure. The new managerial regimes within Volvo now want to regain control of the production agenda. Since the car business was sold to Ford, there has been a discernible shift away from a soft to hard emphasis within Volvo's HR strategy. The evidence suggests that in an increasingly globalising world conditions for 'good work' are under constant erosion as Volvo develops new forms of labour management and begins dismantling its 'good work' philosophy. Labour and product market changes have undoubtedly led Volvo to move away from the 'Volvo Philosophy' – a 'philosophy' based around humanistic values (Volvo, 1996) towards the 'Volvo Way' – a 'way' based around issues of production, sales and management (Volvo, 2002). The employment relationship within the Swedish plants has shifted from one based on consent and co-operation to one in which it is more strained than ever before. The company, according to union activist, is no longer interested in finding common solutions and want to define the HR and production strategy wholly on their own terms and in so doing marginalise the Metal Workers Union, SM. It seems that although 'good work' is still a contested area, the development of the global truck and wider processes of globalisation have placed the agenda very much more in the hands of management.

References

Ahlstrand, R. (2000) *Förändring av deltagandet I produktione: exempel frän slutmonteringsfabriker i Volvo*, Lund: University of Lund Dissertations in Sociology 31.

Anxo, D. and Niklasson, H. (2004) *The Swedish Model in Turbulent Times: Decline or Renaissance*, Centre for Labour Market Policy Research (CAFO), Department of Economics and Statistics, University of Växjö.

Applebaum, H. (1998) *The American Work Ethic and Changing Work Force*, Westport, CN: Greenwood Press.

Axelopolous, M. and Cohen, J. (2003) 'Centralised Wage Bargaining and Structural Change in Sweden', *European Review of Economic History,* **7**, 331–366.

Berggren, C. (1992) *The Volvo Experience: Alternatives to Lean Production in the Swedish Auto Industry*, London: Macmillan.

Berggren, C. (1995) 'The Fate of the Branch Plants – Performance Versus Power', in *Enriching Production: Perspectives on Volvo's Uddevalla Plant as an Alternative to Lean Production* (Sandberg, Å. ed.), Aldershot: Avebury, pp. 105–126.

Blackler, F. and Brown, C. (1978) *Job Redesign and Management Control: Studies in British Leyland and Volvo*, New York: Praeger.

Boyer, R., Charron, E., Jurgens, U. and Tolliday, S. (eds) (1999) *Between Imitation and Innovation: The Transfer and Hybridization of Productive Models in the International Automobile Industry*, New York: Oxford University Press.

Boyer, R. and Freyssenet, M. (2002) *The Productive Models: Conditions of Profitability*, New York: Palgrave MacMillan.

Delsen, L. and van Veen, T. (1992) 'The Swedish Model: Relevant for other European Countries?' *British Journal of Industrial Relations,* **30**, 1, 83–105.

Engström, T. and Medbo, L. (1995) 'Production System Design – a Brief Summary of Some Swedish Design Efforts', in *Enriching Production: Perspectives on Volvo's Uddevalla Plant as an Alternative to Lean Production* (Sandberg, Å. ed.), Aldershot: Avebury.

Engström, T., Jonsson, D. and Medbo, L. (1996) *The Volvo Uddevalla Plant: Production Principles, Work Organization, Human Resources and Performance Aspects: Some Results from a Decade's Efforts towards Reformation of Assembly Work*, Report on Work Environment Fund Projects.

Goetschy, J. and Rozenblatt, P. (1992) 'France: The Industrial Relations System at Turing Point?', in *Industrial Relations in the New Europe* (Ferner, A. and Hyman, R., eds), London: Blackwell, pp. 404–444.

Harley, B., Hyman, J. and Thompson, P. (2005) 'The Paradoxes of Participation', in *Participation and Democracy at Work* (Harley, B., Hyman, J. and Thompson, P., eds), London: Palgrave MacMillan.

Himmelstrand, U., Ahrne, G., Lundberg, L. and Lundberg, L. (1981) *Beyond Welfare Capitalism: Issues, Actors and Forces in Societal Change,* London: Heinemann.

Hultman, L. (2006) *Focus on the Future – Learning from the Past.* Presentation at 'The End of the End of "good work" Conference', University of Boras, March 21–22, 2006.

Jenkins, S. and Delbridge, R. (2007) 'Disconnected Workplaces: Interests and Identities in the "High Performance" Factory', in *Searching for the Human in Human Resource Management* (Bolton, S.C. and Houlihan, M., eds), London: Palgrave.

Johannson, B. (1975) OJ 6638 760205 Dock Assembly VLV – Arendal' paper presented at Volvo internal seminar '*Socio-technical Experience Exchange Workshop*', December 10–11.

Katzenbach, J. R. and Smith, D. K. (1993) *The Wisdom of Teams: Creating the High Performance Organization*, Boston, MA: Harvard Business School Press.

Kjellberg, A. (1992) 'Sweden: Can the Model Survive', in *Industrial Relations in the New Europe* (Hyman, R. and Ferner, A., eds), London: Blackwell, pp. 89–142.

Korpi, W. (1978) *The Working Class in Welfare Capitalism*, London: Routledge.

Lash, S. (1985) 'The End of Neo-corporatism?: The Breakdown of Centralised Bargaining in Sweden', *British Journal of Industrial Relations,* **23**, 2, 215–239.

Linhart, R. (1980) *The Assembly Line*, Boston: University of Massachusetts Press.

Medbo, L. (1999) *Materials Supply and Product Descriptions for Assembly Systems: Design and Operation*, Ph.D. Department of Transportation and Logistics, Gothenburg: Chalmers Technical University.

Misgeld, K., Molin, K. and Åmark, K. (1988) *Creating Social Democracy: A Century of the Social Democratic Labor Party in Sweden*, Pennsylvania: Penn State University Press.

Nilsson, L. (1995) 'The Uddevalla Plant: Why Did it Succeed with a Holistic Approach and Why Did it Come to an End?' in *Enriching Production: Perspectives on Volvo's Uddevalla Plant as an Alternative to Lean Production* (Sandberg, Å. ed.), Aldershot: Avebury.

Persoff, V. A. (1999) *The Disappearance of Social Partnership in Sweden during the 1990s and its Sudden Reappearance in Late 1998,* Paper presented at the ECPR joint sessions Workshop on Concertation and Public Policy, Mannheim, March accessed on October 15, 2005 at www.essex.ac.uk/ecpr/jointsession/paperarchive/mannheim/w19/pestoff.pdf

Pulignano, V. and Stewart, P. (2006) 'Bureaucracy Transcended? New Patterns of Employment Regulation and Labour Control in the International Automotive Industry', *New Technology, Work and Employment*, **21**, 2, 90–106.

Ramsay, H. (1977) 'Cycles of Control: Worker Participation in Sociological and Historical Perspective', *Sociology*, **11**, 481–506.

Sandberg, Å. (ed.) (1995) *Enriching Production: Perspectives on Volvo's Uddevalla Plant as an Alternative to Lean Production*, Aldershot: Avebury.

Schumpeter, A. (1934) *The Theory of Economic Development*, Cambridge, MA: Harvard University Press.

Senge, P. (1990) *The Fifth Discipline: The Art and Practice of the Learning Organization*, New York: Doubleday.

Svenska Metall (1985) *Det goda arbetet*, Stockholm.

Taylor, R. (1989) 'Why Volvo is Planning to Go Back to the Future', *Financial Times*, 9 June.

Thompson, P. (2003) 'Disconnected Capitalism: Or Why Employers Can't Keep their Side of the Bargain', *Work, Employment and Society*, **17**, 2, 359–378.

Thompson, P., Wallace, T. and Flecker, J. (1995) 'It Aint What You Do it's the Way that You Do it: Production Organisation and Skill Utilisation in Commercial Vehicles', *Work, Employment and Society*, **9**, 4, 719–742.

Thörnqvist, C. (1999) 'The Decentralisation of Industrial Relations: The Swedish Case in Comparative Perspective', *European Journal of Industrial Relations*, **5**, 1, 71–87.

Volvo (1996) *The Volvo Philosophy*, Gothenburg: Volvo.

Volvo (2002) *The Volvo Way*, Gothenburg: Volvo.

Volvo (2003) *Annual Report*, Gothenburg: Volvo.

Wallace, T. (2000) 'Societal Effects Meets Sectoral Effects: Work Organisation, Competencies and Payment Systems in the Volvo Commercial Vehicle Division' *The International Journal of Human Resource Management*, **11**, 4, 715–735.

Wallace, T. (2004) 'Innovation and Hybridization: Managing the Introduction of Lean Production into Volvo do Brazil', *International Journal of Operations and Production Management*, **24**, 8, 801–819.

Womack, J., Roos, D. and Jones, D. S. (1990) *The Machine That Changed the World*, New York: Rawson Associates.

Wise, L. R. (1993) 'Whither Solidarity? Transitions in Swedish Public-Sector Pay Policy', *British Journal of Industrial Relations*, **31**, 1, 75–95.

12

The dignity of difference? Experiences of foreign workers in the multicultural workplace

Anastasia von Mende and Maeve Houlihan

What is it like to be demographically defined as different? What is the relationship between difference and dignity? And taking a more applied perspective, what does the idea of dignity mean for 'diversity management' in the workplace? In this chapter, we explore these questions from two perspectives: on the one hand, we examine what is being said about diversity in the management literatures and what organisations and managers seem to be doing about it. On the other, we take a look at the stories and direct experiences of foreign workers in a newly multicultural Ireland. These frontline accounts move us from abstract theory to the lived reality of the migrant worker and offer glimpses of the essence, implications and fragile character of respect for the person manifest in the contemporary workplace.

Before going much further, it is important to consider what exactly diversity is, or more precisely, what is typically meant when diversity is talked about in an organisational context. Clearly, as a broad term encompassing any characteristic that can be used to differentiate one person from another, diversity has many potential dimensions. Among businesses and institutions, the term is commonly invoked in a *demographic sense* to refer to *categorisations* of difference such as gender, age, ability, ethnicity, class and social status, education level, sexual orientation and religious belief. 'Diversity management' has similarly found a place in common parlance, as a loose set of ideas about harvesting synergies and accommodating (or smoothing) differences. The pervasive imprint of business and institutional language on society has seen both terms become widely used, arguably displacing more political notions such as inequality, minority or disadvantage.

We confess considerable ambivalence towards the static nature of a demographic approach to diversity. On the one hand, given an unequal society, 'counting the countable' is an important step towards making material inequalities visible and urgent where they might otherwise be opaque. On the other, however, this categorical way of thinking has tensions and consequences: putting people into boxes, stereotyping, politically correct rhetoric that can be a little stifling or patronising and the simplistic reduction of difference to a metric or 'problem' – something to be counted and managed. We fear that the narrowness of the demographic approach masks the eclecticism and extent of individual difference that defines each and every one of us: differences in personalities, work orientations, communication styles, attitudes to conflict and more. Indeed, it is these very dimensions that come to the fore, as this chapter unfolds. So let us say at the outset that while this chapter engages with a specifically demographic category, we view this as but one dimension of human diversity, and a narrow one at that.

Setting this ambivalence to one side, the specific focal point of this chapter is the multicultural workplace, and from an individual perspective, the experience of 'foreignness'. We single out this dimension partly due to its contemporary prominence as an issue, but more simply as a proximate means of exploring what it is like to be 'other', and of grasping the essential dignity of difference.

Diversity management and multiculturalism

While migration has always been a pattern in the global workplace, undoubtedly the multicultural organisation has come to increased prominence in recent decades. Opened borders, ease of mobility and communication and shifting labour markets mean that today multiculturalism is making the workplace a richer, and more challenging place to be. Migration is part and parcel of globalisation and a world economy now best described as an interconnected mass of multinational companies and multicultural markets (Bond and Pyle, 1998; Milliken and Martins, 1996; Thompson, 2003). And yet the idea that globalised business is the puppeteer pulling so many strings is only half a truth. While the boundary between choice and necessity is not always clear-cut, we feel strongly that the individuality and active agency of foreign workers must be put at the centre of any analysis of the multicultural workplace. At an individual level, people leave their home place in search of better-paying jobs and new opportunities or experiences, to join partners and families or because hardship of some kind or another forced them out of their home country. Whatever their motives, what is certain is that foreign workers are now entering, intermixing and gaining power in workplaces and organisations that were once more culturally homogeneous (Johnston and Packer, 1997; Konrad, 2003; Shoobridge, 2006).

This has implications not only for the way organisations conduct business, but for the way all individuals, native and foreign, experience work. It also raises vital and contentious questions about the extent to which diversity incites or justifies variation in the treatment of individuals at work, about immigration policies and about labour market opportunism. A central question raised by multiculturalism is the evolving nature of work and working conditions, including the rights and roles of foreign employees both compared to those of the native population, and among each other. At the heart of this concern lies the notion that all individuals are equal, regardless of individual difference or origin. Yet, it may not be so easy as to say that all employees should be treated exactly the same and all differences ignored. While diversity management approaches emphasise the right of each individual to be different, by ignoring the fact that diversity usually involves competing rights and perspectives, and by failing to address the causes of difference they risk institutionalising inequality and failing to stimulate change.

The tensions between *assimilation* and *accommodation* approaches to diversity run through migration policy debate and are echoed in organisational practices, reflecting arguments that tread murky waters and are far from clear-cut. Consider, for example, the following scenarios: Should foreign workers be allowed to compete for the same jobs as natives, or is it alright for them to be channelled into areas of labour shortage only, regardless of their capacity and training? Is it fully ethical to employ foreign workers for poorly paid jobs that natives 'won't do', simply because the pay and working conditions exceed those to be found in their home country? Is it fair for foreigners to be overlooked for promotion due to lack of cultural knowledge or linguistic fluency? Is it fair to discount the work experience and education that foreigners have from their home country when they apply for jobs in another country just because it is hard to compare the quality of this experience and education? Should foreigners be allowed special treatment to accommodate their religious, cultural and travel needs? None of these are merely academic questions, as their fierce debate amongst unions, policy makers and civic discussion shows. And yet, the absence of policy in their regard causes its own problems and inequalities. In

2005 for instance, the cases of *Irish Ferries*, *Gama* and *Gate Gourmet* each galvanised attention towards the ways organisations can, in the search to drive down labour costs, exploit legislative gaps and labour market inequalities by outsourcing to less expensive labour markets or locally substituting domestic with foreign workers and discriminating amongst nationality and employment status of workers.

Although critiqued both for excessive political correctness and for the sanitisation of difference, diversity management has since the early 1990s consequently become a focal issue in contemporary human resource practice. Many organisations have developed elaborate diversity schemes, often first arising reactively out of issues of compliance with anti-discrimination laws (Thomas, 1990) and then broadened to meet a variety of strategic business and sometimes moral goals. The result is a blurred and arguably ineffectual positioning of diversity management between the requirements to protect individual rights and the management of organisational objectives. This duality is reflected in the management and organisation literatures, where although scholars have long acknowledged that understanding and management of diversity is important, analysis remains underdeveloped (Nkomo and Cox, 1996).

In joining these debates, we cannot but notice how little voice is given to the experiences of individuals in the diversity management literature, betraying a rather elite, managerialist perspective that many times appears to treat the very people that make up diversity as silent, uninvolved objects of work. This is something we strive to address with this chapter. By focusing on the experience of diversity from the perspective of those at the front end of difference in multicultural organisations, we hear something of the dignity of difference and its frequent neglect. That said, we are also not naïve to the global structural forces that shape the state of this diversity. What we will aim to emphasise, however, is that within these rigid structural walls exist people who live out this dignity of difference every day, and it is this dignity that we feel needs to come to the fore if we are to ultimately understand and seriously engage with diversity, its meanings, questions and consequences.

Where diversity meets dignity

We are particularly interested in how rarely the idea of dignity has been applied to the experience of difference. As an example, in the multicultural organisation literature, very little discussion ventures to explore what dignity means when foreign workers encounter specific issues, such as language and cultural difficulties, the recognition of skills and qualifications, employment opportunities and interactions with customers and colleagues. Yet it is in such day-to-day occurrences that the true fate of difference can be seen, and that dignity is gained or lost.

The goal of this chapter, therefore, is to look at dignity in the myriad of ways in which it is *felt* by foreign workers, using both research and workers' own stories to paint a picture of what *dignified diversity* might signify. We begin by presenting a framework that brings together dignity and diversity, and move on to explore how the two intersect in the workplace.

When the topic of diversity is broached in the literature and by practitioners, it usually treats differences in people (like culture, values, nationality, ethnicity and so on) as variables that either have to be managed, assimilated or removed. This has led to some very mixed results as to whether diversity is effective or ineffective within an organisation, and whether its results are positive or negative. For example, some research shows that diversity can increase productivity (Hartenian and Gudmundson, 2000; Ng and Tung, 1998) and problem-solving (Watson et al., 1993), while others find that diversity leads to greater dislike, mistrust, stereotyping, communication difficulties and interpersonal stress (Fine, 1996; Hambrick et al., 1998), and less cohesion and greater turnover (O'Reilly et al., 1989).

We would suggest that a deep limitation of such research, and perhaps a reason for its inconclusiveness, is that too much attention is put on static demographic differences, at the expense of a fuller engagement with how diverse people work together. The consequence is a limited and partial view of how diversity is actually enacted in the workplace. Differences in people may be given, but such differences only come to light through behaviours and interactions with others (Hambrick et al., 1998). The framework proposed here argues that the outcomes of diversity are better seen as continually evolving processes rather than as point-in-time measurements and draws attention to the microdynamics of diversity manifesting through interpersonal interaction. Seen in this light, equality is a function not only of the organisation's treatment of people's differences, but of the web of interactions and relationships that unfold between and among managers, co-workers and customers, whether native or foreign.

Of course, each of these relationships is deeply embedded in a structural net of labour markets, economic and legal systems and social rules that are not easily separated out, or so easily changed. The hierarchies and boundaries in these structures make inequality an almost inevitable consequence, so we do not mean to suggest that inequality is merely a product of individual relationships or can be corrected by such routes. Yet, within these microdynamics and interpersonal interactions, a story emerges of the enactment of inequality and the challenges to individual dignity that merits closer examination. As people come into contact with each other and social structures, they change and are changed by them. It is in these encounters that we see the dignity of diversity in action, and we thus stress their relevance to the perception and experience of diversity.

The following sections will elaborate on this framework by applying it to various situations that affect culturally diverse people in the workplace. Specifically, we look at dignity as it is experienced in three areas: *relationships with others*, *language and communication* and *the conditions of the job itself*.

These accounts are drawn from foreign workers in a newly multicultural Ireland. With a population of a little over four million, but an estimated 70 million descendents abroad, Ireland has long been known as a net donor of migrants to the world labour market, while ostensibly remaining a relatively homogenous (catholic, white) and 'tight' (Bochner, 2000, p. 233) society, at home. The so-called 'celtic tiger' economic boom of the 1990s and its attendant labour shortages, EU enlargement and liberalised employment laws have changed all this, and for the first time the long trend of Irish emigration has reversed. In the years from 2000 to 2006, Ireland received approximately 350,000 immigrants (CSO, 2005), or close to 60,000 newcomers a year.[1] As a result, approximately 9 per cent of the Irish workforce and 10 per cent of the general population is now foreign-born (Holmquist, 2006). Such newfound cultural diversity makes Ireland an interesting case through which to explore the dynamics and dignities of being different. While the stories told here come from migrants to Ireland, we suggest that they reflect, at least to some degree, the experiences of foreign workers everywhere.

Relationships: Bridging the space between us?

Whether with co-workers, superiors or customers, relationships at work undoubtedly have a tremendous influence on the quality of working life, having the ability to make good work great and bad work tolerable. Dignity at work is strongly tied to the quality of these relationships and, good or bad, determines in large part how foreign workers feel about their work and their experience as immigrants.

In a very practical sense, faced with knowing very few people in a new country, many immigrants find that the workplace provides good opportunities for socialising and making friends and bridging the loneliness of being separated from family and familiarity. One Lithuanian hotel worker in Ireland clearly exemplified this point when she said, 'All my friends work here'. Often such relationships can help give support at work and strongly mark the quality of the work experience, irrespective of the quality of the work. A Chinese worker, for example, who trained as a solicitor in her home country, talks of her experiences while working as a domestic in a mental hospital,

'I made my first Irish friend there. She knew that I was trying to learn about the Irish culture so she taught me a lot. And every time we had tea break, she had me sit down with her, and we always spent lunchtime together'.

It is not easy to reconcile the transition from work of professional status to work as a domestic, yet this is less the focus of her analysis than the relationships she made there. The importance of this human connection becomes even clearer in its absence. Changing to another job where she found it difficult to socialise, this initial connection took on even more importance:

'Sometimes I would call her, and she would tell me to come back so that we could have a small chat. One day I went back and she had prepared some food in the kitchen and gave me a very big hug. I was really moved at that time because you have a hard time during the day time, but when someone gives you a hug and prepares some food and gives you comfort, it is very precious for a foreign person here'.

It is being recognised, appreciated and taken care of that this person appears to value most, as making difficult job situations bearable and sometimes even enjoyable. Research confirms that emotion-based relationships help to facilitate interaction and information sharing among multicultural people, reducing conflict and intolerance and increasing effectiveness, suggesting that peer supportive organisational climates may be more relevant as dimensions of dignity than, for example, job quality (Bacharach et al., 2005). We would not diminish the importance of job quality; however undoubtedly friendship with co-workers was commonly mentioned by our field respondents as one of the key sources of work-related pleasure. For instance, when asked what it was that made her happiest when working, a Latin American cook in a luxury brand hotel simply said, 'It's the interaction with people'.

Clearly, not all relationships at work will run such a smooth and positive course, nor can such a condition be legislated for in diversity management programmes. However, many organisations have been able to successfully create cultures that encourage peer support in general, socialising among co-workers and mentorship programmes, all of which can go a long way to informally help integrate diverse people.

The way people are treated by their supervisors similarly matters. Some research has indicated that relationships between demographically dissimilar superiors and subordinates may be more prone to negative perceptions (Tsui and O'Reilly, 1989), misunderstandings and potentially discrimination. This is perhaps what happened to a Polish man working in a photo laboratory in Ireland. When asked what his worst experience was as a foreign worker, he talked about the time his bosses fired the middle manager who was also a foreigner and who fought hard to better the working conditions of the employees. The two people that were chosen to replace her were the only two Irish people working in the laboratory, however, as this Polish man puts it:

> 'Both were not the most senior employees nor the best employees, to be honest. And the rest of us felt quite cheated, like it wasn't really fair. [Our former manager] was really good to us and they had a totally different way of doing things. They didn't care about us, they didn't even say hello to us. They cared only about the company, they were like programmed robots'.

But foreign workers also recognise and appreciate good managers who support them, help them learn and respect their different choices. One Chinese IT employee talks fondly about her manager and how the manager both adapted to her work habits as well as helped her adapt to the new culture's working style:

> 'Before I was working very late and they didn't accept this, always wanting me to go home early. As time went on and we discussed this, finally [my manager] understood that it was my habit, and she told me that she respected my habit. My manager has tried to do a lot of things to support me. For example, she tried to teach me what people usually do during the daytime, and if I had any problems that I could go to her and she would explain things to me. She's really good, and she supports me day to day, really hand in hand, so I try to follow her suggestions and to mix with people and after a year it's become easier'.

This Chinese worker's story about her manager provides a clear expression of what fairness, equality and dignified treatment means to her. This example shows the power of negotiating the relationship until agreements are reached that satisfy both parties. The positive outcome in this situation is not the result of managing away the person's cultural differences as if they were a problem to solve, nor outright accepting them out of a need to champion diversity, but rather of both sides learning about each other, agreeing to compromise and adapt where necessary, remaining supportive and patient, while standing ground on what is important for each.

Interestingly, customers can often pose the most challenging interactions that foreign workers have to deal with. Research (Harrison et al., 1998) suggests that when people first meet, they are more likely to categorise each other on surface-level traits, such as gender, ethnicity and age, as these provide the most readily available information about the person. The longer people work together and consequently the more they interact with one another, the less important become these surface-level traits and the more salient become deep-level factors such as attitudes, values and beliefs. It is theorised that these deep-level factors represent a more accurate knowledge of the person and that they can lead to greater interpersonal attraction between people (Allport, 1954). As compared with co-workers and supervisors, however, interactions with customers tend to be short-lived one-off occurrences that provide little opportunity for each party to get to know each other. Consequently, it is from customers that many foreigners most frequently report bad and undignified treatment.

For example, one Chinese employee in a fast food restaurant explained that while her co-workers were very nice, her time working there was not enjoyable because she often had problems with customers who would get annoyed with her when she did not understand them and made mistakes, or some of the teenagers who would purposely try to cause trouble because:

> 'they thought that foreigners were easy targets, and sometimes when we worked in the lobby, the area where the customers eat, they would try to cause trouble, making a mess, hitting you. It wasn't violent hitting, but just to annoy you, or they would say some bad words to you. Sometimes we would try to protect ourselves, but if it got worse, we would go to the security people and ask them to do something about it'.

While questions must be asked about the dynamics producing such customer behaviour, the support this employee received from her co-workers and managers in taking her side and quickly dealing with the problem customers is an example of how organisational support for foreign workers can play a key role in protecting employee dignity.

We see in these stories a common theme of respect, its power and its vulnerability. Of course respect whether in the form of considerate friendships with co-workers or understanding and cooperative relationships with superiors is important for all workers, but its presence or absence is heightened in the experience of diversity and plays a key role in affording diversity its due dignity.

Communication: Lost in translation?

Language forms the core of communication, and communication of socialisation. It is through these that we expressively manifest who we are to the outside world, and so they become vital for how we relate to others and how others perceive us. Little research has actually been done on the impact of language in the workplace, but some ethnographic research undertaken in multiethnic organisations (e.g., Ogbonna and Harris, 2006) suggests that language plays an important role in constructing ideas of discrimination and difference at the level of both the organisation and the individual.

Organisations, for their part, play a big part in creating meaning for difference and otherness through their discourses and rhetoric on diversity (Kamp and Hagedorn-Rasmussen, 2004). Many, for example, construct diversity in strategic business terms, emphasising how employees with transcultural backgrounds can use their cultural knowledge to help the company adapt to and access globalised, multicultural markets and suppliers. Others frame it more simply as the need to hire culturally diverse people in order to avoid labour shortages. For example, one hotel manager explained their rationale for recruiting foreign workers, thus: 'we needed to start the new hotel with 250 [staff members], and for the first few months, we were scouring the local market, getting as many local people as we could, but it just wasn't happening and we weren't filling the gaps'. Despite its frequency, however, this type of perspective on diversity tends to objectify foreign workers as mere economic resources. Some companies claim a more personal consideration of the worker, emphasising that each person is a unique and valued asset to the company, and encouraged to learn from each other's differences and challenge each other for their own personal development. Yet in many respects, there is reason to be sceptical. The persistence of discrimination, inequalities and power difference suggests that the rhetoric of diversity can be criticised as sanitising difference, and simply masking or attenuating underlying conflicts (Netmetz and Christensen, 1996).

However, language has more than symbolic importance and can be a very real barrier mediating interpersonal communication and relationships for migrant workers, and thus the quality and equity of their experiences. When it comes to individuals, language and communication is the topic that comes up most frequently in conversations with foreign workers because it is at the heart of most situations they face, from forming social relations to being able to do certain work. The challenge for most foreign workers is of course that they are working in a country where the local language is not their native one, and the consequence of not fluently speaking this language can be considerable.

In terms of personal relations, although most foreigners will interact and form friendships with co-workers from the local country and other foreign countries, many admit that they spend quite a bit of time with people of their own country in large part because of the language and the cultural aspects, such as formalities and humour, which come with it. One Chinese worker, for example, said that she preferred working on her own and found it difficult to associate with her local colleagues because:

> 'it's still a little bit scary for me to talk to people I don't know, especially the local people. I know they're very good and when we have some jobs that we need to cooperate on, they're very kind and very responsible, but I still don't have a very big self-confidence... I just worry that I'll do a bad job of chatting with people, and I'm just still not very confident about my talking abilities'.

A Swiss woman similarly confessed to usually socialising with other French-speaking people at work because it was easier and more comfortable in terms of communicating ideas and sharing jokes. But this is of course not to say that foreigners do not at all mingle with other co-workers, and many examples of friendships between local and foreign workers emerged in this research. Nevertheless, segregation along linguistic lines would seem to be generally accepted by natives and non-natives alike. Some organisations practice local language only policies, such that foreigners are strongly discouraged from speaking their own language, in the belief that others might see it as rude or as a way to gossip unobserved, thus reinforcing the heavily qualified nature of respect for individual difference that diversity management perspectives at times offer.

Professionally, it is quite widely acknowledged that workers not fluent (itself a subjective term) in the local language will face problems in getting certain jobs and promotions, manifestly affecting the opportunities available to foreigners. In the course of discussion about why foreigners do not often get higher-level jobs in Ireland, a recruiter for multilingual positions explained it thus:

'Well it depends where they're from. If they're from the UK, they definitely have the opportunity to get a high-profile job. If you have, for instance, on your CV that you're French, a recruiter will say, "Ok, I can put you in a call centre position". If you're brilliant in something, like you've got a PhD in computer science or whatever, they might put you in a technical support role. If you tell them, "I don't want a call centre job, I want an English job", your English really has to be good, otherwise you would never get the job. It really depends on the language. If you're fluent in a language, then you can get a job, otherwise, you will end up getting something bilingual in a call centre'.

Importantly, many foreigners feel that their lack of language skills gives the local employees a negative impression of their *other* skills and intellectual abilities. In the words of one Polish worker:

'Often people think that if you can't say something in English, it's because you just don't know it. Which is the craziest thing ever, but I've found it quite a lot actually'.

The conflation of communication style differences and even accent with inability to understand or communicate is common, and part of a negative stereotyping that greatly hinders the full appreciation and utilisation of foreign workers' skills in the workplace. An Indian nurse had similar problems when co-workers associated her lack of fluency in English with a lack of understanding:

'They think I'm not competent in communication. I want to make sure that things do not go wrong. Even though I hear, I want to confirm the things they say, so I will ask them questions. But they think in a different way, they think that I didn't follow them, that I'm not keeping up with them'.

In summary, what one comes to appreciate from these stories is how closely dignity is linked to being understood, both profession-ally and socially, which in turn is closely linked to one's ability to express oneself in a certain language. This is a difficult road to traverse given that language skills are generally viewed as the responsibility of the individual. Labour market demands have led some companies to offer language courses or provide multilingual application forms, company handbooks and written safety material. Nonetheless, the dig-nity of difference is vulnerable when the talents of individuals are overlooked simply because their ability to speak the native language is less advanced. Organisations wishing to embrace diversity do well to consider this issue.

Job conditions: Choosing or losing?

So far, we have discussed how foreign workers are affected by the quality of the relationships they have with others at work, as well as the challenges they face in communicating in a language that is not their own. Now we turn to the final piece of this puzzle, which is the job itself and the conditions and choices surrounding it. We find here that often, despite high levels of education and abilities, many foreign workers end up in lower-level and lower-quality jobs that inherently tend to be socially less respected than higher-level jobs. In Ireland, research (Barrett et al., 2005) has shown that many immigrants are *underemployed*; that is, they work in jobs whose skill requirements are below the skill level and educational attainment of the worker. There are likely a number of reasons for this including a lack of recognition of foreign qualifications on the part of employers, and incomplete knowledge about the labour market or language issues on the part of the foreign worker. But what consequences does this have for the worker herself?

In general, it appears that many foreign workers hold a tacit acceptance that starting in a new country entails taking on lower-level jobs for a while, at least until they can better establish themselves and learn about the work environment. And yet this would not always seem justified. One Indian nurse with 14 years of nursing experience back home was forced to start again at the bottom of the hierarchy in terms of job duties (although her years of previous experience were recognised in relation to her salary). Her acceptance of this, though puzzling, is unequivocal:

> 'I was already prepared for going into a new place, a new situation, new environment, so obviously I need to learn from the beginning. So it does not make any difference to me. I was not bothered. I just believe that work should get done'.

A Chinese worker echoes this sentiment but expresses stronger discontent that her hard-won past achievements are often not recognised:

> 'I think that when you're a foreigner, it's always the case [that you work in lower-level jobs] when you start, so I had this kind of mental preparation before I came here. But I didn't realise that you would be looked down on sometimes just because you are a foreigner.

Nobody wants to understand your background and nobody wants to respect you for what you did before'.

Here an important tension emerges with our earlier point about interpersonal interaction, the notion that difference requires the work of effort and understanding on behalf of both parties to the relationship. The closing comments of the Chinese worker above raise a question about how willing native workers and employers are to extend this effort. While comparative improvement in pay or working conditions from home to host country are often put forward as a justification, underemployment raises questions about how fully natives and employers engage with foreign workers as equals, or recognise their potential. And from a resource perspective, it highlights missed opportunities for organisations and host countries to benefit from these skills. Official recognition of qualification equivalencies is an important first step that many organisations and governments are beginning to take to counteract this situation.

While there is every reason to question outcomes such as underemployment, the conscious recognition of certain tradeoffs in the decision to travel for work serves to reinforce the fact that foreign workers are active, conscious choice makers. As one Eastern European man says:

'I had better qualifications than the job that I got, but I thought, I earn good money, the work is close to where I live, so I'm going to stay with it. The people were nice and there was a good atmosphere in the company. I also didn't mind because I knew it would only be temporary'.

It is important to see that underlying this acceptance a clear equation is operating in relation to personal dignity and the surrounding conditions of the job. This equation weighs up certain inequalities against key dimensions already touched upon (good relationships, communication and being respected), but also money and other practical considerations, and notably, as we see from the Eastern European gentleman above, another key dimension of human dignity, hope. Hope for the future, that a better position can eventually be had. In the words of one worker: 'You do think that things will get better, so with this hope and confidence, you can survive those hard times'.

However, such stoicism does not eliminate vulnerability and clearly foreign workers do not always have the means to speak up and ask for better conditions when work situations are not good. Since few have either the financial cushion or social support necessary to go without employment for a while, there is a greater risk attached to losing a hard-won livelihood, and hence a greater propensity to tolerating unfairness or inequality. Going back to the story of the Polish worker in the photo laboratory who felt the new managers treated the employees badly and did not do their work properly, he explains that:

> 'the Polish and other non-Irish people were afraid to say that [to the upper managers] and get fired because for them it would have been a loss of income and along with that their way of living'.

This suggests perhaps that foreign workers can be prisoners to, as well as authors of, their choices, particularly those economic aspects of the equations that may have brought them to where they are. Whether the risk to them is real or not, the perceived threat can be compounded by cultural differences. A Chinese worker says, for example, that:

> 'the thing about Chinese people is that they don't like to express themselves a lot. So when bad things do happen, they don't have a very good channel to address it'.

She goes on to say that this is a problem especially for people in lower-level jobs:

> 'because [employers] have a lot of people waiting outside the gate to work in those jobs. Nobody cares about this. It's a worse situation in that case'.

Again, this reinforces the point that foreign workers need to be heard and afforded the space to express themselves and be recognised. Dignity in this case means having a voice to negotiate their side of the deal. Given the circumstances they find themselves in, foreign workers demonstrate a great willingness to accept jobs that many locals may themselves not want nor be able to do. But with that comes a responsibility from the employer to provide them with decent working conditions, and especially opportunities for speaking up and for bettering their lot at work.

Final thoughts

The stories and anecdotes shared over the last few pages not only give some factual accounts of the experience of difference in the multicultural workplace, they offer significant doubt to the notion that difference is a static and unchanging thing. While these accounts would lead us to question the degree to which diversity is truly being addressed in organisations despite the prominence of its rhetoric, we suggest that diversity management's simplistic construction of difference is no answer. Policies on diversity that stop at the level of categorising and attenuating demographic differences would seem to offer little by way of addressing these narratives, instead focusing managers on cultural stereotypes, not offending, fulfilling ratios and dodging discrimination legislation. Little wonder then, that there is so little time and energy left to consider the richer picture of difference, or to harvest its opportunities.

To Pless and Maak (2004), diversity is,

> 'first and foremost, a cultural question and thus a question of norms, values, beliefs and expectations. As such, it is an ethical question and determined by some very essential founding principles of human coexistence' (p. 130).

In this chapter, we have listened to the voices of diverse individuals expressing their dignity, and the many challenges to it. We would conclude that dignified coexistence means fair treatment for the individual, whether foreign or native, as an individual and in relationship to others. We have emphasised the enactment of dignity through interpersonal interactions and the dimensions of language and work quality.

In particular, we have come to conclude that the agency and choices of the individual must be put at the heart of this analysis. While we might wish for a fairer world and unequivocally reject the exploitation of foreign workers, we have through this journey learned to respect the motivations and choices underlying their experiences. We have heard from foreign workers a pragmatic view of their role in the workforce and the equations that underlie their choices. In large part, it is economics that brought them to where they are, be it that the company needed such workers or that workers were looking for better job opportunities abroad or a combination of both. As part of this equation, they reconcile differences between their position in the job market and those of natives with the fact they are new to the country and lack, at least in the beginning, essential language skills, cultural acumen, social networks and job market knowledge. This they know, so for them dignity is not so much about being treated the same, but about being respected for their situation in life and what they can in fact contribute. It is about the availability of supportive social relationships, among co-workers, with superiors, local people and people from their own national and linguistic groups; about having skills and qualifications recognised; and when the job is bad or working conditions poor, it is also about being heard and being given hope that things can change. From listening to the voices of the individuals contributing to this chapter, most of all we are drawn to conclude that it is the age old issues of respect, communication and work quality that will do most to engage with the dignity of difference.

References

Allport, G. W. (1954) *The Nature of Prejudice*, Cambridge, Massachusetts: Addison-Wesley.

Bacharach, S. B., Bamberger, P. A. and Vashdi, D. (2005) 'Diversity and Homophily at Work: Supportive Relations Among White and African-American Peers', *Academy of Management Journal*, **48**, 4, 619–644.

Barrett, A., Bergin, A. and Duffy, D. (2005) *The Labour Market Characteristics and Labour Market Impacts of Immigrants in Ireland*. Discussion paper no. 1553, Bonn: Institute for the Study of Labor.

Bochner, S. (2000) 'The Majority Experience: An International Commentary', in *Cultivating Pluralism: Psychological, Social and Cultural Perspectives on a Changing Ireland* (MacLachlan, M. and O'Connell, M., eds), Dublin: Oak Trees Press, pp. 219–239.

Bond, M. A. and Pyle, J. L. (1998) 'The Ecology of Diversity in Organizational Settings: Lessons from a Case Study', *Human Relations*, **51**, 5, 589–623.

CIA World Factbook: United States (Updated: September 7, 2006) Available on the World Wide Web at: https://www.cia.gov/cia/publications/factbook/geos/us.html

CSO (2005) *Population and Migration Estimates,* April, Dublin: CSO.

Fine, M. G. (1996) 'Cultural Diversity in the Workplace: The State of the Field', *The Journal of Business Communication*, **33**, 4, 485–502.

Hambrick, D. C., Canney Davison, S., Snell, S. A. and Snow, C. C. (1998) 'When Groups Consist of Multiple Nationalities: Towards a New Understanding of the Implications', *Organization Studies*, **19**, 2, 181–205.

Harrison, D. A., Price, K. H. and Bell, M. P. (1998) 'Beyond Relational Demography: Time and the Effects of Surface- and Deep-Level Diversity on Work Group Cohesion', *Academy of Management Journal*, **41**, 1, 96–107.

Hartenian, L. S. and Gudmundson, D. E. (2000) 'Cultural Diversity in Small Business: Implications for Firm Performance', *Journal of Developmental Entrepreneurship*, **5**, 3, 209–219.

Holmquist, K. (2006) 'What Will it Mean to be Irish Two Decades into the 21st Century?' *The Irish Times*, 11 March, News Features.

Immigrant Council of Ireland (2005) *Background Information and Statistics on Immigration to Ireland*, Dublin: Immigrant Council of Ireland.

Johnston, W. and Packer, A. (1997) *Workforce 2000: Work and Workers for the 21st Century*, Indianapolis: Hudson Institute.

Kamp, A. and Hagedorn-Rasmussen, P. (2004) 'Diversity Management in a Danish Context: Towards a Multicultural or Segregated Working Life?' *Economic and Industrial Democracy*, **25**, 4, 525–554.

Konrad, A. M. (2003) 'Special Issue Introduction: Defining the Domain of Workplace Diversity Scholarship', *Group & Organization Management*, **28**, 1, 4–17.

Milliken, F. J. and Martins, L. L. (1996) 'Searching for Common Threads: Understanding the Multiple Effects of Diversity in Organizational Groups', *Academy of Management Review*, **21**, 2, 402–433.

Netmetz, P. L. and Christensen, S. L. (1996) 'The Challenge of Cultural Diversity: Harnessing a Diversity of Views to Understand Multiculturalism', *Academy of Management Review*, **21**, 2, 434–462.

Ng, E. S. W. and Tung, R. L. (1998) 'Ethno-Cultural Diversity and Organizational Effectiveness: A Field Study', *The International Journal of Human Resource Management*, **9**, 6, 980–995.

Nkomo, S. M. and Cox, T., Jr. (1996) 'Diverse Identities in Organizations', in *Handbook of Organization Studies* (Clegg, S. R., Hardy, C. and Nord, W. R., eds), London: Sage Publications, pp. 340–356.

Ogbonna, E. and Harris, L. C. (2006) 'The Dynamics of Employee Relationships in an Ethnically Diverse Workforce', *Human Relations*, **59**, 3, 379–407.

O'Reilly, C. A., Caldwell, D. F. and Barnett, W. P. (1989) Work Group Demography, Social Integration, and Turnover', *Administrative Science Quarterly*, **34**, 1, 21–37.

Pless, N. M. and Maak, T. (2004) 'Building an Inclusive Diversity Culture: Principles, Processes and Practice', *Journal of Business Ethics*, **54**, 129–147.

Shoobridge, G. E. (2006) 'Multi-Ethnic Workforce and Business Performance: Review and Synthesis of the Empirical Literature', *Human Resource Development Review*, **5**, 1, 92–137.

Thomas, R. R., Jr. (1990) 'From Affirmative Action to Affirming Diversity', *Harvard Business Review*, March/Apr, 107–117.

Thompson, P. (2003) 'Disconnected Capitalism: Or, Why Employers Can't Keep Their Side of the Bargain', *Work, Employment and Society*, **17**, 2, 359–378.

Tsui, A. S. and O'Reilly, C. A. (1989) 'Beyond Simple Demographic Effects: The Importance of Relational Demography on Superior-Subordinate Dyads', *Academy of Management Journal*, **32**, 2, 402–423.

Watson, W. E., Kumar, K. and Michaelsen, L. K. (1993) 'Cultural Diversity's Impact on Interaction Process and Performance: Comparing homogeneous and Diverse Task Groups', *Academy of Management Journal*, **36**, 3, 590–602.

13

Short stories from industry

This is a chapter comprising six individual reflective pieces that consider dignity and its role in corporate life. Two of the pieces are written from the perspective of people working in senior roles in various organisations who attempt to address issues involved in dignity at work in their own workplace, with the ultimate aim of creating 'cultures of respect'. In the third piece, a practitioner considers how money as a motivator may be a missing dimension when considering dignity at work. In the fourth and fifth pieces, we hear compelling personal stories that shed light on the devastating effects of denials of dignity at work. And, finally, the concluding section of this chapter is made up of a selection of 'voices' – people from all walks of life talking about their experiences and definitions of dignity at work.

1. The Co-operative Group: a case study in building a culture of respect

Amanda Jones

Most people know the Co-operative Group as their local store that provides top-up convenience shopping. Few are familiar with the scale and size of the whole Group. The Co-operative Group is an association of people united voluntarily to meet common economic, cultural and social needs through a jointly owned, democratically controlled enterprise. The Group focuses on supporting the needs of its membership and customers within the communities in which it trades. It has a wide and diverse set of businesses in both Retail Trading and Financial Services employing circa 70,000 people. The Group's approach to the provision of goods and services is based on strong business performance and under-pinned by open and honest values and principles together with an ethical approach that enhances the lives of our people, members, customers and the communities in which we trade.

The Food Retail division is the largest business within the Co-operative Group, pioneering *Fairtrade* and clear labelling as well as a whole range of ideas to protect the environment. Co-operative Pharmacy is the UK's fourth largest pharmacy providing healthcare services within the community. *Travelcare* is the UK's largest independent travel agent approaching customer service with a 'right to know' policy based on openness, honesty and impartial advice and no ownership links with any holiday company. *Funeralcare* is the UK's leading funeral director dedicated to providing help and support to bereaved families. It also manages two coffin factories and a national memorial masonry service. *Farmcare* is the UK's largest commercial farmer and the Group also owns a shoe business, home stores, an electrical online service, a significant property business, has a joint venture with Scottish Power to run a wind farm and sources nearly all of its electrical power from green services.

As can be seen, the Group has a diverse business portfolio and, therefore, a diverse employee base. The Group's core principle is to provide services that are built on ethical principles which, we recognise, requires the commitment and energy of its employees. To respond to and engage employee diversity effectively, we know it is important to create a culture of respect for everyone. Given the wide recognition of the Co-operative Group's core principles, it would be expected that we would have an ethos of treating our colleagues with respect; that, quite simply, it would be the right thing for us to do. This is certainly the case but we also recognise that there are significant business reasons for being proactive and effective in this arena; it is part of how we enable our brand values, how we engage our people and how we deliver better services to our customers. These are core issues for all UK organisations to consider.

A basic starting point, and what we see as a fundamental aspect of creating a culture of respect, is to eradicate workplace bullying. The extent of bullying and harassment across the UK and the corresponding costs to UK businesses is really quite shocking. One in eight UK employees, that is 3 million employees, has been bullied in the last five years; half of them say bullying is commonplace and a quarter say it is getting worse. Bullying costs the UK £30 billion per annum through absence and that amounts to over £1,000 per working adult. An employee experiencing bullying becomes up to 50 per cent less effective, even if they do not take time off. Bullying leads to poor health, low morale, low productivity and poor attention to health and safety. The cost of replacing an employee who leaves because they are bullied is circa £5,000 and can be as much as three times annual salary. Grievance processes will cost businesses up to £3,000 and employment tribunals up to £1 million. The business argument is compelling, whether you look at the cost of getting it wrong or not getting it right. Disengaged people, people who cannot face the thought of work or cannot concentrate on it, do not help UK businesses be successful. If challenged, none of us want to work in an environment like that and, hopefully, none of us want to manage an environment like that.

In response to the needs of an increasingly diverse workforce, the Co-operative Group launched its *Respect Works* programme in early 2005. The whole programme is about creating the right environment, one where all of our employees would want to work and not simply a programme that responds to bullying and harassment. The name itself is designed to be positive. In context, we are saying that *Respect Works* for you, for me, for all of us. It is about changing people's behaviour to create a positive atmosphere. This is a cultural shift that will take time and continual investment, needing to be refreshed and sustained to maintain momentum.

As the programme has been rolled out, we have been very careful to say that it is not about political correctness. We do not want to take the fun or natural human engagement out of the workplace. Nor is it about stopping managers managing their employees but it is about the way in which we engage with each other. For Group employees, it is about self-accountability and taking ownership for the way in which we do things rather than just what we achieve. It is about getting people to understand the impact that their behaviour has on others and to work toward changing that behaviour in order to create a positive environment. It leads to a broad understanding of what is acceptable and what is not and it creates an operational framework in which acceptable behaviour is understood, recognised and encouraged.

Creating a culture of respect is most certainly a fit with our internal brand. This is not just about changing logos and fascias or how our stores look but about creating an internal culture that values diversity which, in turn, creates an effective external service for a complex set of businesses. In other words, we want to build the right employee experience to establish a great customer experience. *Respect Works* is also a foundation stone programme that allows us to generate an environment where a diversity of talent may flourish. Respect does work as it holds the potential to create a productive, effective, enjoyable environment that builds on the Co-operative Group's core ethical principles whilst also strengthening business results through its effective engagement of people.

The Group's approach to implementing *Respect Works* started with a review of the end-to-end process. This involved the implementation of a process that would articulate the Group's commitment to creating a culture of respect, making it clear to people what was expected of them and giving people a clear and confidential process to raise complaints and get support. Finally, the process looked at how we would measure improvements and take further action.

There is a statement in our Diversity policy that makes it clear that we will not tolerate bullying and harassment in any form. *Respect Works* goes that step further in encouraging an environment for people to work together, for people to understand their impact and their roles and responsibilities. This is reinforced through the various engagement interventions which are refreshed on a regular basis in order to make it part of the very fabric of the way we work. For the first time across our diverse businesses, we also have one clear process that encourages informal resolution, where appropriate. This process is about creating an atmosphere where people can talk openly and constructively. Building a culture of respect provides multiple routes to raise complaints and receive support. If people feel uncomfortable talking to one particular person, then they have other support routes they are able to access. It also provides a front-end process to existing grievance and disciplinary procedures in an attempt to find resolutions before processes becomes formalised and relationships break down. We have also established *Respect Work* champions across the businesses – people who are knowledgeable about the process and could help and guide people to get support.

The most important change is the development of a range of interventions to get people thinking, challenging themselves and others in a powerful, fun and memorable way. This allows people to observe the impact that they can have on others without realising it. The intention was to break down existing mindsets, create a safe environment for people to ask questions and to challenge their own thinking. We use drama-based scenarios, targeting them at senior managers, with the intention of encouraging them to champion, challenge and question the environment around them. We do not offer them answers; we want them to start asking the questions. Off-the-shelf packages do not work with senior groups of managers so we developed tailored, relevant scenarios about real situations and a method of responding in contexts that those involved will recognise and relate to. As a result, we have developed a flexible range of training responses for different businesses depending on what delivery mechanism works for them. These scenarios are based on relevant, meaningful examples for our businesses, such as those that occur in our offices, stores and funeral homes.

Building a culture of respect is an evolutionary process. Our *Respect Works* champions now sign-post the process but in the future we hope that they will be able to counsel employees. Critically, we use our employee opinion survey and other trend data to refresh the programme year on year. A top–down, bottom–up approach that fits with our business ethos and objectives is working. We have created the challenge in our senior people and offer everyone the tools and support to challenge behaviour that does not fit with our core principles and help our business be successful.

2. Dignity at work: the Royal Mail commercial case

Frank Hogan

In 2003, the incoming Royal Mail chairman Allan Leighton put 'Dignity at work' at the forefront of Royal Mail's commercial business strategy. The key issue for Royal Mail was the compelling evidence of a pattern of erosion of people's dignity through bullying and harassment by colleagues, customers and managers. Bullying and harassment not only causes great suffering for its victims, it also incurs huge financial losses for business. Indeed, the cost of bullying and harassment to UK industry is estimated to be more than £2 billion per annum. This figure is primarily based on increased staff absence and replacement costs for those who leave as a result of bullying and harassment. It does not take into account lower productivity, negative publicity and increased legal costs, which would all pose additional financial expense. But, of course, the real cost of bullying and harassment is the damage it does to people's dignity, affecting:

- relationships (both at home and at work);
- health and well-being;
- performance;
- morale; and
- self confidence.

In a service-based industry, predicated upon the quality of relationships, this type of malaise cuts at the very heart of sustainable competitive advantage.

Royal Mail's Diversity and Inclusion Team was tasked with tackling the issues. They introduced a new dedicated policy to root out the bullies, including a 12-step investigation process and a national database for tracking complaints. Nearly 200,000 employees were trained in diversity issues and a telephone helpline was introduced. A number of independent harassment investigators were appointed, along with in-line *Diversity Champions* in the most problematic units. Significantly, throughout the country, a host of 'Dignity and Respect at Work' groups were established to provide both a voice for front-line staff and an impetus for action. In effect, the whole community was galvanised towards zero tolerance. The key aim of the diversity training was to encourage an open and honest approach to interpersonal conflicts at work. We set out five key principles:

1. We will make it easy for people to complain;
2. We will support them when they do complain and afterwards;
3. We will investigate complaints thoroughly and within a set timescale;
4. We will deal with the perpetrators appropriately; and
5. We will take significant steps to change the culture of harassment in the organisation.

To protect people from 'vexatious' claims, we added provision for each case, when completed, to be assessed as to whether the complaint was brought in bad faith.

So what does the evidence tell us? First, the cases suggest that dignity is most harmed when there is a sense of it being a 'zero-sum game'; that is to say when people do something to an 'other' which has the effect of increasing their own sense of worth at the expense of the other. It follows that the most successful interventions are ones that break this mould. For example, the figures show that, currently, around 80 per cent of cases concern 'banter' between employees. In light of this, the diversity and inclusion team developed a DVD to highlight the potential damage that this can cause in the workplace. This is currently being shown to all managers, many of whom have decided to show it to their staff.

Second, Royal Mail has conducted research into employee opinion over several years. The 'Have Your Say' survey canvasses opinion from all employees once a year, asking a range of questions which cover both how people are treated and how they feel about the organisation. Correlations of differing aspects of dignity with various questions in the survey support the importance of dignity. A key premise is people who are treated with dignity at work will enjoy their work. Themes of communication, involvement and opportunity for discretion emerge strongly from the data collected. Interestingly, harassment by manager was on average half that of harassment by colleagues and customers. The best managers, it would seem, are those who are most able to present market demands as an opportunity for achievement, rather than a drudge of delivery to 'unreasonable' demands. In short, by switching the locus of control to the individual, a manager can create the opportunity for a dignified response.

The bullying and harassment database allows Royal Mail to see, at a very general level, the incidence of different types of allegations. This information allows the business to target interventions towards tackling the most common causes of complaints. What the database shows us is that in terms of real incidents, there are various ways in which dignity may be perceived to be undermined. This leads us to suggest that, just as the term 'intelligence' is now understood to go beyond IQ and to comprehend such broader concepts as 'emotional' and 'kinaesthetic intelligence', so dignity can also be derived from multiple origins: dignity is as diverse an issue as the people around us.

Perhaps most importantly, the Royal Mail Database shows a number of asymmetries of perceived power, the abuse or absence of which are perceived to erode people's sense of dignity. These potential asymmetries can be turned round from negative concepts to positive models of the expression of dignity at work:

- to be valued;
- to be listened to;
- to be respected;
- to be treated fairly;
- to get recognition for achievement; and
- to take pride in work.

One can extend these further into even more positive sets of opportunities for people to make choices and so to find deeper meaning in life:

- the opportunity to achieve;
- the opportunity to speak their mind; and
- the opportunity to grow.

It is in the provision of these opportunities that Royal Mail is moving away from the old 'master–servant' model of the employment relationship, where the role of the servant is to comply with the ascribed commercial wisdom of the master; and towards the idea of the 'servant–leader', where the role of the leader is to provide opportunity for the employee to be successful. This switch in the locus of 'service' from the front-line employee to the leader requires leaders themselves to be much more like 'coaches' in their approach. As such, they give ownership of performance and development back to the individual, and in this way the individual can express their dignity at work. This is consistent with Rosabeth Moss Kanter's assertion (2005) that the role of leaders is 'to ensure accountability, cultivate collaboration, and encourage initiative'.

We can also learn about the way in which the process of addressing dignity can itself add or subtract. Sometimes, it seems that people approach cases more with a potential lawsuit or employment tribunal claim in mind. Individuals often expect unlimited resources to be put into substantiating the truth of the matter, and anything less than a 'full independent public enquiry' is seen as a 'cover up' if it does not give the complainant a desired result. This quasi-judicial approach creates a pressure to attend to process which can be purposeful, but can also be destructive. Often, there is little likelihood of being able to get to the truth of a matter, especially where it is one persons' word against another. In these situations, the manager's role is to give people the dignified opportunity to accept the ambiguity and repair the relationship. This requires considerable skills of empathy and the ability to mediate ambiguity. The pressure in this case is to attend to relationships, which in itself can be destructive if it leaves ambiguities unclosed.

Putting these two concepts, attention to process and attention to relationships, together we can create a landscape of business response to dignity erosion (Table 1).

What this schema shows is the need to attend to both 'process' and 'relationships' in order to achieve sustainable improvement, achieving a sense of restorative justice. To manage process without attention to relationships positions the manager as simply a judge and jury and risks the creation of grudges and retribution. To manage relationships without attention to process risks people having unresolved ambiguities and uncertainties that may present later as anxiety and absence. The concept of restorative justice derives from the 'Truth and Reconciliation Commission' work in South Africa. If it can be successful in that most tumultuous environment of sustained indiscriminate inhumanity, then it should be something we can learn to use in tackling indignity in UK industry.

Table 1 A landscape of business response to dignity erosion

	Attention to relationships	
	Low	High
Attention to process		
High	Assign blame and punish	Restorative justice (acknowledge contribution and repair relationship)
Low	Go through the motions	Mediate the ambiguity

In 2002, Royal Mail was suffering from high sickness absence rates estimated at an average of 7 per cent, although the actual figure was probably higher than this due to underreporting. The range of sickness absence also varied significantly across the business, from a low of 4.9 per cent to over 18 per cent in the worst unit. While this was the result of many factors, bullying and harassment were major causes. Since 2002, there has been an over 30 per cent reduction in the reported level of harassment. Whilst Royal Mail acknowledges that any harassment level is unacceptable, it is an improvement that is encouraging. Even more spectacularly, absence is now reduced to around 5 per cent. The benefits of this for the employees is clear, however, even more compelling are the benefits for customers and stakeholders. The Dignity strategy has been part of Royal Mail's recovery plan that has seen the company vastly improve performance – from losing £1 million per day to making £1 million per day, and from poor quality to best ever Quality of Service. And all this whilst facing full competition for the first time and significant volatility of the marketplace.

In terms of the future, the Dignity strategy has created a wave of softer skills amongst managers that make it a self-sustaining process. The need for this is consistent amongst modern leadership literature: 'How did you become more focused on others?' is one of Robert E. Quinn's pivotal questions for leaders (2005). In a recent series of training events for the most senior leaders in Royal Mail, facilitated by coaches from South Africa, the people were encouraged to greet each other by using the courteous Zulu term 'Soborno'. This translates literally as 'I see you'. It says far more than this. It acknowledges the existence of the other person. Without assessing them, it assigns to them value and worth from the fact that we see them. In 'soborno', by assigning worth without judgement, we give dignity.

3. 'Show us the money!'

Adele Geoghegan

The job advertisement marked the beginnings of the psychological contract to which I would soon subscribe. A leading global airline organisation was recruiting Reservations Sales Agents for a new pan-European call centre in Dublin. Successful candidates would possess excellent customer service and telephone skills, hold industry experience and speak at least two languages fluently. The salary of just under €14,000 was low even then – nine years ago in Celtic Tiger Ireland – though ballpark for call centres of its category. It would be a 'foot in the door', I reasoned, an opportunity to develop skills I had gained while working abroad, and a starting salary and first step to merit-based progression and reward.

In fact, I was luckier than most of the new hires. I spent just six months 'on the phones' before being promoted to a supervisory role, and a year later I was managing the centre's European Frequent Flyer division. While on the phones, and later from my vantage point as manager, I saw much evidence of unhappiness around pay vis-à-vis accelerating performance expectations. A standard inbound call centre menu applied: a constant stream of calls from frequently irate customers, a tightly confined physical environment, shift-work and strict productivity goals culminating in the requirement to take up to 100 calls per day; simultaneously achieving direct sales goals, switching from language to language as call flow dictated and subject to monitoring at will. All to be delivered with a smile. However, people were not always smiling. With reward limited to a roll-over contract and a maximum €600 pay increment, 'overwhelmed and underpaid' became an apt descriptor for the sentiments of many.

As the start-up rapidly grew, cutting over new markets and third-party business, many more front-liners joined the ranks, increasing anonymity, fragmenting work and further limiting development opportunities in an already flat organisation. The centre seemed to descend quickly to sweatshop grade, and a sense of negativity was palpable. Was this an affront to dignity? I sensed that it was. But as a novice call centre manager, in order to perform my job believably and well I had to adopt the manager's mantra: it was survival of the fittest; people were only here for the short-haul anyway; if so-and-so could do it cheerfully, why could not the rest, and so on.

Consequences of demoralisation were more difficult to dismiss. Sabotage (releasing calls, answering on 'mute') and burnout seemed unfortunate outcomes for skilled human capital in short supply – those who initially go above and beyond to satisfy escalating demands for 'emotional labour' critical to sustainable organisational success. But it becomes: 'I'm not paid enough to take this . . . ' High attrition and ample anecdotal evidence imply that this dissonance is not an isolated phenomenon. But can pay (rather than job design) be considered a central issue? Or a dignity issue? And is there any real alternative? Experiences throughout my professional and academic career indicate 'Yes'.

It can be argued that low pay, particularly in the call centre context, is a fundamental affront to dignity. Recently the 'McJob' concept has reinforced the link between low dignity and low pay. Coupland (1991) defined this as 'a low-pay, low-prestige, low-dignity, low-benefit, no-future job in the service sector'. But it goes back further. Call centres are said to be the modern-day manifestation of scientific management: constituents of performance are tightly prescribed and measured exactingly against the 'one best way' to conduct a call, close a sale and so forth. But the 'complete mental revolution' that Taylor envisaged – sharing productivity gains fairly for the benefit of management *and* workers – remains a mandate which many centres have yet to address. My experiences suggest that they could quite feasibly do this by *extending measurement metrics to units of reward*.

The matter of money

Notoriously, pay has been discounted for decades as a hygiene factor and mere short-term extrinsic 'satisfier'. On the surface, 'good wages' may seem purely extrinsic. Yet, at a deeper level, monetary rewards may also affect employees' emotional and familial well-being. Tang et al. (2005) relate 'worship' of money positively to achievement, power and organisation-based self-esteem, indicating that extrinsic and intrinsic motivators need not be exclusive. Extrinsic rewards can also increase intrinsic motivation if perceived as providing information about competence. Crucially, this is where dignity becomes pointedly contingent on pay. It is a statement of our value – to the organisation, to society, even to ourselves.

The interpretive paradigm views the meaning of money as being socially constructed, with its importance increasing concurrently with the social status and power that it is able to buy (Ardalan, 2003). One benefits not just from the material value of reward, but also from the boost in self-esteem that recognition associated with monetary compensation affords. The rise of consumerism, representing a more materialist society, means that the instrumental value of money has increased, because put simply, money can buy more and confer greater status. Conversely, there are key areas in which buying power has diminished that relate to our basic needs, and dignity may clearly be compromised if we cannot meet these. I need money not just because I am hungry or cold, but to satisfy a range of other needs whose means of realisation is commercialised. The media monster screams at people *'this is what you should be getting, this is the new standard!'*, but many are left far behind. Consumerism combined with low pay keeps 'profit centres' oiled, but the front-liners who shape them may well feel deprived, conscious of the indignity of building profits, but not sharing gains. Meanwhile, managers lament the demise of the traditional work ethic – the willingness to work now for later returns – however, they forget one important parallel trend which may justify demand for everything 'instant'.

The 'transactional contract'

The main criticism of money as positive 'KITA'[1] (Herzberg, 1966) is that it is merely a short-term motivator. But this has become less relevant with growing recognition that jobs are now short term. The changing nature of the psychological contract also means that there is less time now for 'hearts and minds', with a focus on 'lean and mean' techniques such as downsizing and job simplification. With contracting and outsourcing bringing a continuous widening of the 'peripheral/core', can one not argue that money may assume more importance as a substitute for security?

This seemed evident in my later experience of managing students employed part-time in a small Telesales call centre. These contracted employees unapologetically *un*subscribed to the commitment ethos, but were extremely driven by money. Paid lucrative commission based on clear measurable outcomes, the primary focus was on optimising sales revenue and thus personal earnings. Recognising that their stay was temporary, and merely facilitative of wider life goals, they were content with a straightforward version of the psychological contract – a simple effort-money exchange. Result? A climate of high energy, respect and mutual dignity. The material outcome of which was a cumulative 350 per cent revenue increase with sustained profitability over four years.

Granted, the above example relates to telesales which produces very specific measurable outcomes. Not all call centre work is quite as easily quantifiable; nonetheless most models feature tight prescription, measurement and control as given. In the information age, it has never been easier for managers to quantify value and if we accept the old adage 'what gets rewarded gets done' (Skinner, 1953), we can view pay positively as a yardstick to measure and reward desired behaviour. Increased work simplification and automation mean there is less and less excuse for ambiguity in determining and measuring the constituents of work effectiveness. Thus, there are clear opportunities for managers to *use* the fact that pay is a motivator rather than fight the inevitable. Indeed, it is argued that there is no motivational value in pay equality and that rewards must necessarily be clearly linked to performance (Nadler and Lawler, 1977). Nevertheless, one must accept some initial problematic in this proposal: internalising this concept may involve a radical paradigm shift for some managers – movement from the idea of pay as a *negative fixed cost* to one of pay as a *neutral variable percentage of profit*.

My experience suggests that such pay configurations can be widely applied, requiring only consensus and clarification on performance sought and mechanisms to reinforce and fairly reward desired behaviours. Moreover, if well-designed, they will *increase* net revenue for *both* employer and employees, coming closer to Taylor's original ideology.

Still, employers are often reluctant to keep their side of the bargain (Thompson, 2003). The emphasis shifts to facilitating employability, yet employers often shy away from investing in education or any meaningful transferable skills for employees in case they may later need to divest human capital. Thompson sees this new social contract as practically embodying the end of the bond between human and corporation, with the resulting 'engagement' representing compliance at best. Increased education means heightened – or perhaps merely changed – expectations. Employees, recognising the altered contract, increasingly demand: 'show me the money!' – and can we really blame them?

The future

The irony is thick in meetings where an organisational development (OD) consultant, often the best-paid person in the room, repeats the 'money does not motivate' mantra to willing managers, the best-paid people in the organisation (Ledford, 1995). Of course, this belief never leads to a reduction in managerial incentives or executive pay. Ledford believes that OD researchers have traditionally avoided the nitty-gritty of progressive pay systems due to discomfort with technicalities. But he appeals to managers to ask themselves truthfully how careers now look when many rungs on the ladder have been removed by de-layering, and how organisations can reward sustained performance without offering promotions?

As Lazear (1998) puts it, 'Money isn't everything, but it is the best metric'. And indeed the intrinsic motivators we have relied on heavily in the past may not be practicable or even acceptable for long before one cynically demands 'show me the money!' It is time to exploit the instrumentality of money instead of demeaning it.

There will always be people who work for the intrinsic value of work itself. Whilst upholding that concept, I dare to argue that the circumstances affecting the motivational force inherent in pay have changed radically, thus affecting dignity. This has occurred in the face of (a) growing consumerism, which accelerates the instrumentality of pay and (b) declining job security which increases instrumentality and heightens compensatory value.

Herzberg (2003) more recently reiterates the disparaging attitude towards employees evident in his earlier KITA metaphor, bemoaning lack of obedience in today's workers who he says must now be asked 'three times to stop spitting'. He does not address the disparity between spiralling executive salaries and his perceived need to curtail everyone else's; nor does he question the macro influences of consumerism or declining job security, which this commentary has raised. Widening education and media access mean that people are not as naive as Herzberg may believe. A philosophy that would enhance dignity and rebalance the psychological contract does not stop at saying 'our employees are our greatest asset'. Putting this into action by paying workers equitable salaries may be a true means of dignity at work in the future.

4. The personal paradox of supporting dignity at work

Marina Meehan

My parallel experiences both as an advisor on human resource (HR) policies and procedures on the correct application of dignity at work policies and as a woman who has repeatedly experienced various degrees and types of bullying and harassment in three different organisations in the last eight years (experiences that have fundamentally undermined my own sense of worth, self-respect and dignity) has inspired me to entitle this contribution 'personal paradox at work'. I believe that things happen in life for a reason. The episodes of bullying and harassment I have experienced at work were very unpleasant and life changing but I believe that they have, ultimately, made me a stronger person, resulting in me undertaking a 'spiritual healing from within' programme that inspires and rejuvenates me on a daily basis. I am pragmatic enough to know that I would not have done this had I continued on a high-flying HR career path.

When I began my healing journey, I read a book *Who Moved My Cheese,* in which the question was asked 'what would you do, if you weren't afraid?' This question resonated with me, and I often use it when employees are struggling with the idea of making a formal complaint, or with the belief that they have a choice to do nothing. It is a good starting point for facing personal demons and to come to terms with the consequences of an action being taken. This was something I faced alone. I was not fortunate enough to meet anyone that was able to helpfully support and guide me when I was in the thick of events.

I have worked in HR management for the last 25 years, and as I sit here in a new job working as a senior learning and development person in a fabulous organisation, the thought of writing about my experiences with regard to bullying and harassment fills me with doom and gloom. With this in mind, I am going to focus on what I personally learnt about how individual dignity can be undermined both as an HR practitioner and as a victim, which will hopefully enlighten the reader and enable them to understand the implications from various perspectives.

Reflecting on denials of dignity at work

In the early 1990s, I worked as a personnel manager in east London for Tesco Supermarkets. When I reflect on my experiences as a newly fledged staff manager, I realise that I encountered bullying and harassment on a daily basis – bad behaviour that adversely affected me and a wide range of staff. For example, it was commonplace and, seemingly, accepted that the white store manager could openly make racist comments to the black workforce, until one day a young student decided to take his frustrations out on the manager by physically beating him up. As a consequence, the company had a major investigation and the store manager was put on 'action short of dismissal-suspension' for a month and the student was re-assured that the company did not endorse racism at any level within the company.

I cut my teeth in that role and learnt that HR is a lonely place in any organisation. HR may appear on the surface to be the employees' champion but as a combination of legislative issues and performance-linked pressures increase our workload we are also expected to be subject matters experts as well as independently minded. I would love to say that times have changed and that due to the rising amount of legislation and greater education of people in the work relationship bullying and harassment behaviours centred on race would not happen in 2006. In my experience, however, I believe behaviours that may manifest themselves as an affront to people's dignity have merely become much more covert, as individuals become adept at using their power to subtly control people and situations in the workplace.

My own personal experience of denials of dignity at work commenced in earnest when I took the decision eight years ago to accept a HR Directorship in a big global company – working in their European headquarters in Ireland. I made a massive assumption that the Celtic economy would have impacted on the cultural mores in the organisation and that the need for equality and diversity was a fundamental principle that was not up for debate. I discovered how wrong this assumption was when I found myself reporting to a South African manager who would only actively engage with a male on my team.

I seemed to spend endless amounts of time having to justify my existence in the role and investing extra effort into gaining respect for my value in the organisation.

After five months, I was called in by my boss, the operations Director, and told my services were no longer needed and that I should take the week to clear my desk and go. One could argue, looking from the outside in, that this was not bullying, that it was more a case of fit and alignment within a global organisation and I would have to agree. That is the reality. I have brokered the signing of a number of compromise agreements for people in the higher echelons of organisations, when it is deemed that they no longer 'fit'. However, what was important to me was the way in which I was treated, how I was made to feel – the emotions unleashed in me as I dealt with a situation that left me in a strange country, with no job, no friends and no future. Therefore, the first observation that I would like to share was the overwhelming feelings and emotions that episodes of bullying and harassment create. These manifest themselves in different ways and in the extreme can result in loss of health or even suicide and are fundamentally an affront to human dignity. The feelings of shame, embarrassment and rejection were physically observable in my demeanour as I struggled to come to terms with such a challenging event in my life.

The second time I was bullied I headed up a team of 10 professional HR people in a 700 strong workforce. I had been in the company for 12 months and believed I was doing a good job – at least nobody had told me anything to the contrary. I came into work one day to discover all the management team, included the main board, were off site to plan the HR strategy for the next two years. No one had told me. Feelings of inadequacy and vulnerability that had haunted me in my previous workplace came rushing back as I struggled to come to terms with this exclusionary behaviour and I did a lot of soul searching to see whether I might be the catalyst that creates such situations. My sense of isolation was swiftly followed by the issuance of a list of eight unobtainable and entirely unrealistic objectives – objectives that I was told I had to achieve in six weeks or my position would be reviewed. It took a retired HR Director to tell me I was being bullied, I had gone to him for help and guidance and was advised that the company obviously wanted rid of me. This was corporate bullying at its worst. However, on this occasion, the experience brought something else out in me: my ability to fight and stand up for what I believe. I received legal advice, donned my best red outfit and informed my boss that the bullying would not continue and that I would leave, but on my terms. And that is exactly what I did.

The third and final time I experienced a denial of dignity at work, I had been asked as HR director to investigate my 'boss', who had been accused of sexually harassing a senior female employee. I carried out the investigation and followed the internal procedures to the letter, naively believing that my boss could maintain his objectivity in our relationship whilst I did my job. I worked with senior members of the company board, and between the three members of the group it was agreed that the 'boss' was guilty of the charge. However, he was the CEO of a multidollar public organisation; there was no one higher than him in the company. As the board floundered as to how to resolve it, he single-handedly threatened all the male managers in the management team that if they talked to me or worked with me at any level their futures would be in the balance. Consequently, I had lots of days with nothing to do and my professional integrity was in taters as I found myself powerless to defend the interests of the wronged employee. This was a bitter lesson to learn as I realised that even if you have the evidence, the witness statements and a clear case for the company to answer there are no winners, only losers. Once again, I donned my red outfit and separated from the company, though it took me two years to get a job of the same status.

And now . . . ?

The red outfit hangs, neglected, in the wardrobe. In the light of my experiences and a review of what I thoroughly enjoy, I have recently made a successful transition into an OD role that draws on my creative and innovative talents. The challenge I have set myself is to create something positive from previously negative experiences and become the number one benchmark in Ireland for the most effective learning, development and education practices that will establish PayPal as the number one employer of choice.

5. Sean's story

Corry de Jongh

What follows is the account of an employee, Sean, who experiences an undermining of his dignity at work. This is a real, and not unique, story. Although acted out and lived in the workplace, this story is told and heard mostly in the private domain because of the stress and shame attached to it for the individual as well as the organisation's defensiveness, represented by their unwillingness and inability to hear such stories.

Sean is a conscientious, loyal employee of a large insurance company. Over the eight years since he joined as a salesman, he has been known as an effective and committed team member, who achieves a consistently good performance record. Four years ago, he was promoted to team manager. He is a good-humoured, personable fellow who is well liked by all in the company. He is happily married, with two young children.

Recently some major re-structuring took place in the company. Sean's boss, George, who had always managed his department with great skill and concern for his staff, was promoted to a more senior position. The new manager, Neil, younger and more ambitious than his predecessor, has a more authoritarian style of management. Responding to new, more aggressive policies of the new group management, Neil put in place a new system of performance appraisal. At the same time that Neil took up office in the department, Sean's assistant became ill and Neil replaced her with a less experienced staff member.

Sean begins to feel increasingly pressurised by Neil who is hinting at reorganising the whole sales department. Sean feels put down and undermined by Neil at management meetings and after every encounter with Neil, Sean feels uneasy and upset. He shares his disquiet with a friend in another department who confirms for him that it is not just his imagination that Neil indeed does behave in an intimidating and aggressive manner. Sean is a union member and has a word with the union representative but does not want to take any further action and risk escalating the situation. He is afraid to broach the issue with Neil directly and by now he dreads going into work in the morning. Awake at night, Sean ruminates over how he can improve the situation. Tired in the morning, his concentration is flagging and his in-tray is piling up. The more he misses his deadlines, the more despondent he becomes. Critical commentary increases, he feels more inadequate and a vicious cycle starts. Sean shares his worries with his wife, Anna, who suggests after many late night discussions that he takes a break, or considers changing job. He hates taking time from work but feels so low and is so tired that he cannot bring himself to go to work any longer. There are days when Sean feels that life is not worth living. Anna notices that recently he has been drinking more. His daughter tells him in no uncertain terms he is no fun anymore.

Finally, he goes to see the family doctor. She recommends sick leave because of stress; she prescribes medication and suggests counselling. Back home, Sean calls Jean in the HR department who urges him to avail of the company-sponsored employee assistance program (EAP). He makes an appointment to talk with someone the same day.

Sean takes four weeks sick leave due to stress. He spends time with his family, reflects on his situation, speaks to some colleagues and attends six counselling sessions. With his counsellor, he discusses how to address the problem in work and looks at the options for his future career in the company. His anxiety subsides but returns again shortly before he is due to return to work. Nothing much has changed in work. He meets with one of the HR managers he likes. He learns that Neil is temporarily moved to a different department, and Sean feels comfortable enough working with his replacement. However, Neil is to return in the near future. Sean does not know what conversations took place between HR and Neil, and he does not trust he can work for Neil again. Nevertheless, for the moment, Sean feels he can cope better with work pressures, he feels safe while Neil works in another part of the building but is aware that the situation could worsen.

While originating from within the work place, Sean's distress has spilled over into his family life, into his conversations with friends and eventually into the doctor's surgery and counsellor's office. Nobody, speaking in a private capacity, will dispute that his manager Neil should have treated Sean with more respect. No one likes to be put under excessive pressure or feel berated and criticised by his or her manager, particularly not in front of colleagues. That kind of behaviour erodes one's sense of dignity and personal integrity. Yet, this kind of behaviour can become widespread in organisations when not addressed effectively in what Frost (2003) refers to as 'toxic' organisations. In Sean's firm, this behaviour is occurring frequently and affecting his colleagues in various ways. It is seldom talked about in the organisation and kept safely 'under wraps'.

Sean sees himself and is perceived by others as a committed employee. For him, this had always been a source of pride and a positive aspect of his sense of self, of his identity. His firm reaped the benefits over the years, and Sean had always expected that if a problem arose he would be 'looked after'. However, when he talked about his distress to another, more senior, manager he did not feel supported, which was disappointing for him. He began to feel depressed and behave in an anxious, moody manner. This was in turn interpreted and framed as Sean being 'stressed', 'burnt out' and eventually 'ill'. Sean's increasing distress now takes on a life of its own and becomes disconnected from its source: his manager's callous and insensitive behaviour. A downward spiral is set in motion and what began as an organisational problem is effectively outsourced for personal 'healing'.

Every one in Sean's story has a different voice as each holds a different position with its own 'script'. Every 'actor' in this story or (if you prefer) every stakeholder in this event is embedded in a network of relationships of which Sean is also part. Each individual role is coloured with its own prescriptions for organisational, professional or family behaviour. If we look at each of them in turn as part of their larger relational networks, if we explore the position they hold within these and the dilemmas they experience as a result of this position, more complex perspectives emerge.

Sean is a junior manager in the organisation and is by the nature of his position less authoritative than Neil. His sense of dignity tells him not to accept this behaviour and to fight back, but he also knows that he is not an equal partner in any dialogue or confrontation with senior management.

Neil is himself under considerable pressure to meet the new company targets. He is young and ambitious and his career is on the line. Neil himself receives little support and lacks the necessary people management skills. He is not aware of how his insensitive behaviour has diminished Sean's sense of dignity in work.

The HR manager is concerned about Sean's account and suggests counselling in the hope that he can learn to cope with more work pressure. As part of management, she needs to conform to the new business plan and to get employees to meet the new sales targets. She resolves her dilemma by sending the problem away!

The union representative advises Sean that he does not have a strong case and that a positive outcome is unlikely. He himself has a poor relationship with management who deliberately try to sideline the trade unions. Sean is discouraged and feels more powerless after this conversation.

Anna, his wife, and the kids want Sean 'back'. He values their perception of him as husband and dad as much as he values his boss's appraisal of him as a worker. He does not want to let them down. They want to help but have no power over the work situation. Their level of support at home is crucial for Sean to restore some of his dignity.

The counsellor's and the GP's framing of the problem is important for Sean's dignity; neither is in a position to exert any influence over the work situation and both may feel that Sean's firm has 'dumped' their problem on them. 'Pathologising' will make it worse while enabling him to act may restore a sense of dignity.

All these voices are important facets of Sean's story. Each actor with their framing of the problem, the actions and reactions, the conversations with and about him, in and outside the workplace all contribute to a greater or lesser extent to Sean's sense of dignity in work.

The responses of the various stakeholders in Sean's predicament as described above are characteristic of an organisation, which lacks a clear culture of support for human values and support for employees. Despite a stated policy to the contrary, Sean's experience tells him that in this firm profit comes before people. Three months later, Neil is due to return to his former position. Sean waits to see how matters develop, before he gives up or leaves. He hopes that Neil has changed; management hopes that Sean can cope better and that the issue is dealt with by having a talk with Neil; Neil himself has become aware of Sean's distress and feels sidelined when moved to a different department for a few months; HR is still uncomfortable with Neil's behaviour but is satisfied to have contained the situation; the union rep continues to battle with management to improve on implementation of the 'dignity at work' policy; the GP continues to prescribe anti-depressants for employees in a similar situation; the counsellor continues to help employees to cope with undignified treatment in work, while bemoaning privately the lack of human values in the corporate world. Sean's family is happy that he is back in work and seems to be 'ok', but they are concerned that the same will happen again.

And so the story continues...

6. Voices

Sharon C. Bolton

The following section of this chapter presents the voices of people from industry – some just starting out in work, some retired and some in senior management positions, others in blue-collar work. This source of insightful data is provided by people who were invited to express their views regarding dignity at work as part of the Economic and Social Research Council-funded project 'dignity in and at work'.[2] People have taken the time to write sometimes long and poignant accounts of how dignity has been denied to them and others shorter but insightful definitions of what dignity means to them. The 'voices' are deliberately left without any supporting narrative or interpretation. They tell their own stories and help to fill the human void in our understanding of dignity at work.

Male, 54, Engineer

'Being treated with respect – the little things; like people calling you by your proper name, also trusting you to do the job properly, not taking advantage and stopping paid over-time but expecting you to work anyway and dipping into people's pensions and understanding that employees are human beings and that they have families and worries other than their jobs and need time sometimes to sort their lives out'.

Male, 75, Retired MD

'Having a voice in work – unions used to have the power to offer people dignity at work. Even as a senior manager I used to be able to see that and work with it and though it wasn't always easy we knew how things worked and where we stood and things got done and it seemed fair somehow. In a way it meant I didn't have to worry if I was doing the right thing by the people who worked for me – the union did that for me. I don't know how young managers actually manage now. I remember quite fondly all the shop-stewards I used to have battles with!'

Male, 46, Line manager

'Managers can give or take dignity away from employees. So I lead by example – do as I do, not do as I say. The shop floor deserves more respect than to see me swanking about throwing my weight around'.

Female, 50, Clerical officer

'Hierarchies are a fact of life but wherever you are in the hierarchy you deserve respect'.

Female, 38, Secretary

'Dignity at work is mutual respect at work'.

Male, 64, Tool Maker

'There isn't any dignity in work anymore. When I was an apprentice being around for years meant something. People respected the older workers and relied on their experience. Now you're made to feel on the scrap heap as soon as you pass 50. I'm glad I'll be retiring next year – as long as the bastards don't get their hands on my pension! The funny thing is it's not the youngsters who don't respect you – they're a good bunch of lads. It's the bloody managers!'

Male, 23, Management Trainee

'Dignity at work to me means that not only are your work responsibilities and actions respected, both in terms of required work and
also extra work you do, but also that the individual and human
aspects of your actions are respected'.

Female, 50, Personal assistant in health care setting

'My "lack of dignity" in the workplace stemmed from belittling,
harassment, rude comments made in front of people, and in the end
physical abuse which led to a grievance. This started within one
month of starting the post and remained until my redeployment four
years later (in process now). No one knew how to deal with the
situation especially as I was the first person to bring it to light after
so many years of bullying from the same person!'

Female, 42, Cleaner

'Dignity at work? It's people like you saying good morning, asking
me how my kids are, thanking me for hoovering your office and
asking me questions like what do I think Dignity at Work is'.

Male, 36, Parent

'Dignity is dependent upon an even more basic question: What is
a human person? How we see human persons affects how we treat
them'.

Male, 41, Senior strategist, public sector

'By the time we have a situation that meets a definition of bullying it
is (generally) too late to reach a totally satisfactorily outcome – the
damage has been done. If "we" set out to provide an environment
and culture of dignity any need to use grievance procedures will
disappear'.

Female, 56, Accounts clerk

'My job was dismantled without any reference to me, responsibility
was taken from me, I had no control over what was happening to
me. I was completely powerless, stripped of all dignity'.

Male, 29, Clerk

'It is every person's right to be treated with respect and dignity, regardless of their race, creed or colour. We also have a habit of forgetting the person's age. The person in question might be a young person (10 year old) or (15) or possibly older, age does not come into it, we should still respect the person after all they are human. When you look at someone what do you see first? Is it the colour? Is it the sex? Is it the age? These and other questions we need to answer'.

Female, 46, Administrator

'I think dignity at work means feeling that your contribution is of equal value, which should be reflected in your salary, and consistently applied policies to ALL staff'.

Female, 30, Teaching assistant

'Dignity at work? I don't get paid enough to have dignity at work!'

Male, 59, Engineer

'I can tell you what *in*dignity at work is – when my wife was dying of cancer and my employer still insisted I did call out or I would lose my job'.

References

Ardalan, K. (2003) 'Money and Academic Finance: The Role of Paradigms', *International Journal of Social Economics*, **30**, 6, 720–740.

Coupland, D. (1991) *Generation X: Tales for an Accelerated Culture*, London: St Martin's Press.

Frost, P. (2003) *Toxic Emotions at Work*, Boston: Harvard Business School Publications.

Herzberg, F. (1966) *Work and the Nature of Man*, New York: Staples Press.

Herzberg, F. (2003) 'One More Time: How Do You Motivate Employees?' *Harvard Business Review*, **81**, 1.

Kanter, R. B. (2005) *Confidence*, New York: Random House.

Lazear, E. P. (1998) *Personnel Economics for Managers*, New York: John Wiley & Sons.

Ledford, G. E. (1995) 'Pay as an Organization Development Issue', available at: http://www.aom.pace.edu/odc/newsletters/SUM95.htm

Nadler, D. A. and Lawler, E. E. (1977) 'Motivation: A Diagnostic Approach', in *The Organizational Behavior Reader* (Kolb, D. A., Osland, J. S. and Rubin, I. M., eds), New Jersey: Prentice Hall, pp. 125–135.

Quinn, R. E. (2005) *Moments of Greatness*, HBR Jul–Aug.

Skinner, B. F. (1953) *Science and Human Behavior*, New York: Free Press.

Tang, D., Tang, T., Luna-Arocas, R. (2005) 'Money Profiles: the Love of Money, Attitudes and Needs', *Personnel Review*, **34**, 5, 603–618.

Thompson, P. (2003) 'Disconnected Capitalism: or Why Employers Can't Keep Their Side of the Bargain', *Work, Employment and Society,* **17**, 2, 359–378.

Notes

Prelims

1. Philadelphia Declaration, available at http://www.ilo.org/public/english/comp/civil/standards/ilodcr.htm
2. Dimensions and Divisions of Dignity in and at Work: A Participative Workshop, ESRC Social Science Week 2005, supported by ESRC Grant RES-000-22-1048.
3. Dignity *in* and *at* Work project supported by ESRC Grant RES-000-22-1048.

Chapter 1

1. Ehrenreich (2001) gives similar accounts of low-paid work in the USA.
2. According to National Statistics-Standard Occupational Classification (NSOC), 'Care work', that is, child care, and health care assistant are categorised as 'personal services' and cleaning as 'elementary occupations'. http://www.statistics.gov.uk/methods_quality/soc/ structure.asp.

Chapter 2

1. I am assuming sexual identity can be subsumed under cultural identity here. However, some cultural identities may not be worthy of respect. For example, the identity of white supremacists is based on hatred and stigmatising of their others and is therefore unworthy of recognition. In refusing unconditional respect or dignity to others, they lose their claim to conditional respect for themselves.
2. The particular behaviours that are considered dignified or undignified varies culturally, but I suggest that there are common features, and Hodson's research on meaning and satisfaction at work also suggests that concerns about dignity and respect are common across gender and 'race' (Hodson, 2002).
3. As we shall see, the phrase is likely to mean something different in the context of durable inequalities.

4. This of course, does not mean a sense of humour is incompatible with dignity.
5. It is noteworthy that hospitals now display ward mission statements which include a commitment to respect patients' dignity and also display notices stating that abusive behaviour from patients or visitors will not be accepted. These suggest that awareness of the need to respect dignity at work is growing.
6. "The wise and virtuous man is at all times willing that his own private interest should be sacrificed to the public interest of his own particular order or society" (Smith, 1759, VI.ii. 3.3).
7. See Charles Taylor's related distinction between unconditional and conditional recognition (Taylor, 1994).
8. It is not that employers particularly *intend* to grant respect unequally when they treat different workers unequally, for their construction of jobs of unequal quality are often motivated by much more prosaic, economic concerns, but that is not likely to make those at the bottom feel any better.
9. Obviously, these are strongly gendered occupations and gender would be likely to add a further difference here, but it is the difference that skill makes that I am focusing on here. See Gorz, 1983.

Chapter 3

1. I am following Mary Douglas (1966) for my initial understanding of dirt, though this is partly set aside at the end. In *Purity and Danger* (1966), Douglas defines dirt in terms of misplacement or misclassification. Following William James, her basic definition of dirt is that it is 'matter out of place'. She writes: 'Dirt is a by-product of a systematic ordering and classification of matter, in so far as ordering involves rejecting inappropriate elements'. 'It is a relative idea', she has written, 'shoes are not dirty in themselves, but it is dirty to place them on the dining table; food is not dirty in itself, but it is dirty to leave cooking utensils in the bedroom, or food bespattered on clothing; similarly, bathroom equipment in the drawing room...' Many analysts have used Douglas' ideas about the nature of dirt, sometimes to illuminating effect (see Davis, 1983; Bauman, 1989).
2. Clearly we can overestimate how much cleanliness is good for us. Louis Pasteur is reported to have said: 'I would rather a child ate bread that has been dragged through the dirt, than be brought up on an over-sterile diet' (Leith, 1996).

Chapter 6

1. All names have been changed.

Chapter 7

1. This chapter is based on work supported by the U.S. National Science Foundation, Innovation and Organisational Change and Sociology Programs under Grant 0112434. Any opinions, findings and conclusions or recommendations expressed in this material are those of the author and do not necessarily reflect the views of the National Science Foundation.
2. Lists of the ethnographies included, as well as those considered but excluded, are available from the author on request and at http://www.sociology.ohio-state.edu/rdh/Workplace-Ethnography-Project.html.
3. The codesheet, coding protocol, data and reliability reports are available at http://www.sociology.ohio-state.edu/rdh/Workplace-Ethnography-Project.html. As with any content analysis project, we may have made errors in the interpretation of the texts or in the coding of the data. The data, however, are available for public scrutiny and analysis, and we welcome suggestions, criticisms, and alternative views on the recorded data.

Chapter 12

1. It is interesting to point out that in proportion to the population, this is a rate of immigration over six times higher than that of the United States (CIA World Factbook: United States, 2006; Immigrant Council of Ireland, 2005).

Chapter 13

1. KITA – Herzberg's 'Kick In The Ass' metaphor. The author maintains that money could be used as a short-term mechanism for *making* someone do something, but not for *making them want to* do it.
2. Research supported by an Economic and Social Research Council (ESRC) Grant (no: RES-000-22-1048).

Index

CPSIA information can be obtained
at www.ICGtesting.com
Printed in the USA
LVOW04s2130081215

466017LV00003B/19/P